IMAGES
of America

JEFFERSON COUNTY

IMAGES
of America

JEFFERSON COUNTY

Elise D. Chan,
Curator of Collections
Jefferson County Historical Society

ARCADIA
PUBLISHING

ISBN 978-0-7385-3547-0

Published by Arcadia Publishing
Charleston, South Carolina

Printed in the United States of America

For all general information contact Arcadia Publishing at:
Telephone 843-853-2070
Fax 843-853-0044
E-mail sales@arcadiapublishing.com
For customer service and orders:
Toll-Free 1-888-313-2665

Visit us on the Internet at www.arcadiapublishing.com

Contents

Preface

For several years, I had a dream of publishing a book which would feature the many priceless postcards and other photographs in the archives of the Jefferson County Historical Society. The objective was to share the best of this vast treasure trove of photographs with the public in an affordable manner, something which had never been done before. We were so pleased when Arcadia approached us about doing a book for their wonderful Images of America series, because it seemed to be the ideal venue to showcase the best views from our collection. The huge job of writing and compiling this work was turned over to our curator of collections, Elise D. Chan, and we know you will like the result.

Fred H. Rollins
Director
Jefferson County
Historical Society

Introduction

If you use your imagination, you might be able to see the silhouette of one of the presidents of the United States, Thomas Jefferson, in the profile of the county. Nestled between the Adirondack Mountains to the east, Lake Ontario to the west, and the St. Lawrence River and Canada to the north, Jefferson County is a place of history and scenic beauty. Jefferson County was created by an act of the state legislature on March 28, 1805. Watertown was made the county seat.

Farming continues to be an important occupation. Even until the 1950s Jefferson County ranked third in milk production among all counties in the United States. In the 1800s, the Black River was the sole source of power for the booming industries such as sawmills, paper mills, and cotton mills. The famous Thousand Islands of the St. Lawrence River continue to provide visitors with panoramic sights and nautical recreation. Deepwater harbors provide boaters with scenic and serene anchorages. Jefferson County relies heavily on tourism, and the peaceful tranquillity of the county offers visitors the opportunity to relax and enjoy the beauty of the countryside.

It was not until after the Revolutionary War that settlement by the New England pioneers commenced. Up until this time, Jefferson County had been a frontier wilderness, occupied only by Iroquois tribes. Among the first to settle was Lyman Ellis in 1797. Ellis planted and harvested corn in the present town of Ellisburg. Six months later, Noadiah Hubbard established a settlement in the hills of Champion. The French nobility, fleeing persecution from the French Revolution in their native country, settled throughout Jefferson County, particularly in the northern section. It was a result of this turbulent time in world history that the North Country became the home of James LeRay de Chaumont and Joseph Bonaparte, the ex-king of Spain and brother of Napoleon Bonaparte. Other individuals, primarily from New England, soon began settling into the county. Henry Coffeen, Hart Massey, and Zachariah Butterfield built log cabins on the present site of Public Square in the city of Watertown. They were especially attracted to this region because of the mighty Black River and its ability to power their flour and sawmills.

New England pioneers began coming to the county and settling by the hundreds. By 1805, the townships of Adams, Brownville, Champion, Ellisburg, Lorraine, Rodman, Rutland, and Watertown had been created. Even with the settlement that was taking place in the county, there was still no easy way to get from Utica to Watertown. With the establishment of stagecoach lines, it still took eighteen to twenty hours of travel through densely wooded and sparsely settled terrain to get to Watertown via Utica. The hardships, isolation, and difficulties faced by the early pioneers made them self-reliant and resilient to the perils they often faced during their settlement of the county.

Jefferson County is proud of the fact that many local individuals rose to great fame or prominence in state and world affairs. Roswell P. Flower became governor of New York State in 1891. John Foster Dulles became the secretary of state under President Eisenhower. Robert Lansing, the uncle of John Foster Dulles, was the secretary of state serving in President Wilson's cabinet. There were many local residents elected into the Congress of the United States as well. Jefferson County is also the birthplace of the king of merchandising, Frank W. Woolworth. Inventions such as chloroform and the percussion-cap rifle were both invented by Samuel Guthrie, who resided in Sackets Harbor. Robert Hitchcock's invention of the Hitchcock Lamp, a kerosene lamp that burned brighter and longer that any before it, and James Liddy's invention of the box-spring mattress made life more comfortable for people living in Victorian America.

Jefferson County has much to be proud of. Its rich heritage and scenic beauty can be enjoyed today by visitors and local residents alike.

Acknowledgments

I would personally like to express my sincere appreciation to the following people who, with their unending encouragement and interest, kept me dedicated and confident throughout the project. My gratitude goes to Fred H. Rollins, executive director of the Jefferson County Historical Society, for coming up with the initial conception of the book and enthusiastically assisting me with the challenges I encountered. Alex Duffy provided his memories of early Watertown that were indispensable and greatly appreciated. I am grateful to Mr. and Mrs. Robert Brennan for the photograph of the Sackets Harbor Railroad Station and for their help in finding answers to the tough genealogy questions. George Bonadio and his early recollections of his father's business, the "Six For Five Postcard and Shoeshine Parlor," were not only essential, but also delightful. Thanks go to the *Watertown Daily Times* for permission to reprint the photographs by David Lane so that the images can be enjoyed once again by everyone. Jerry Anderson from the Carthage Free Library, Elizabeth Case (Town of Antwerp historian), and the staff at the Macsherry Library in Alexandria Bay provided me with their time and knowledge. Thanks to William P. Hills, Emerson Laughland (City of Watertown historian), John B. Johnson, John B. Johnson Jr., Harold B. Johnson, Sally Stevens, Jeanne Stanley, and Mrs. Barbara Haller for their kind assistance in proofreading the manuscript and offering their suggestions and knowledge. The staff at the Jefferson County Historical Society including Elaine T. Bock, Melissa Widrick, and Judy N. George also read the manuscript and offered their ideas and opinions.

One

Main Streets

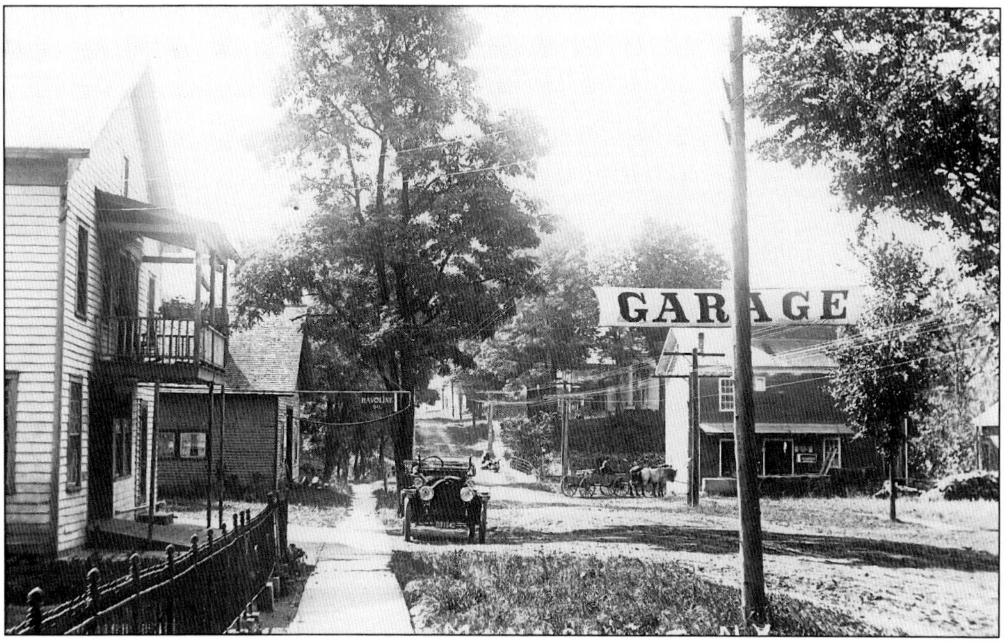

Mannsville, *c*. 1910. Mannsville's location on the Rome, Watertown & Ogdensburg Railroad line provided it with early business opportunities. By 1825 Mannsville had a post office, sawmill, hotel, schoolhouse, and three dwellings. By 1851, when the railroad was completed, businesses in the town proliferated and the small town became a strategic location within the county.

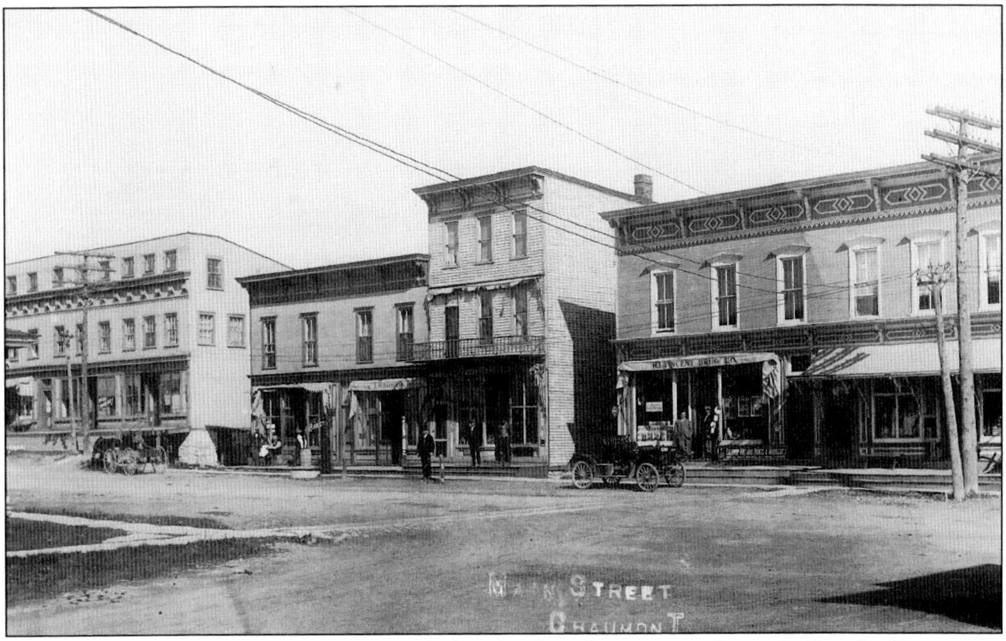

Chaumont, Main Street, *c.* 1910. Named after the French aristocrat James LeRay de Chaumont, who settled the area along with his French compatriots after the French Revolution, the town of Chaumont was established in 1800. Chaumont quickly became known for its abundant fishing industry, which was based on the bay upon which the town is situated.

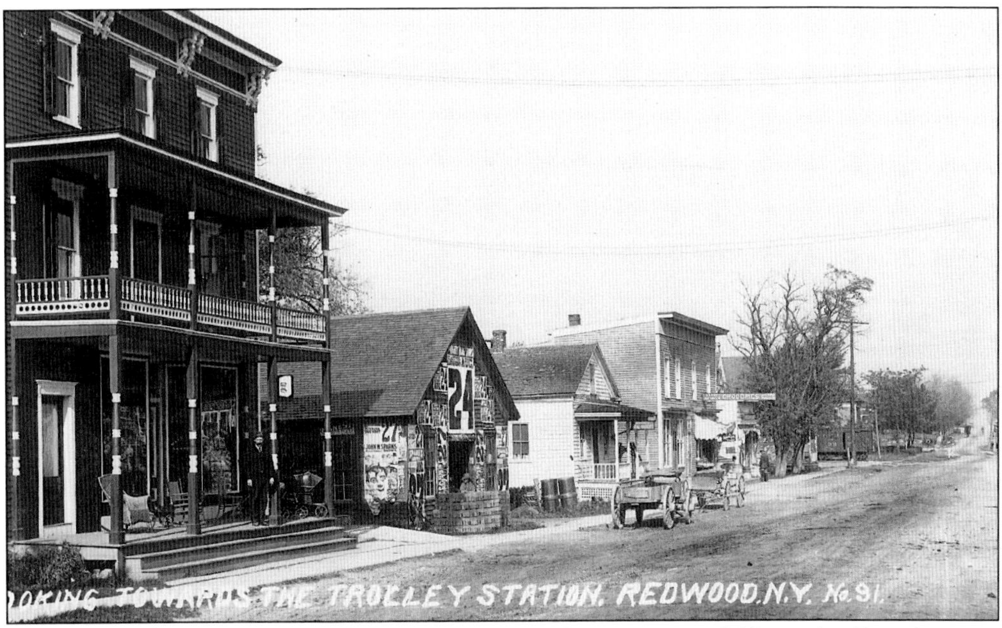

Redwood looking toward the trolley station, *c.* 1910. An extension of Alexandria Bay, the town of Redwood became known throughout the nation for its production of beautiful Redwood Glass. The town had large deposits of sand that were vital in the glass production.

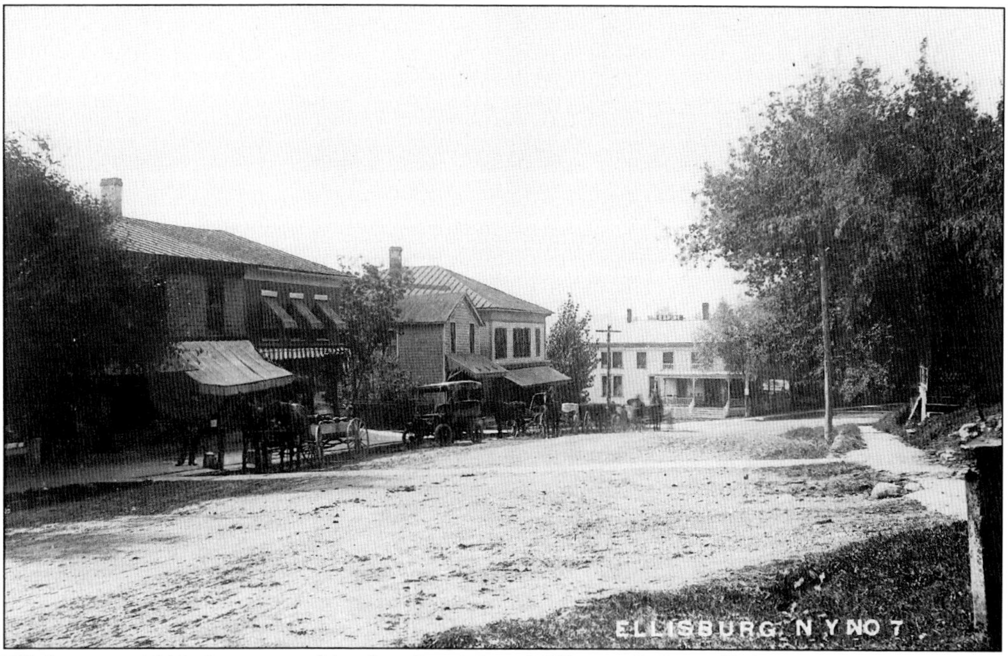

Ellisburg, *c.* 1910. Lyman and his brother Marvel Ellis settled in Ellisburg in 1797 after their sojourn down Sandy Creek. Ellisburg is celebrated as one of the very first locations to be established by the New England pioneers.

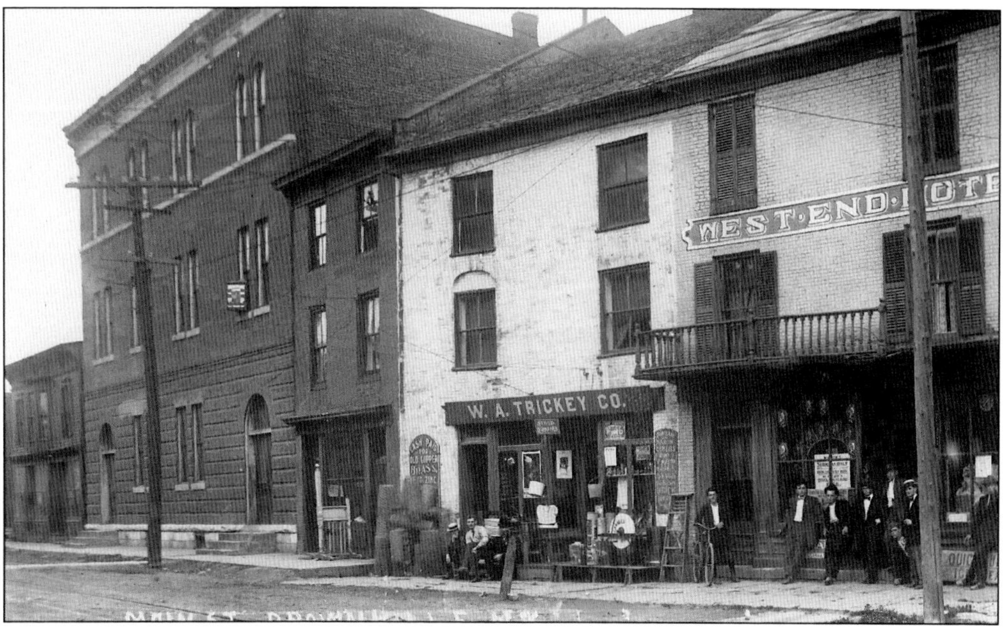

Brownville, Main Street, 1909. Navigating his way on the Black River, Jacob Brown established a homestead in Brownville in 1799. By 1820, Brownville was an established industrial town with cotton, paper, and woolen mills as well as various machine shops.

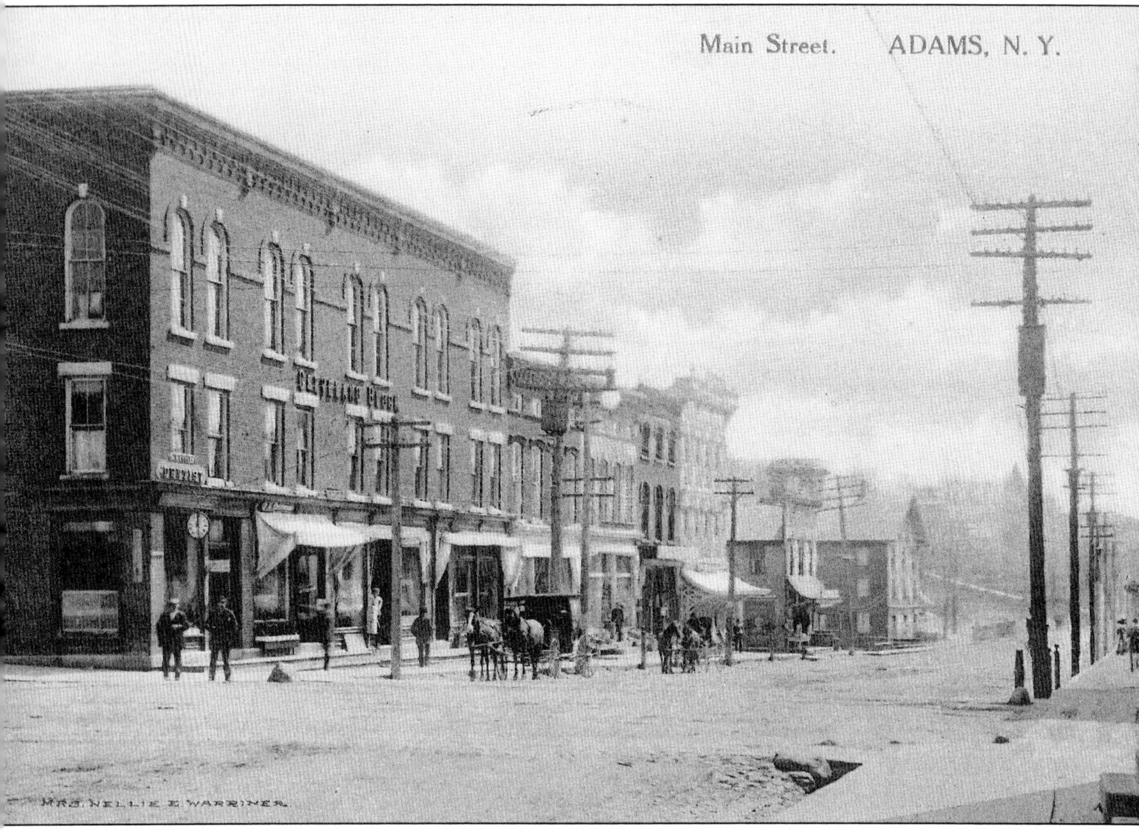

Adams, a view of Main Street looking south, *c.* 1910. Simeon DeWitt, in his 1802 survey of Adams, remarked, "The town has every good quality: mill seats, springs of excellent water, fine timber . . . limestone, fine soil and loam in general." It is not surprising that the purchase of land in the town of Adams by Elisha Phillips in 1798 was the precursor of land transactions in the rest of Jefferson County.

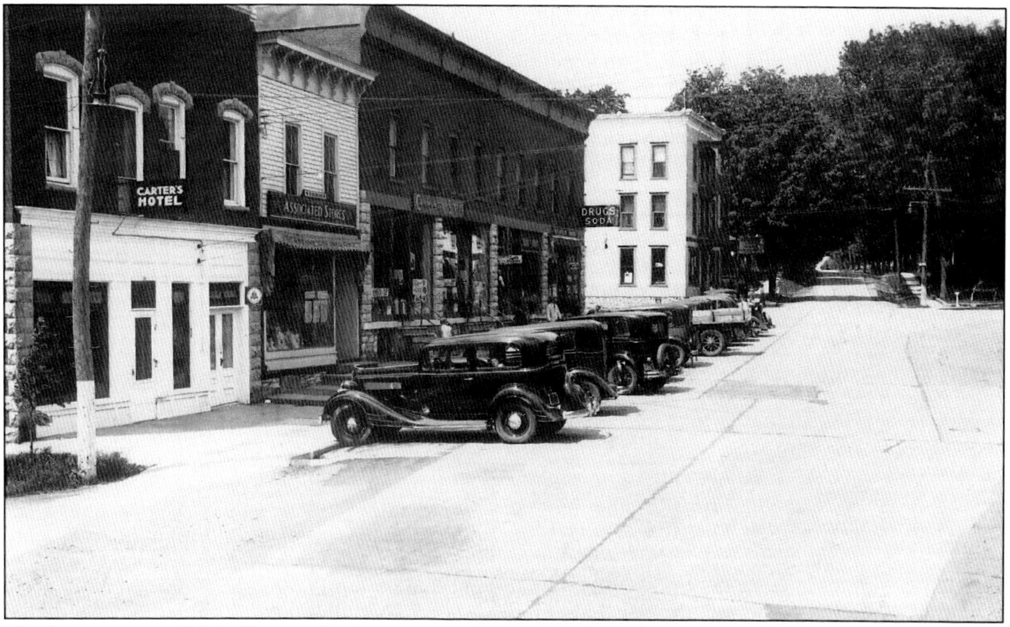

Black River, c. 1930. Originally known as the town of Lockport, the village of Black River is pleasantly located on both sides of its namesake.

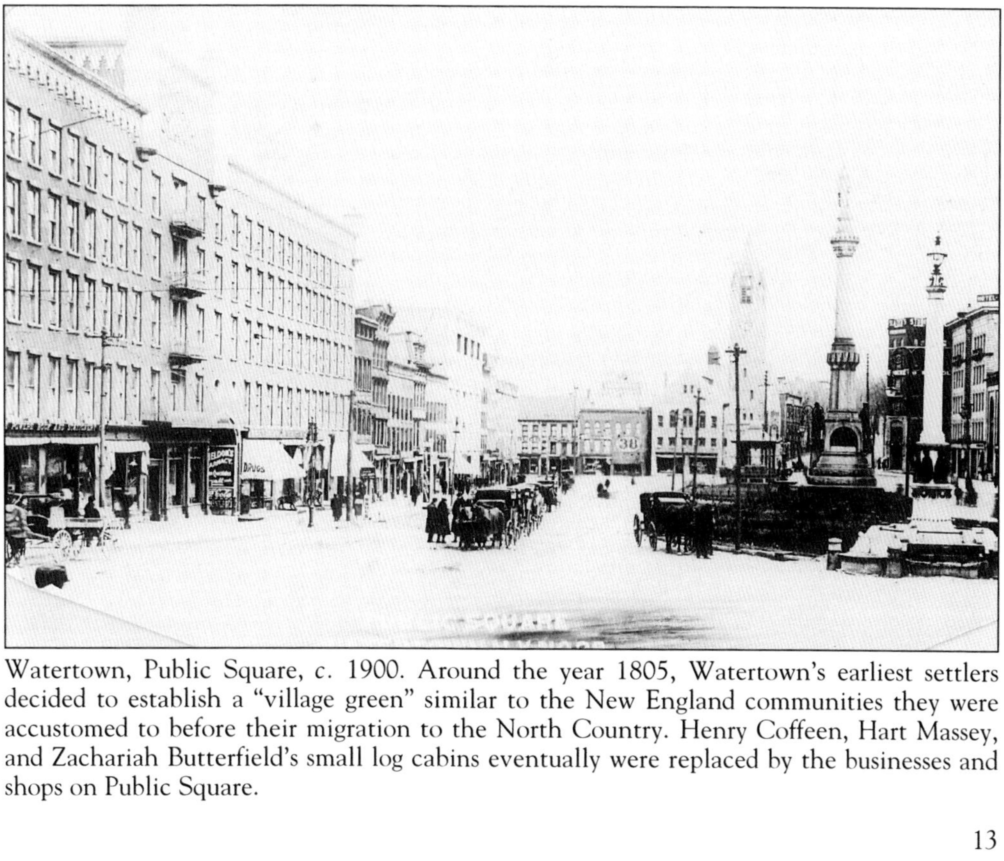

Watertown, Public Square, c. 1900. Around the year 1805, Watertown's earliest settlers decided to establish a "village green" similar to the New England communities they were accustomed to before their migration to the North Country. Henry Coffeen, Hart Massey, and Zachariah Butterfield's small log cabins eventually were replaced by the businesses and shops on Public Square.

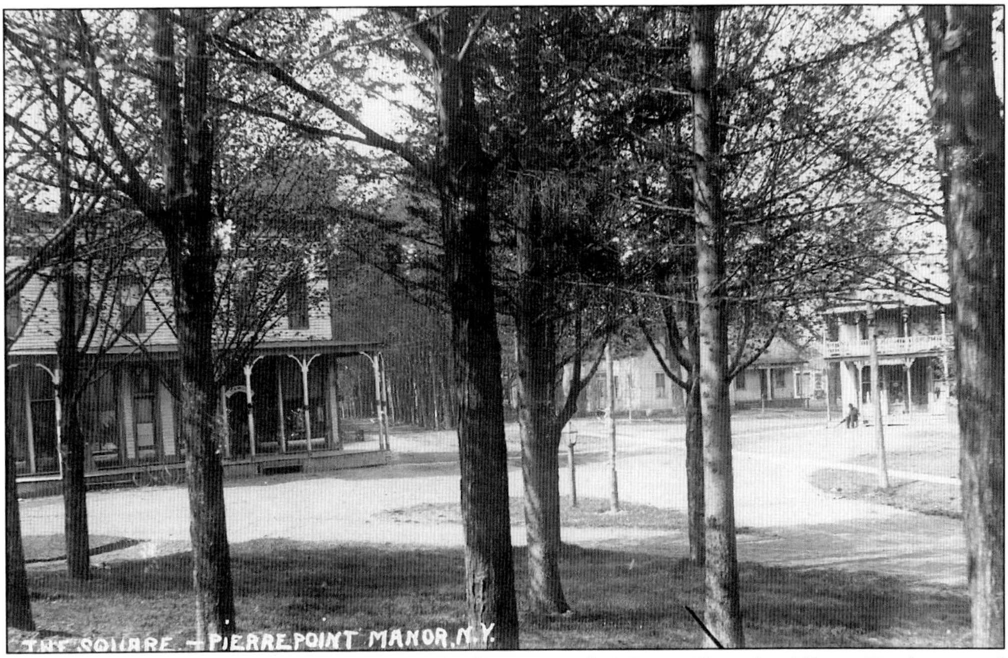

Pierrepont Manor, the Square, *c.* 1910. By way of Adams, Joseph Allen, Pardon, and Arnold Earl travelled through dense forests to settle in the town of Pierrepont Manor. This town later became known for its resident Marietta Holley, an established author of the early twentieth century.

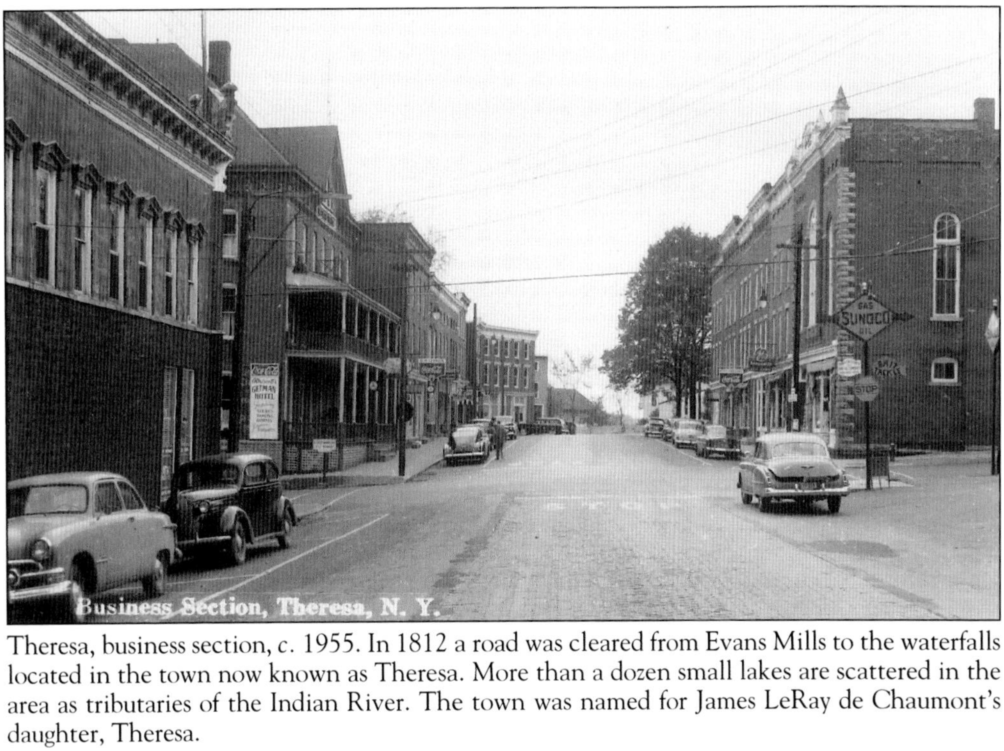

Theresa, business section, *c.* 1955. In 1812 a road was cleared from Evans Mills to the waterfalls located in the town now known as Theresa. More than a dozen small lakes are scattered in the area as tributaries of the Indian River. The town was named for James LeRay de Chaumont's daughter, Theresa.

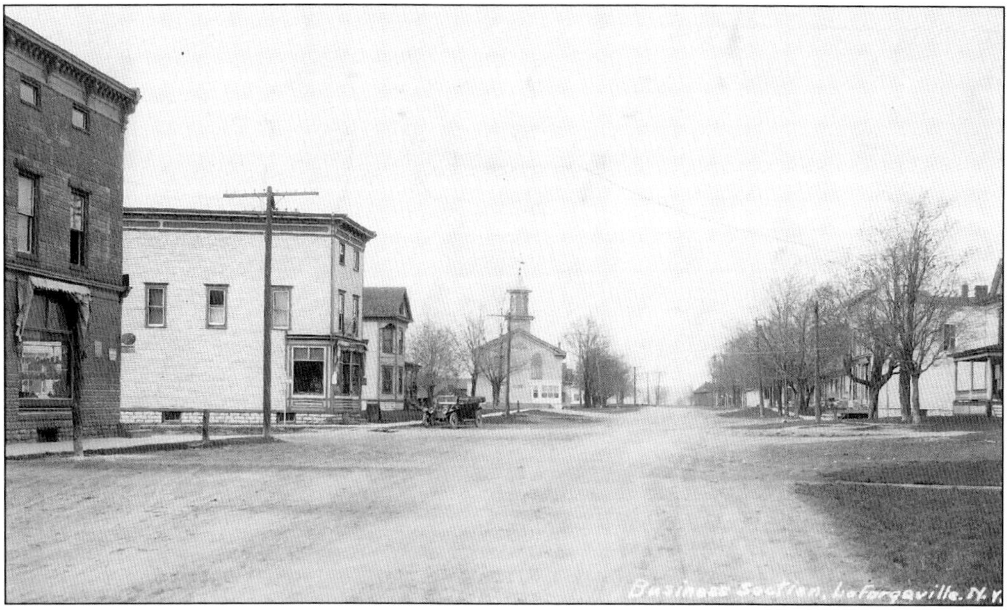

LaFargeville, business section, *c.* 1915. Reuben Andrus settled in the area now known as LaFargeville in 1816. Several other pioneers joined him in the early years, and they built taverns, sawmills, a distillery, and a store. It was not until 1823 that a French mercantilist, John LaFarge, purchased much of the land known today as LaFargeville.

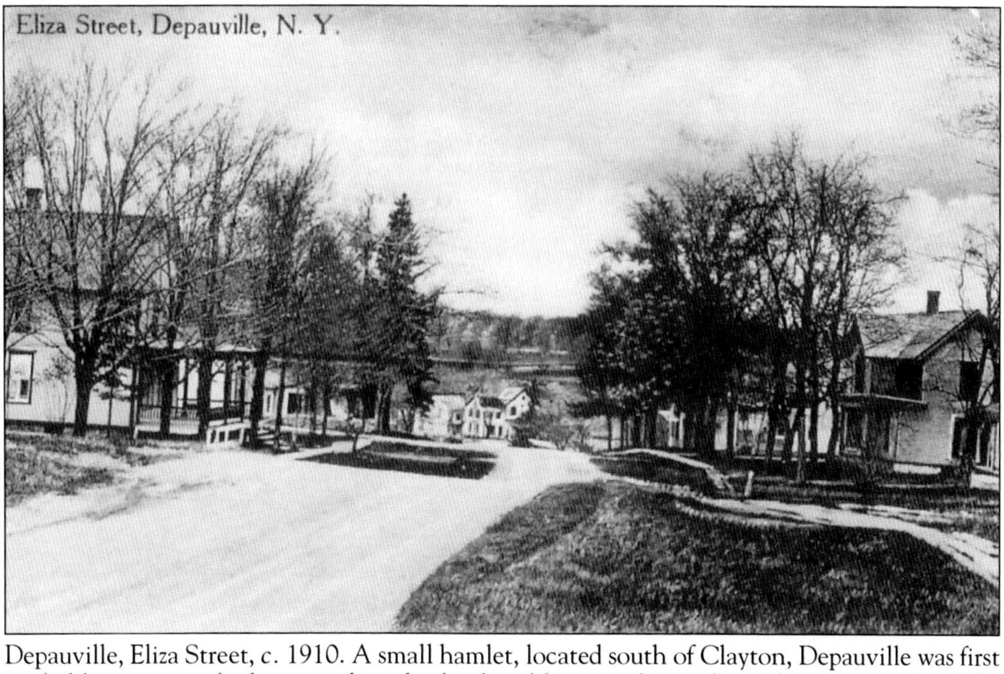

Depauville, Eliza Street, *c.* 1910. A small hamlet, located south of Clayton, Depauville was first settled by squatters looking to clear the land and harvest the timber. They soon utilized the waterpower generated by the Chaumont River, or Catfish Creek, which consequently became the name synonymous with the area.

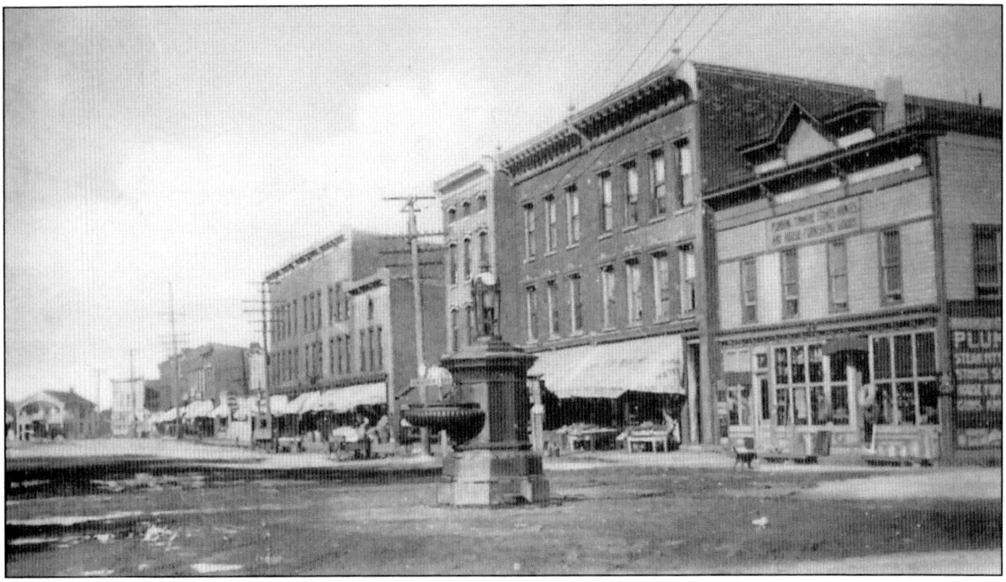

Clayton, Main Street, c. 1905. Located on the St. Lawrence River, Clayton remains a popular spot for summer vacationers and locals alike.

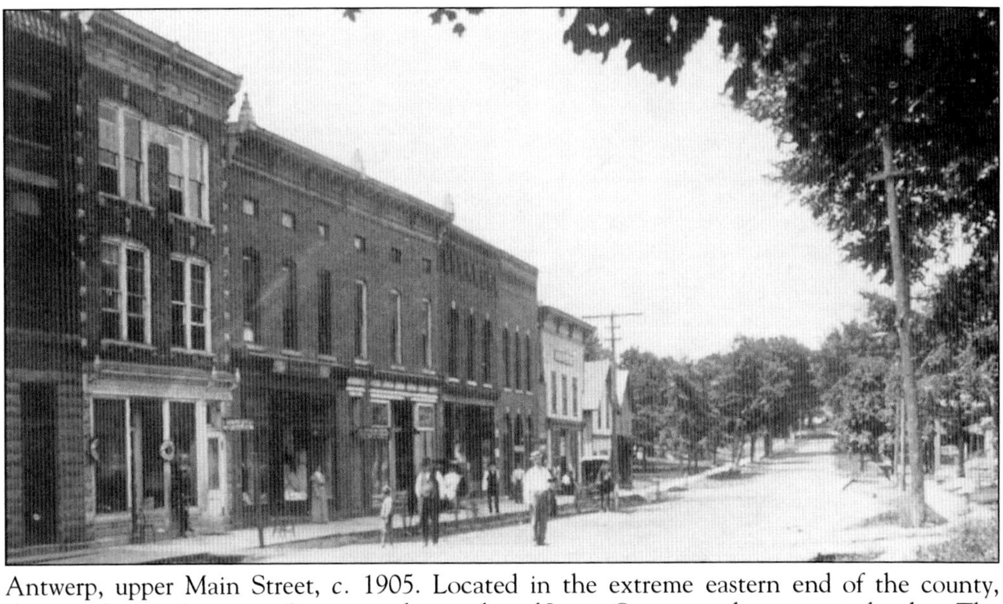

Antwerp, upper Main Street, c. 1905. Located in the extreme eastern end of the county, Antwerp has St. Lawrence County to the north and Lewis County to the east as its borders. The town had rich deposits of limestone and iron ore that were mined in the mid-1800s. Iron ore mining quickly became the biggest commercial industry in the history of the town.

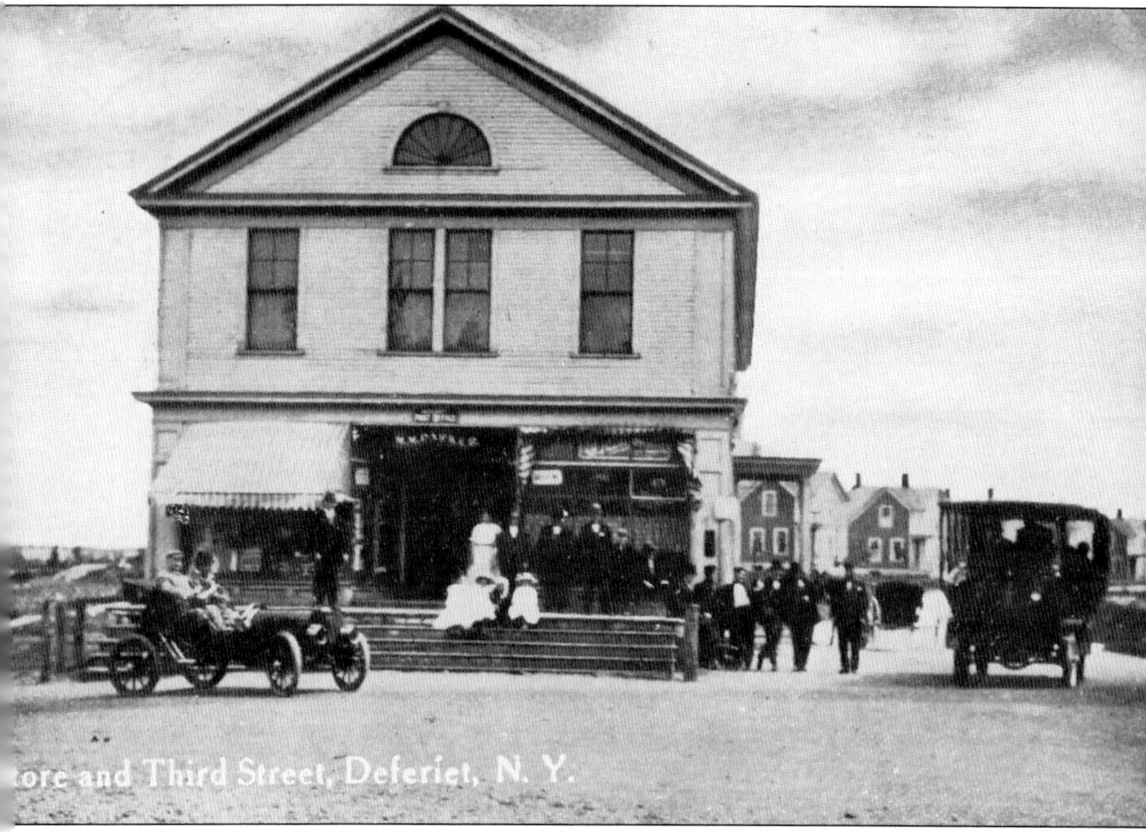

Deferiet, Third Street, *c.* 1915. At one time Deferiet was truly a company town. When the St. Regis Paper Company began production of paper in 1911, almost all those who lived in the town worked at the factory. The company owned many of the homes where the workers resided. The store of M.M. Park & Company served the needs of everyone living in the community.

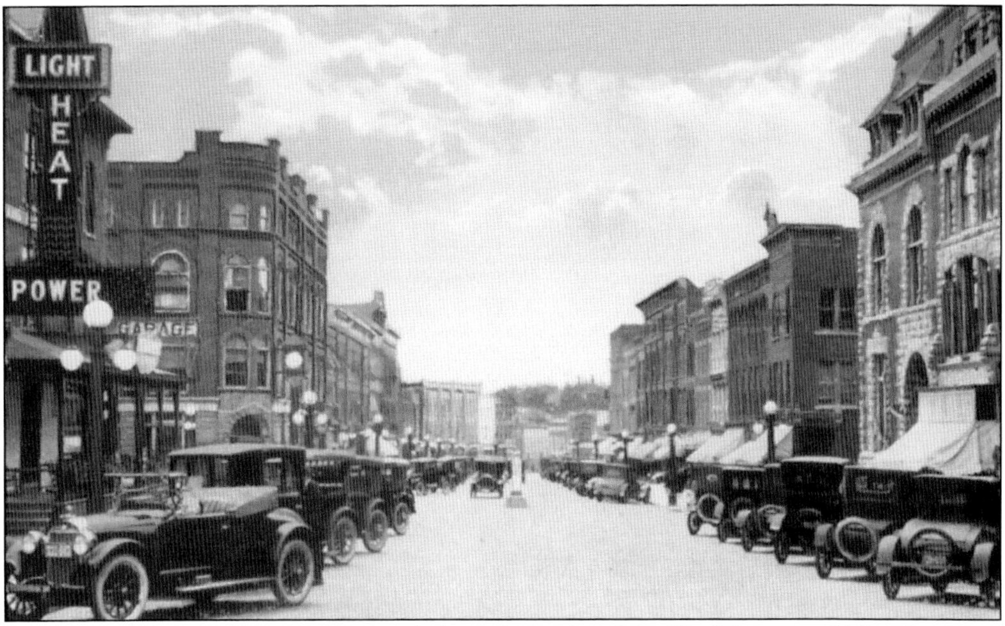

Carthage, State Street, c. 1920. Located along the banks of the Black River and 16 miles east of Watertown, Carthage became the hub of railway traffic. The lines of the Rome, Watertown & Ogdensburg and Carthage & Adirondack railways all intersected in the town.

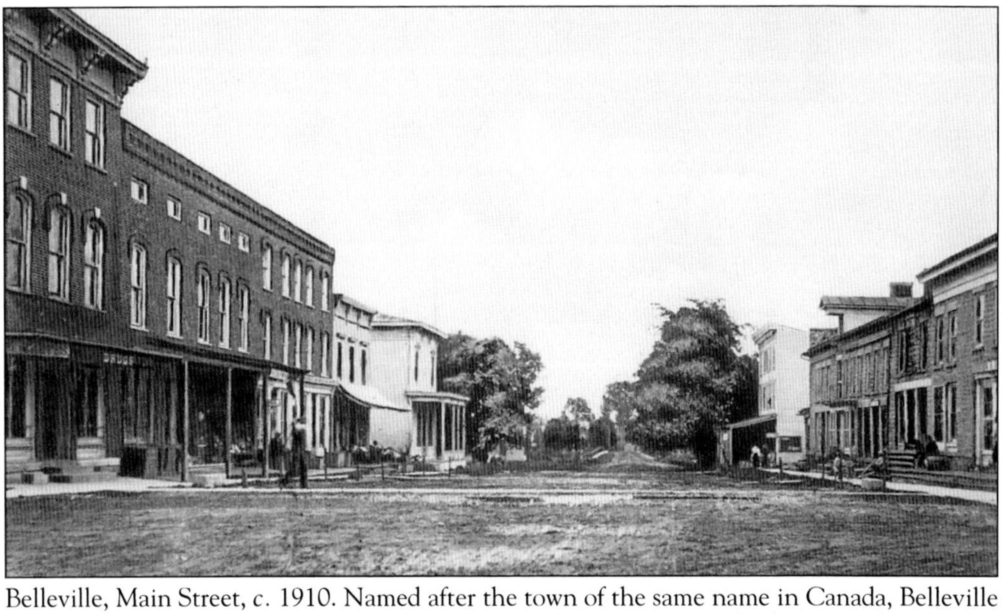

Belleville, Main Street, c. 1910. Named after the town of the same name in Canada, Belleville became one of the most desirable places to live in Jefferson County. The limestone building on the right was built in the early 1800s. It was the home of many different activities, including a bakery, tinsmith shop, village jail, harness store, lawyer's office, post office, and ice cream parlor, before being torn down.

Two

Business and Industry

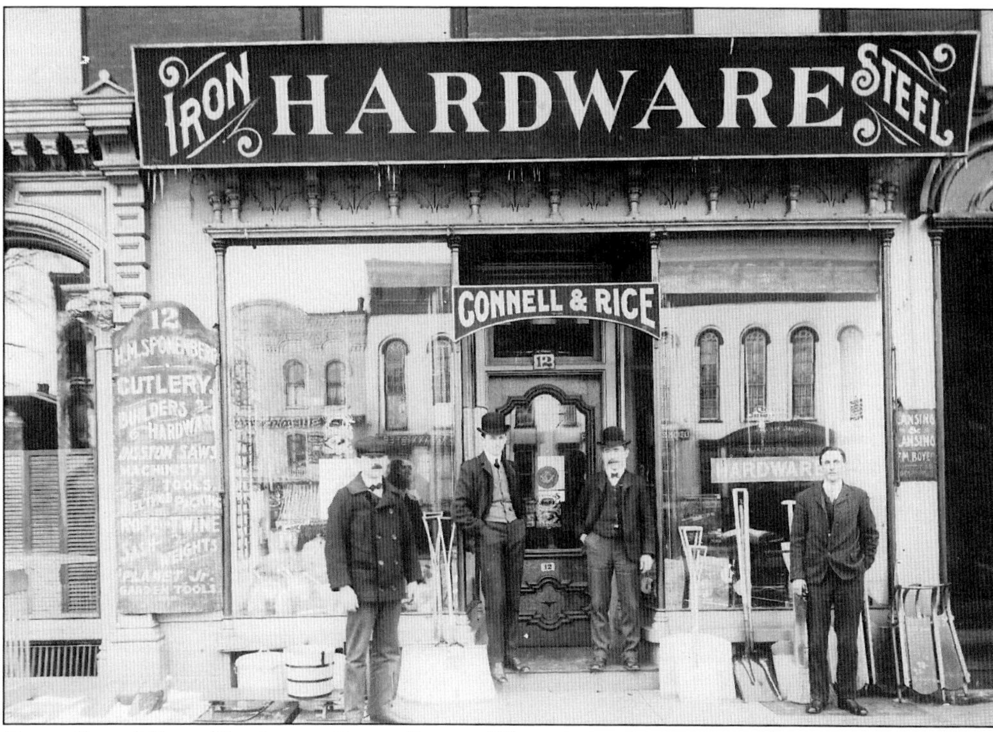

Connell and Rice Hardware, Court Street, Watertown. Located in the center of thriving downtown Watertown in the late 1800s, Connell and Rice were mercantilists dealing with hardware, paints, and tools.

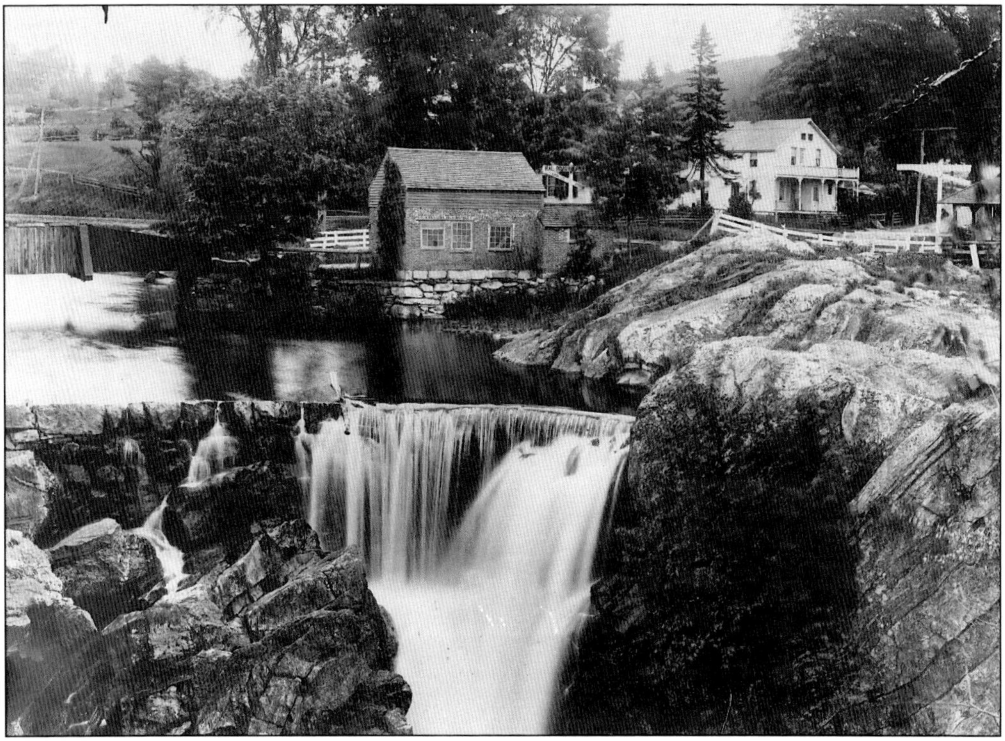

Sarden's Mill, Redwood. Fine glass wasn't the only product made in Redwood in the 1800s, the town also had a proliferation of sawmills and gristmills. Sarden's Mill was located in Redwood, below Cottage Hill.

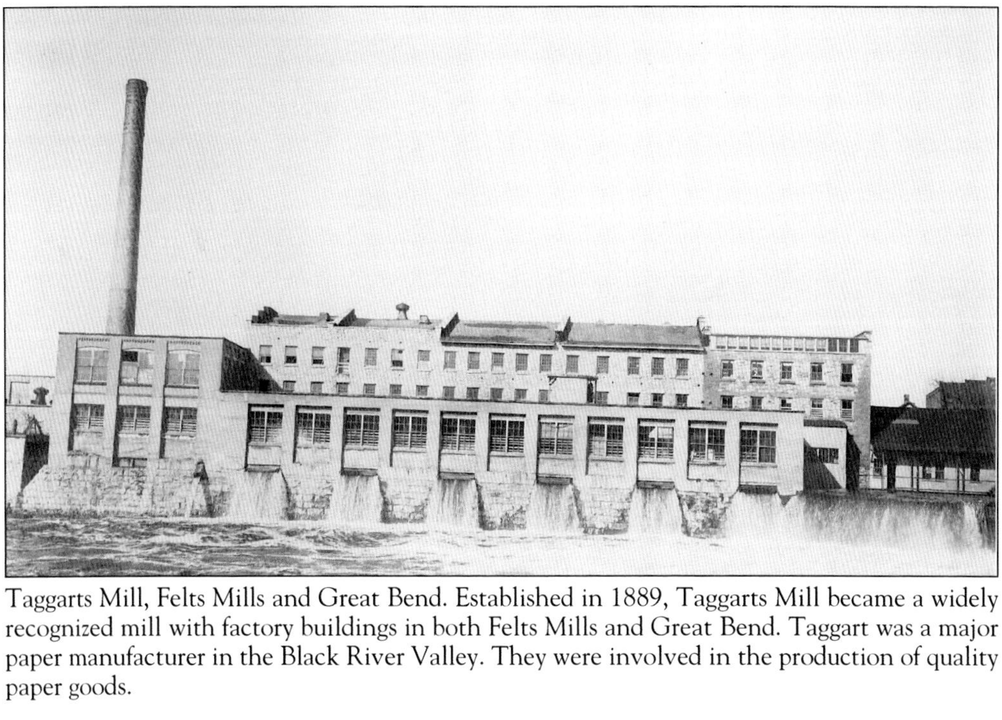

Taggarts Mill, Felts Mills and Great Bend. Established in 1889, Taggarts Mill became a widely recognized mill with factory buildings in both Felts Mills and Great Bend. Taggart was a major paper manufacturer in the Black River Valley. They were involved in the production of quality paper goods.

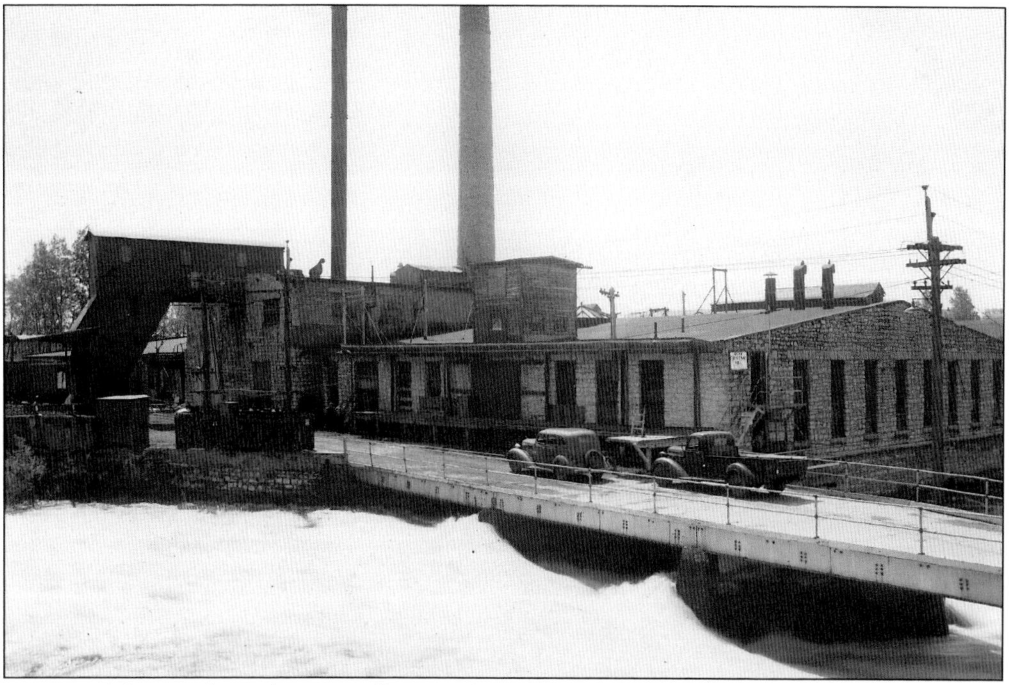

Dexter sulphite, pulp, and paper mill. Considered one of the most extensive industrial plants in the region, the company was incorporated in 1887. It obtained much of its wood from Canada and would send its products (mostly newsprint) throughout the United States.

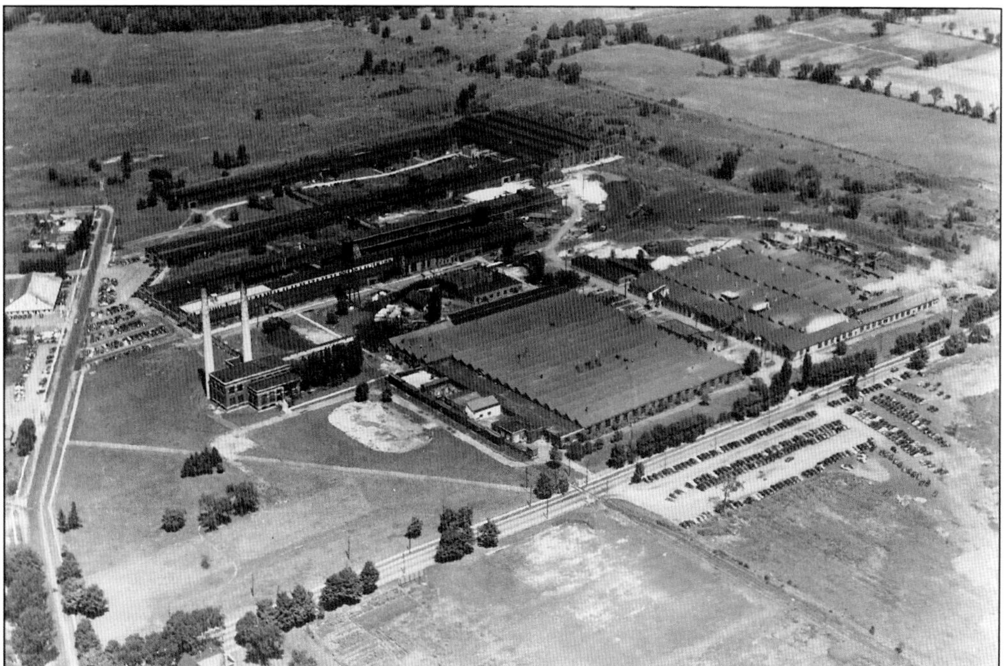

New York Air Brake, Watertown. This important manufacturing center, originally known as the Eames Vacuum Brake Company, manufactured railway power brakes and appliances for the nation's railroad cars.

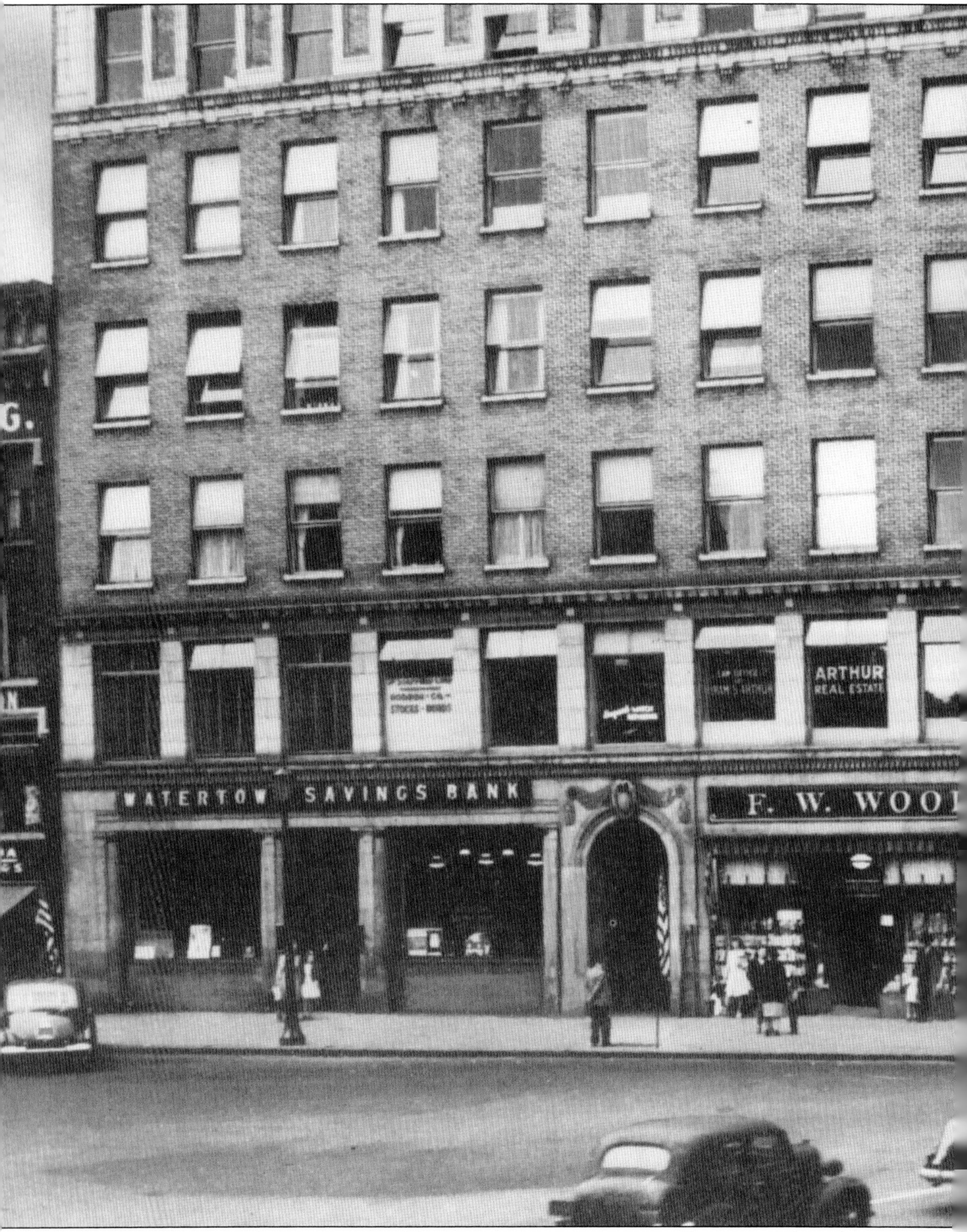

Woolworth 5 and 10¢ store, Public Square, Watertown. Frank W. Woolworth and his conception of the "five and dime" store originated in Watertown. Woolworth set up a small table with nickel and dime items in 1878 within the store of his employer at the time, W.H.

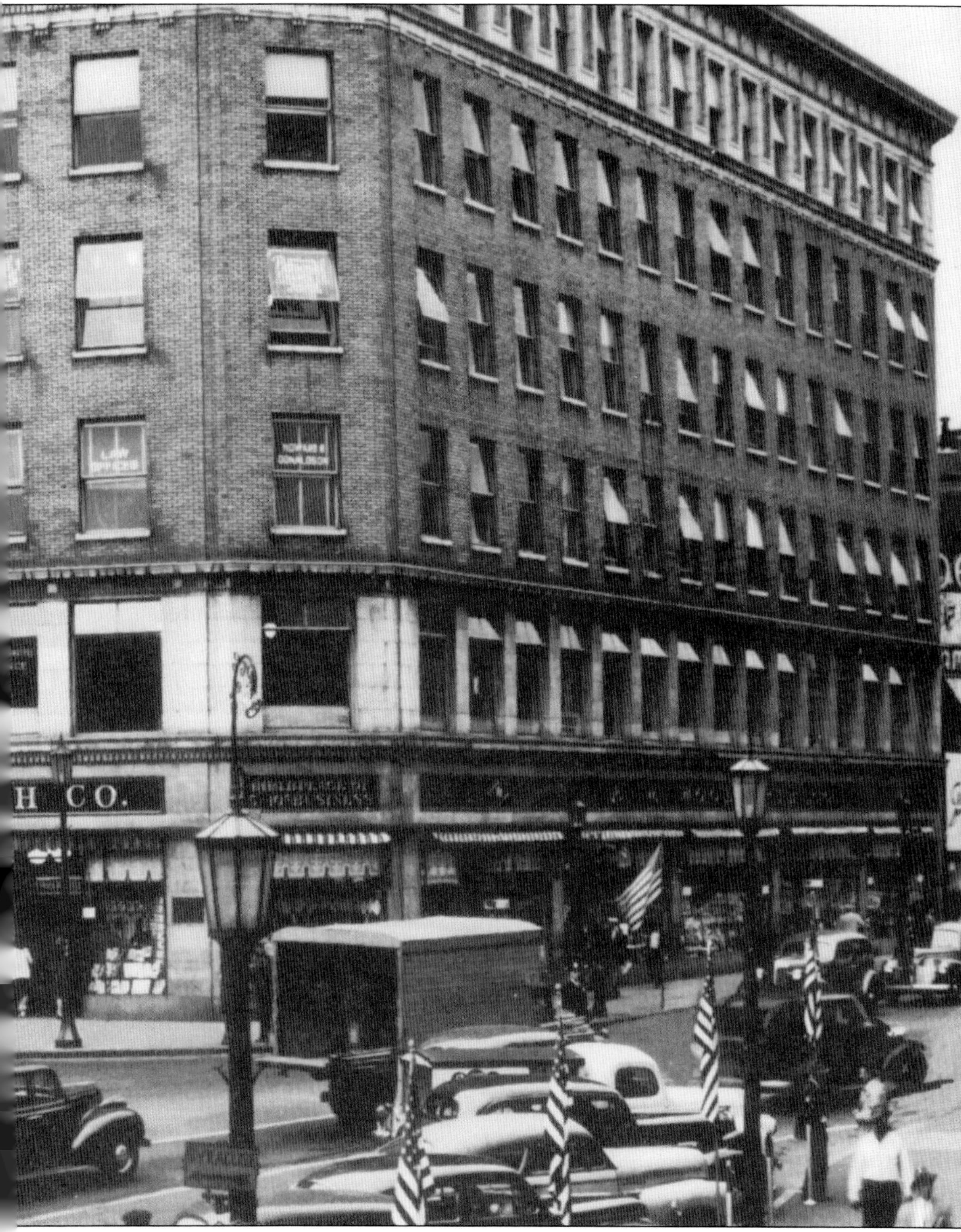

Moore. The popularity of this table, with 5 and 10¢ items, inspired Woolworth to start his own business, which soon became nationally known.

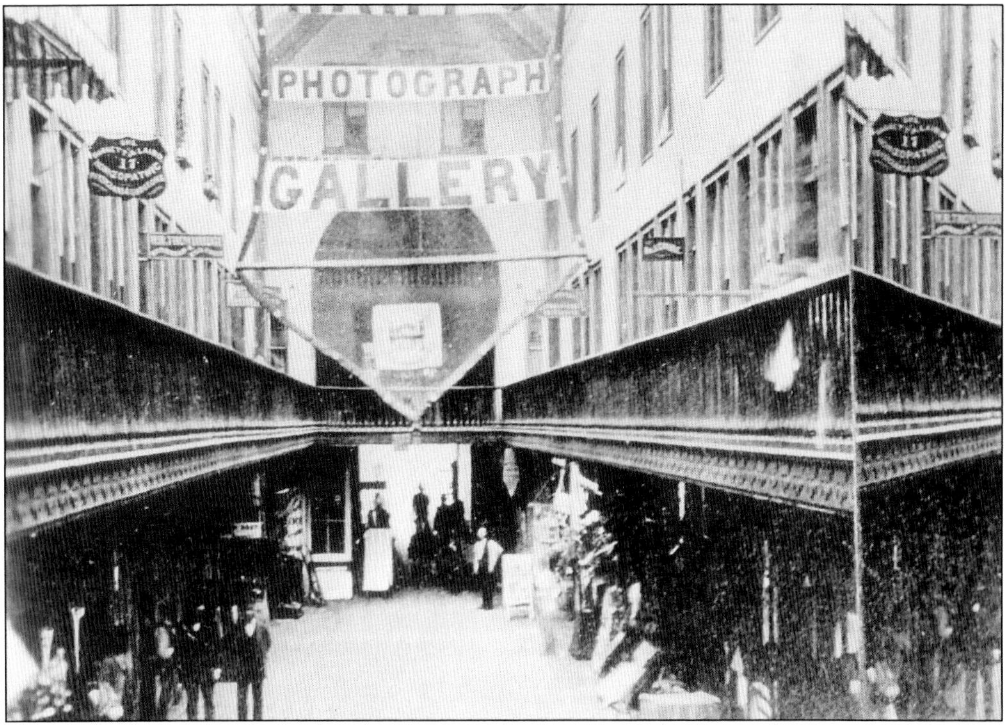

The Paddock Arcade, Public Square, Watertown. Built in 1850 and known as the glass-covered street because of its elegant amber-colored glass ceiling, the Paddock Arcade is the oldest continuously-run covered mall of its kind in the country. The Paddock Arcade was built for $15,000 by Loveland Paddock, a mercantilist and president of the Black River National Bank. It was the site of the first telephone office for the city of Watertown and was quite an elaborate and popular structure.

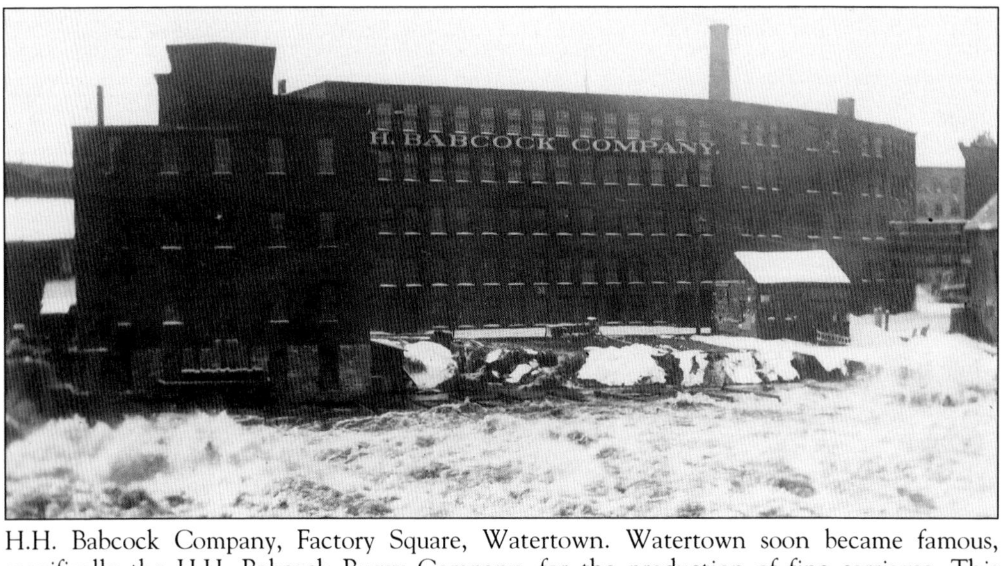

H.H. Babcock Company, Factory Square, Watertown. Watertown soon became famous, specifically the H.H. Babcock Buggy Company, for the production of fine carriages. This business started in 1845 making water pumps and windmills. The company later evolved into the production of automobiles in the early 1900s.

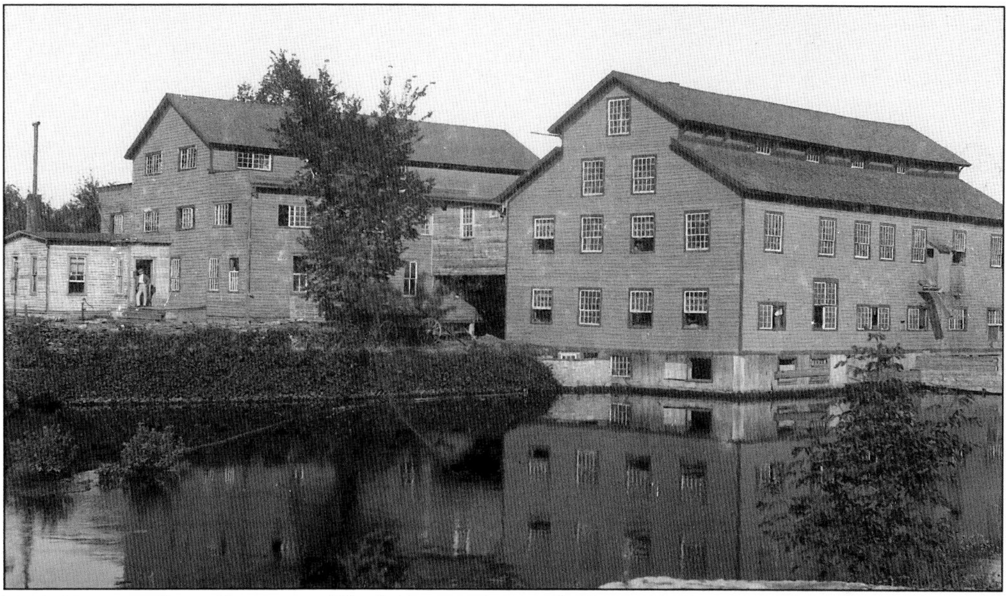

H.C. Dexter Chair Company, Black River. Originally known as Poor, Dexter & Company in 1881, the name was changed to H.C. Dexter Chair Company in 1890. A number of buildings on either side of the Black River housed factories involved in the making of fine dining chairs, fancy chairs, and rockers.

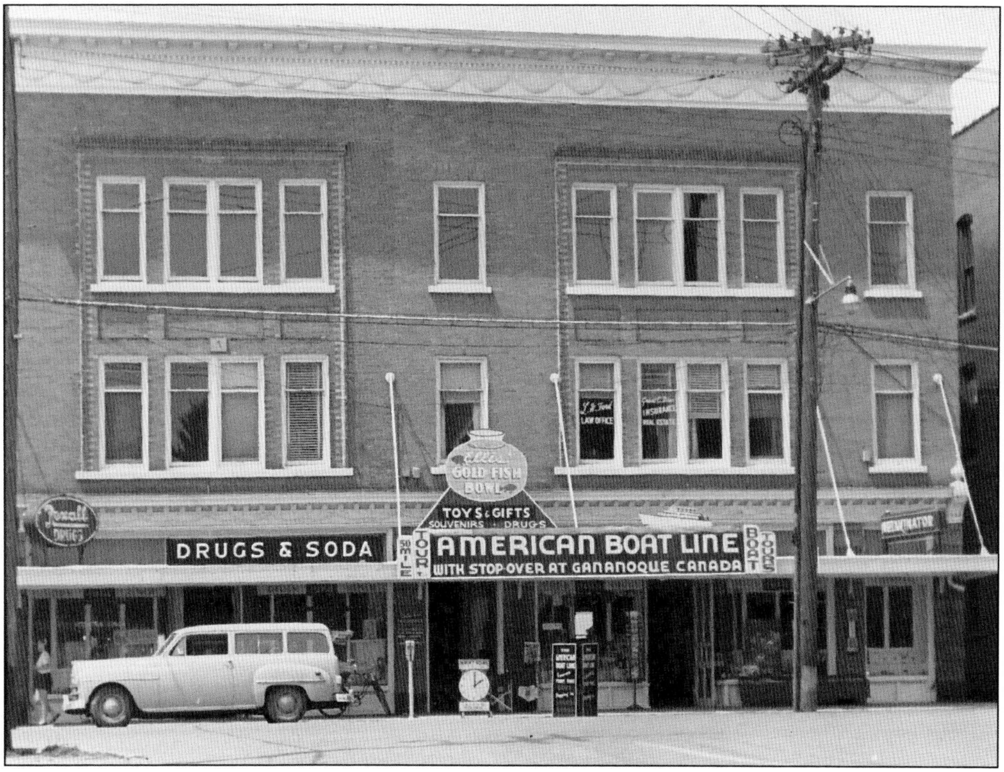

Ellis' Goldfish Bowl, Clayton. A variety store located in the center of the town, Ellis' Goldfish Bowl sold everything from souvenirs to boat tickets for trips through the Thousand Islands.

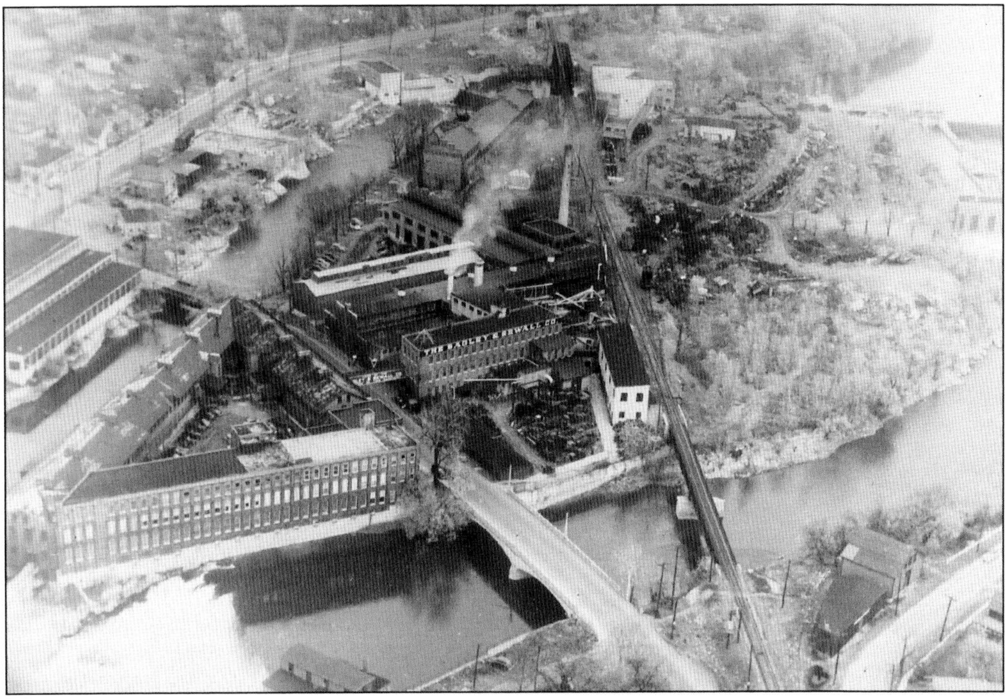

Bagley and Sewell Company, Watertown. A company started by George Goulding in 1823, Bagley and Sewell were manufacturers of everything required in the production of paper and pulp mill machinery as well as general founders and machinists. The entire manufacturing process from this industry was originally powered by the mighty Black River.

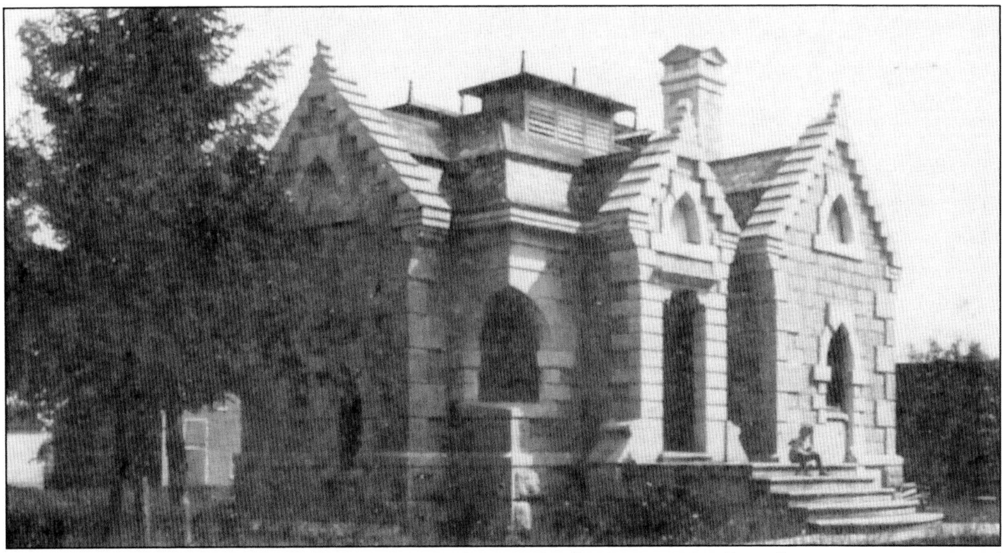

The Copley office building, Chaumont. Built in 1872 by Hirum Copley, the structure was used as the headquarters for the family's lumber and limestone business. Copley had many interests in addition to his quarry business, for he was the Chaumont village president and was also instrumental in the establishment of the Alexandria Bay Steamboat Company. The building was later acquired by Adams and Duford, another limestone business that used the structure as office space.

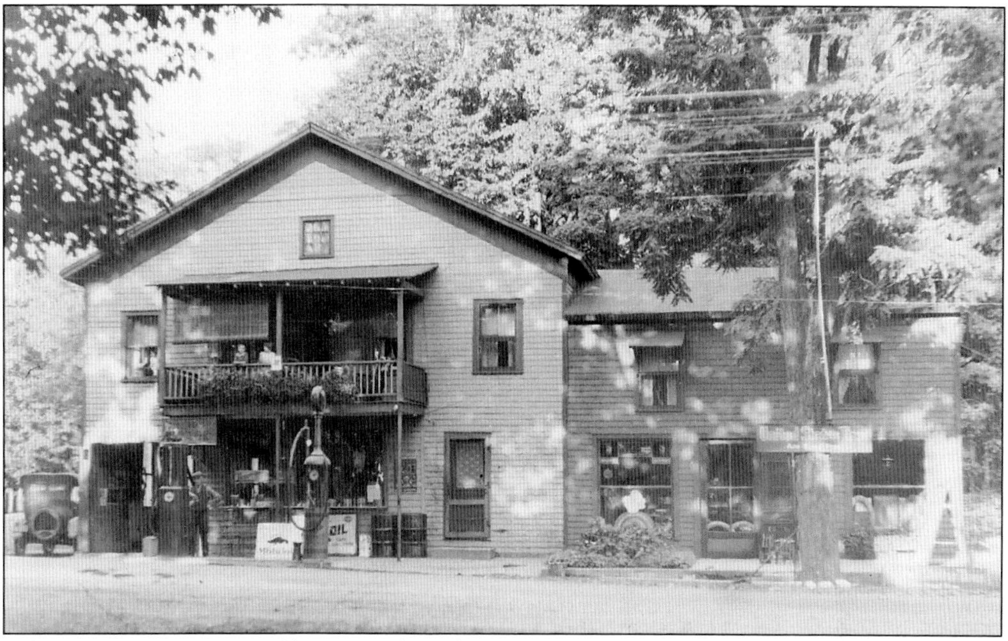

Gibeau Garage, Mannsville. Owned and operated by Charles B. Gibeau, this garage in Mannsville was an important stop for any new car owner in the 1920s. As the horse and buggy popularity was replaced by gasoline-powered automobiles, this garage became a necessity. Gibeau also owned a hotel in Mannsville.

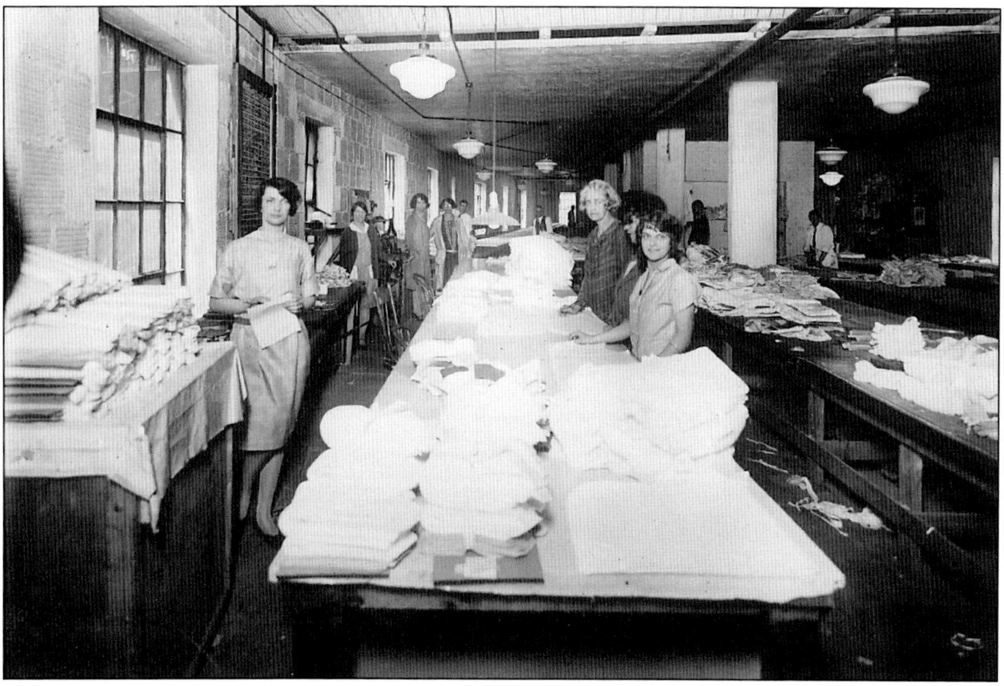

Sweetser Shirt Company. In the late 1920s and early 1930s, Watertown was bustling with shirt manufacturers. The Sweetser Shirt Company, located in the Buck Building on State Street, employed two hundred young women.

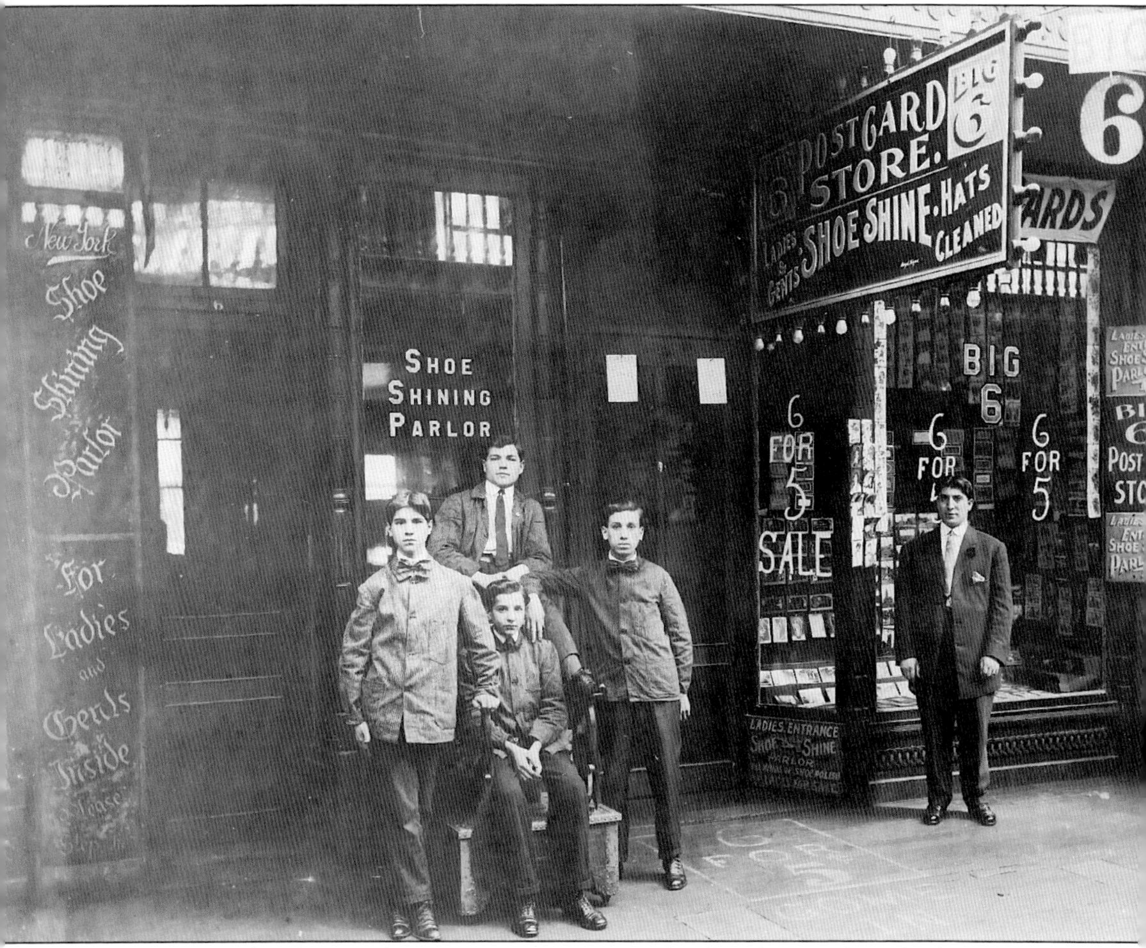

The Big Six shoeshine parlor, Watertown, *c.* 1906. This shoeshine parlor, which was commonly called the Big Six because of the six postcards for the price of five that you could buy while having your shoes shined, was located in the Paddock Arcade. It was owned and operated by Frank Anthony Bonadio. Bonadio went from being a barefoot, penniless newspaper-boy to a wealthy businessman partly because of his motto: "modern methods win." His shoeshine parlor was furnished with the most modern-day machinery.

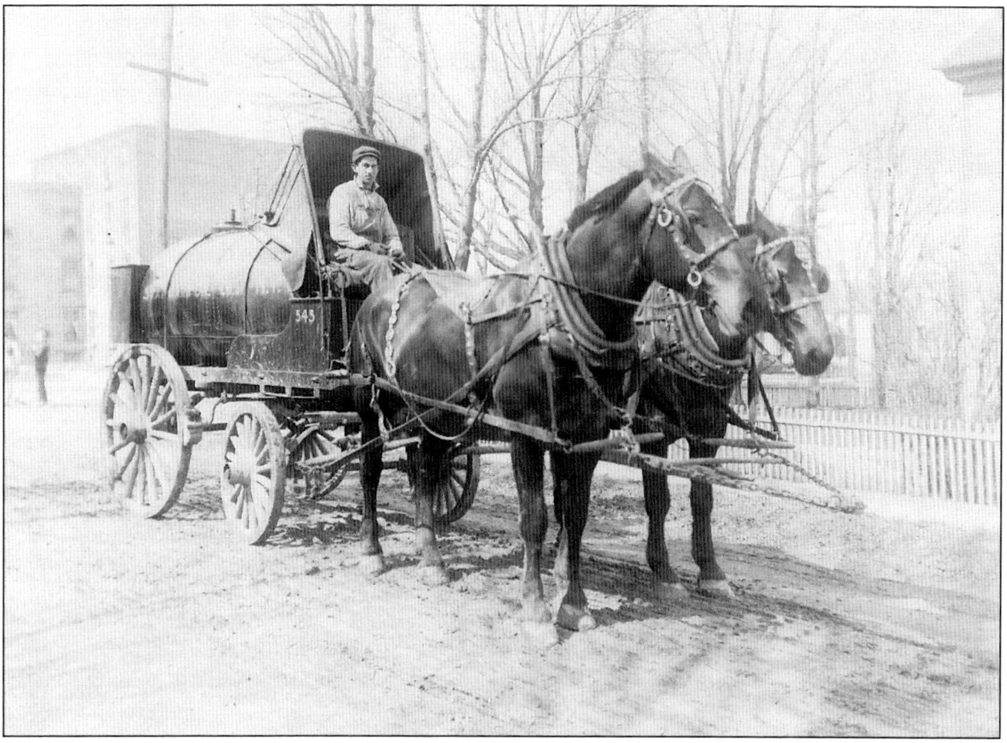

Brownell's Oil Delivery Company, *c.* 1910. Specifically known for his delivery of kerosene, Burt Brownell (seated) furnished the gas that kept the homes of Watertown illuminated. Later in his career, Brownell's oil delivery became part of Standard Oil Company.

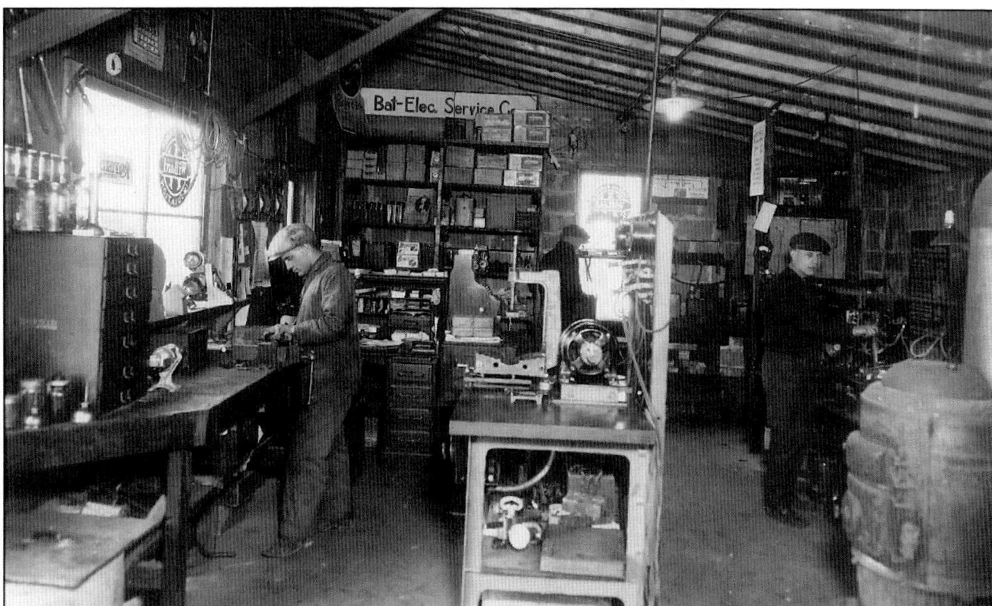

Parson's and Sweeney Battery Shop, Watertown, *c.* 1923. Located on High Street in the city of Watertown, Parson's and Sweeney Battery Shop sold and repaired batteries for the local residents.

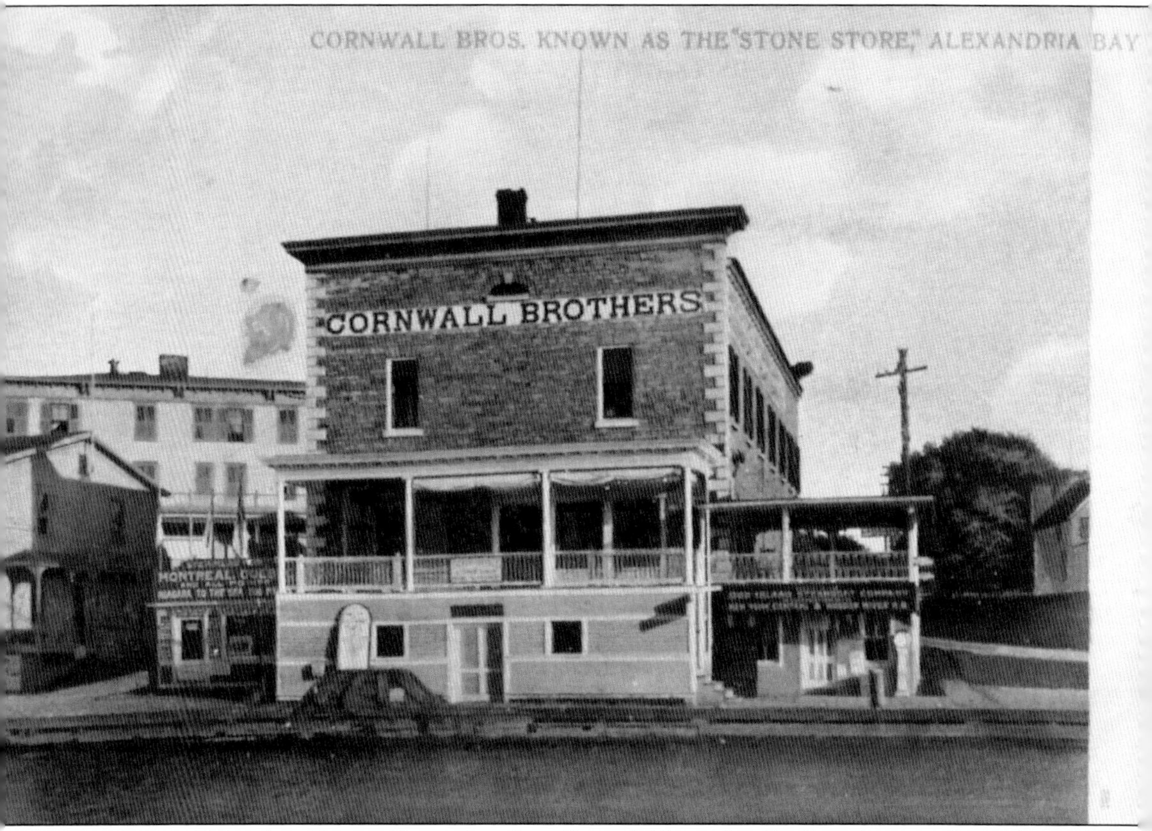

Cornwall Brothers Store, Alexandria Bay. One of Alexandria Bay's earliest settlers, Alexander Cornwall went into business with Lyman A. Walton operating a general store on the upper wharf. Later on, Cornwall Brothers was established to include Alexander's sons in the business. Cornwall Brothers became the largest and best known store in northern Jefferson County. The store is now the site of the Alexandria Township Historical Society.

Three

Public Parks and Buildings

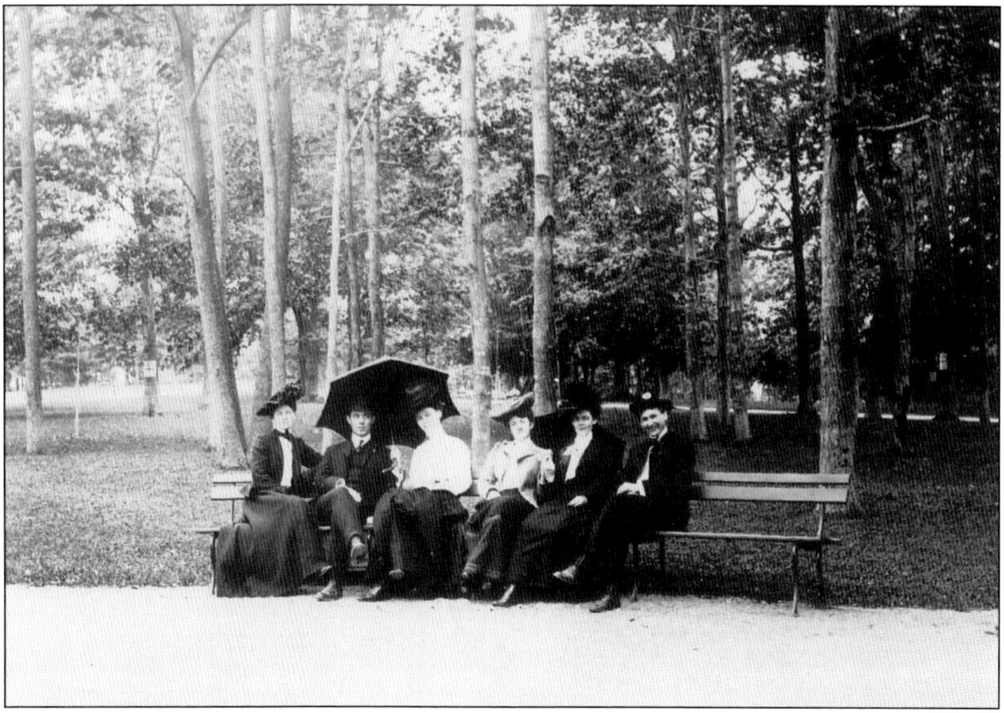

Thompson Park, Watertown. Early in the twentieth century, the New York Air Brake Company's John C. Thompson gave Watertown the land for a municipal park. Thompson Park was designed by the noted authority of landscape-architecture at the time, John C. Olmsted. The Olmsted family were better known as the designers of Central Park in New York City and the Emerald Necklace of Boston, Massachusetts.

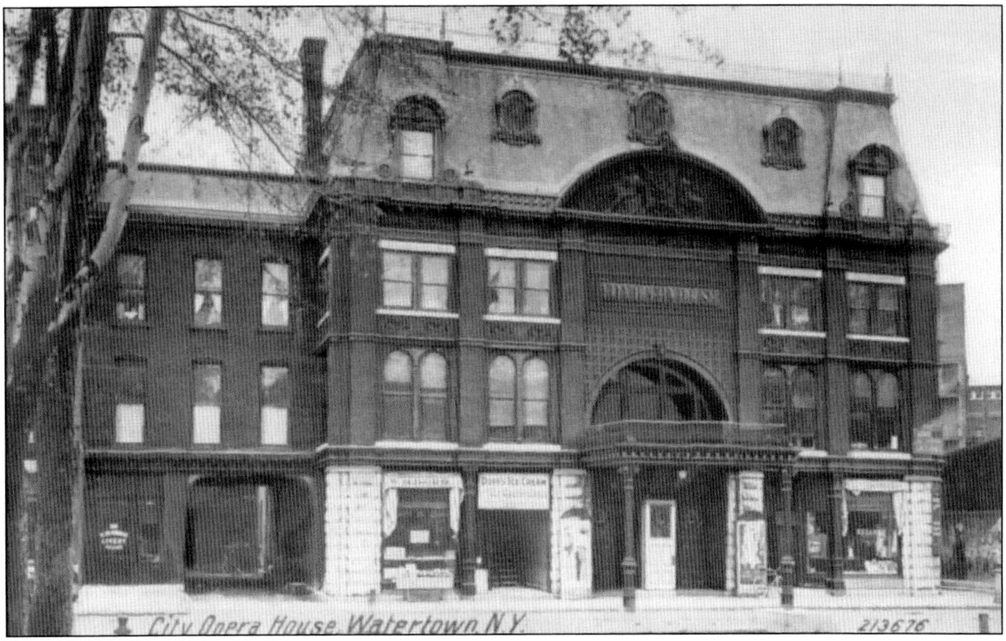

City Opera House, Watertown. The City Opera House opened to the public on January 4, 1886. It was known to be one of the finest theaters in the country for a city of Watertown's size.

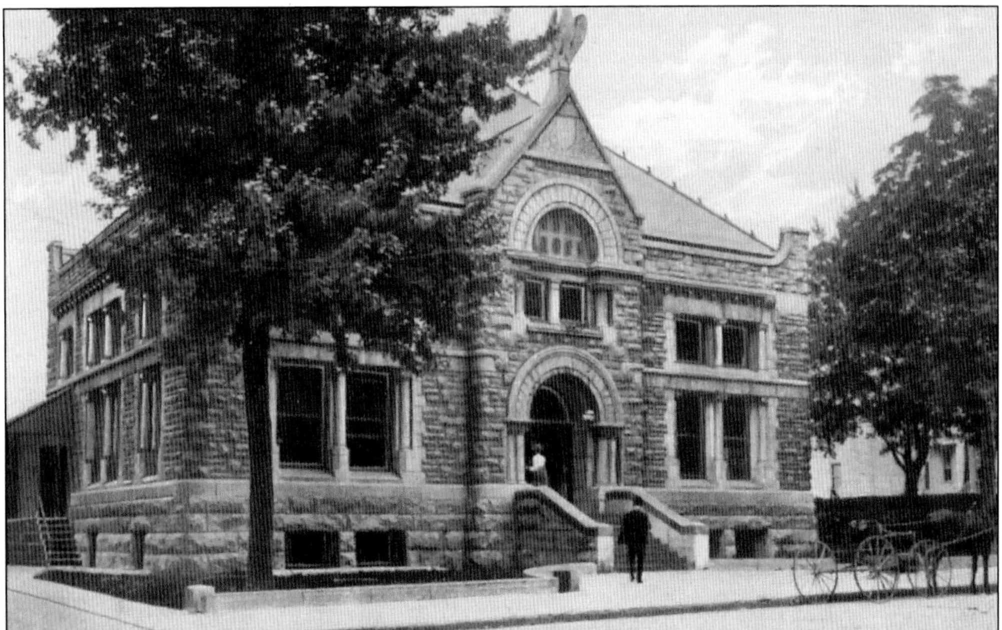

Watertown Post Office, Watertown. Prior to the construction of this post office in 1892, the location of the post office would often change with each appointment of a new postmaster.

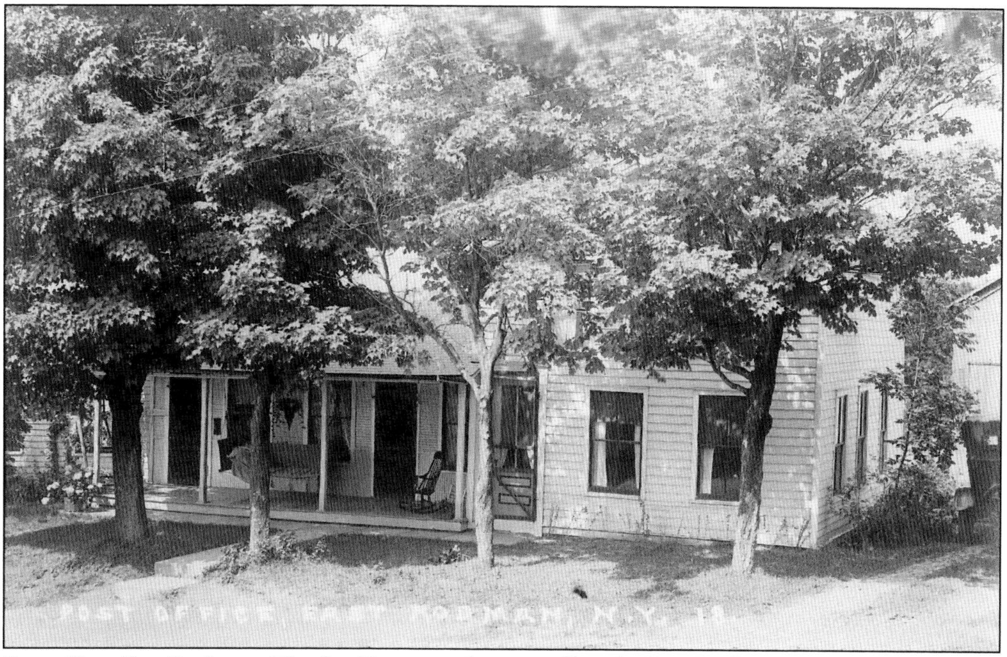

Post office, East Rodman. This building was the post office for East Rodman from 1840 to 1926.

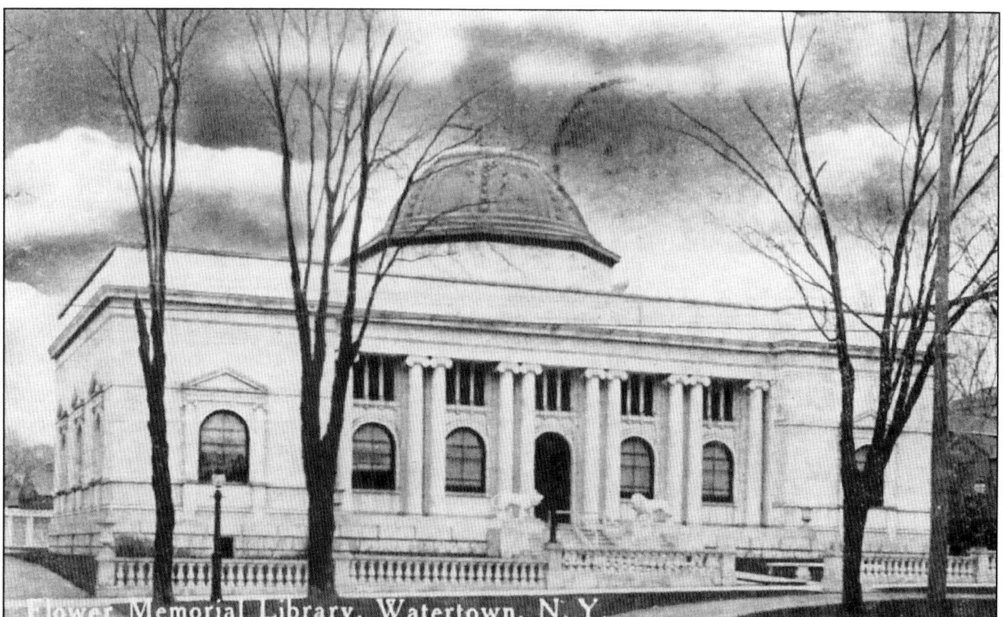

Flower Memorial Library, Watertown. In memory of her father, Governor Roswell P. Flower, Emma Flower Taylor had this beautiful library built on Washington Street in 1903.

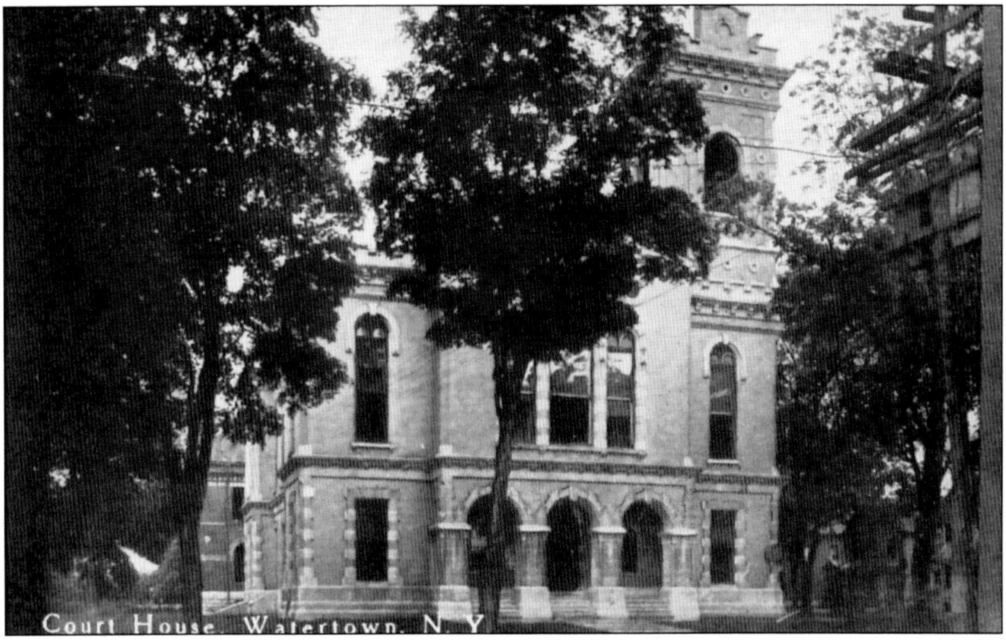

Jefferson County Courthouse, Watertown. Situated on what was once spacious grounds, the courthouse, enclosed by a handsome iron fence, was erected in 1862 at a cost of $50,000.

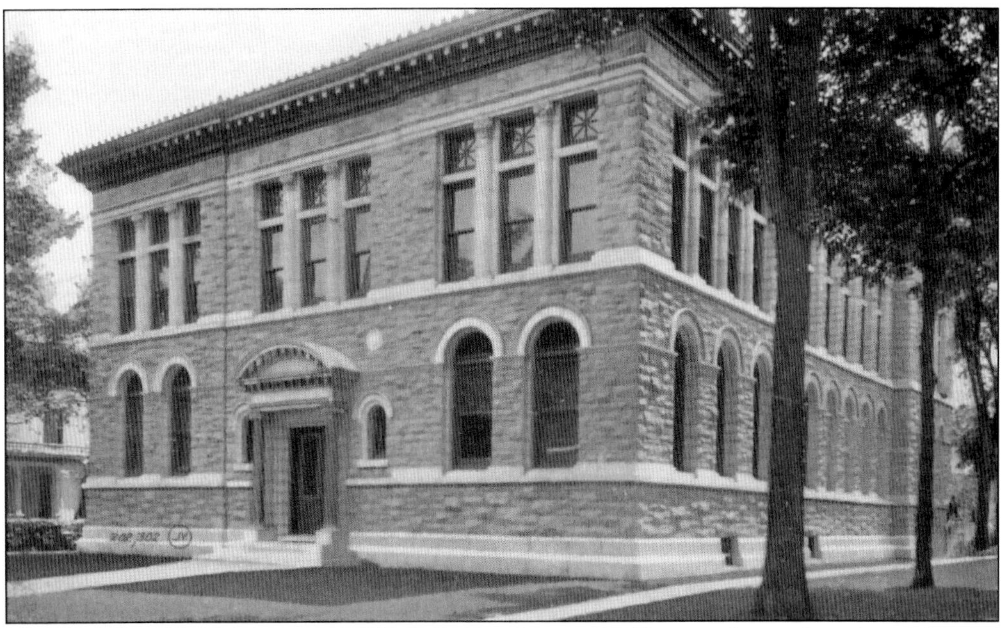

The county building, Watertown. The Jefferson County Building was located on Arsenal Street between the county courthouse and the residence of Governor Roswell P. Flower.

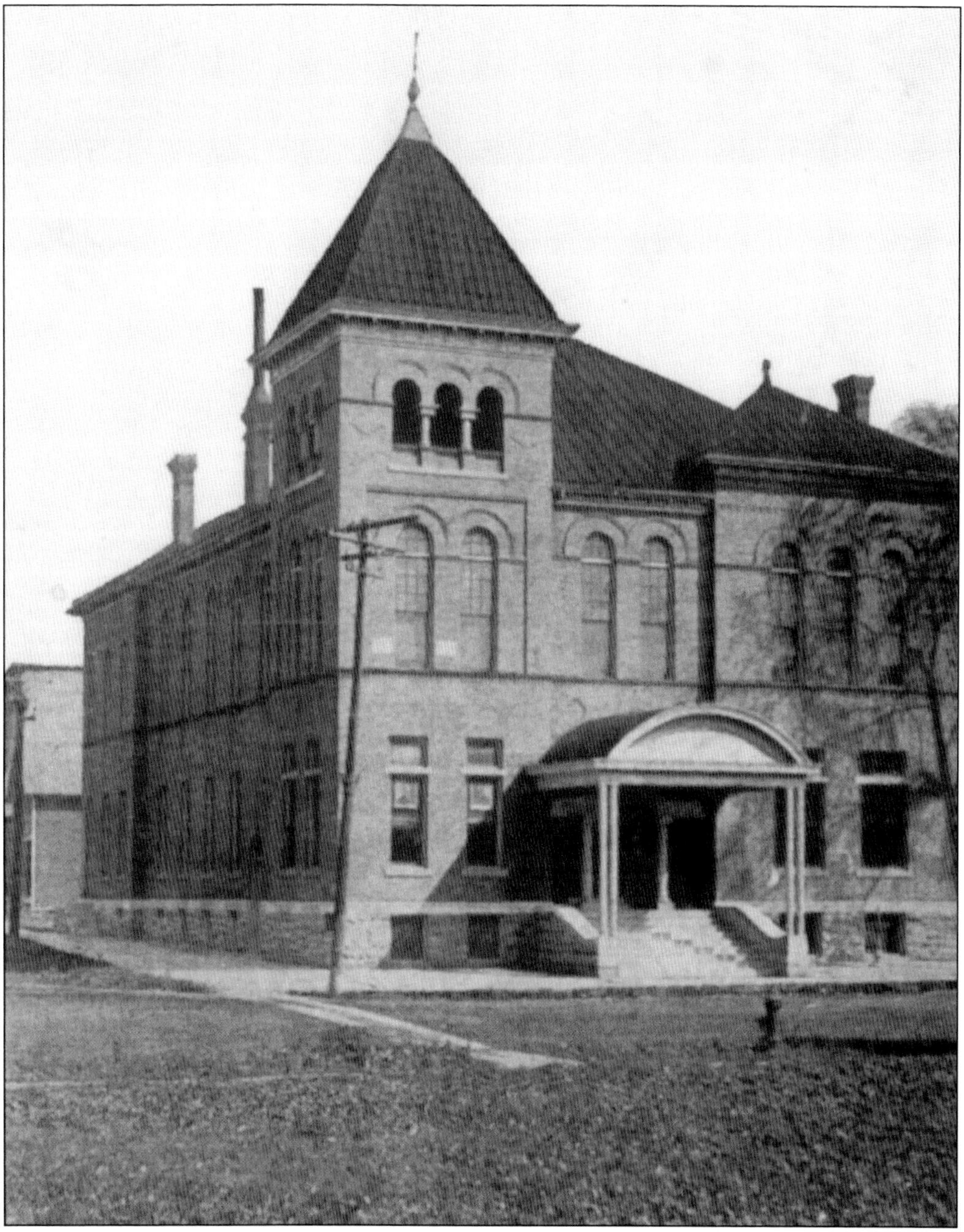

Town Hall, Antwerp. Located in the northernmost portion of Jefferson County, the village of Antwerp was first settled in 1804 by General Lewis R. Morris. The building celebrated its one hundredth birthday in 1997.

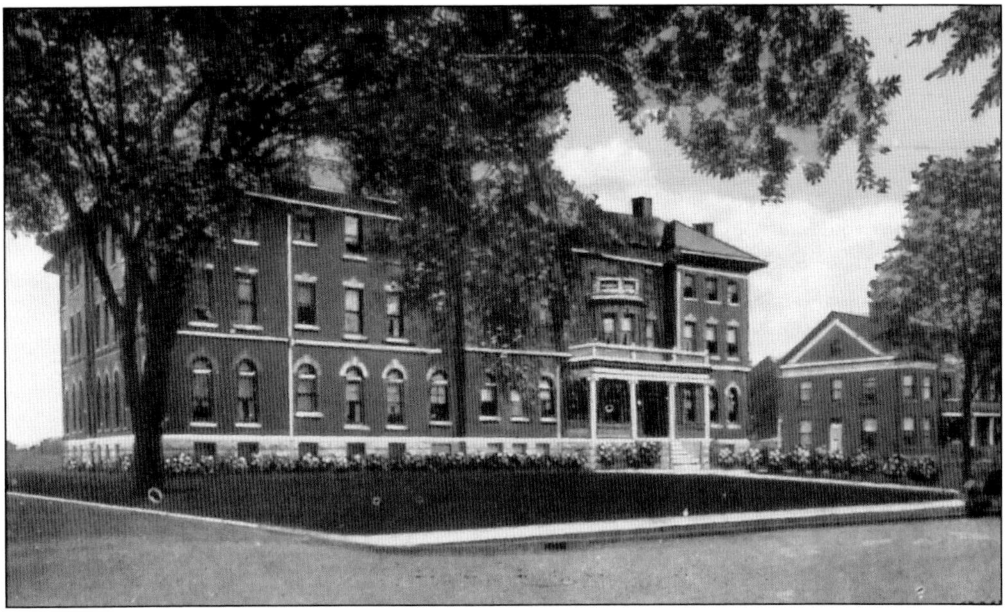

City hospital, Watertown. The hospital was established in 1881 under the auspices of the Trinity Church and Grace Church. Today, the original building is part of a larger complex known as the Samaritan Medical Center.

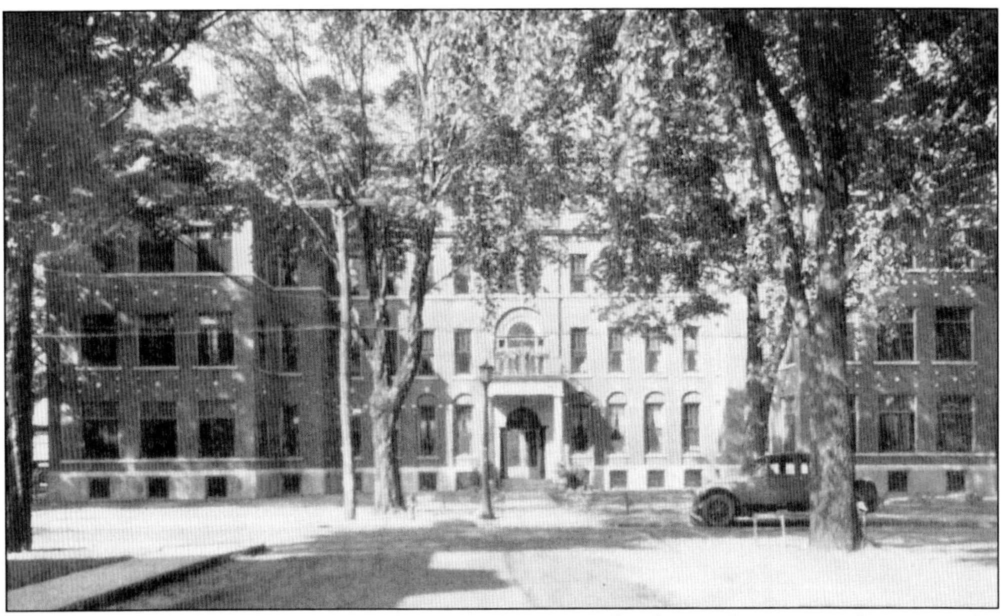

Mercy Hospital, Watertown. Located on Stone Street, this hospital was once known as St. Joachim's Hospital.

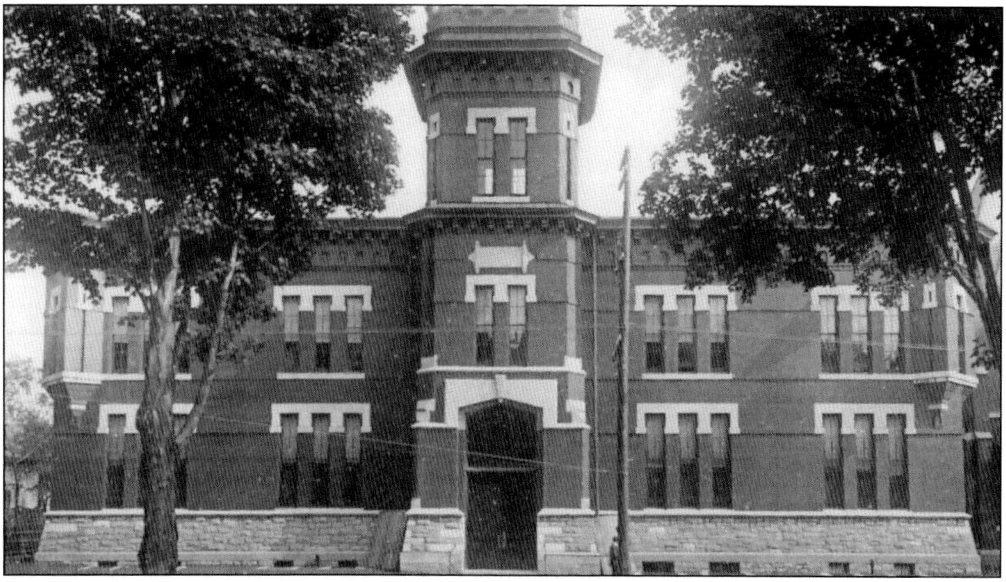

Armory, Watertown. First built in 1809, Watertown's armory was located on Arsenal Street. At the time, the site of the armory consisted of dense forests and few dwellings. The building was constructed at a cost of $1,940.99. A portion of the ammunition located in Utica was transferred to Watertown following the armory's completion. The building pictured here was erected in later years to replace the original.

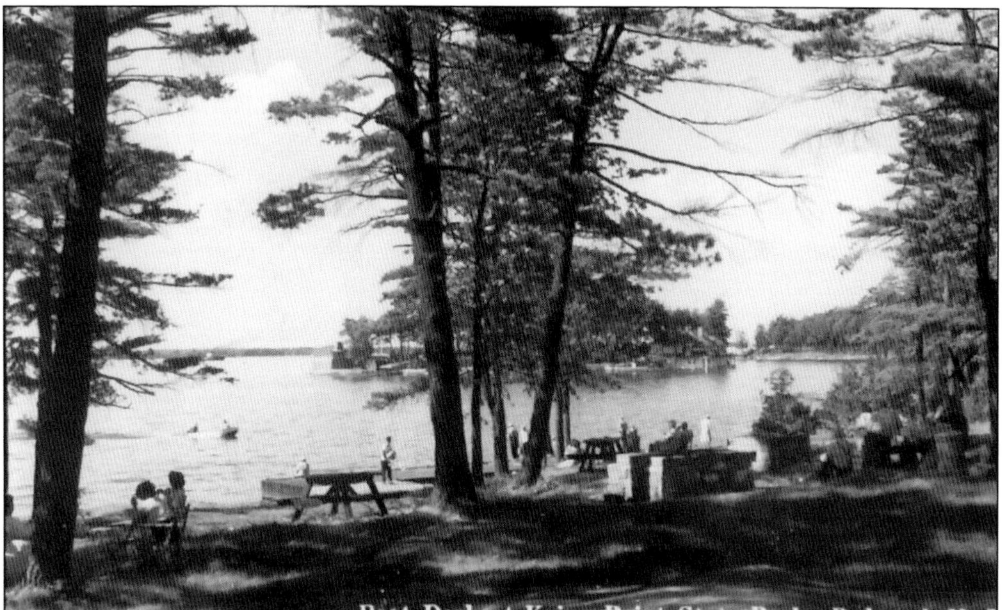

Kring Point State Park, Redwood. Kring Point State Park was a place of recreation and leisure. A popular spot to launch the boat, picnic, or swim, the park offered hours of entertainment for all.

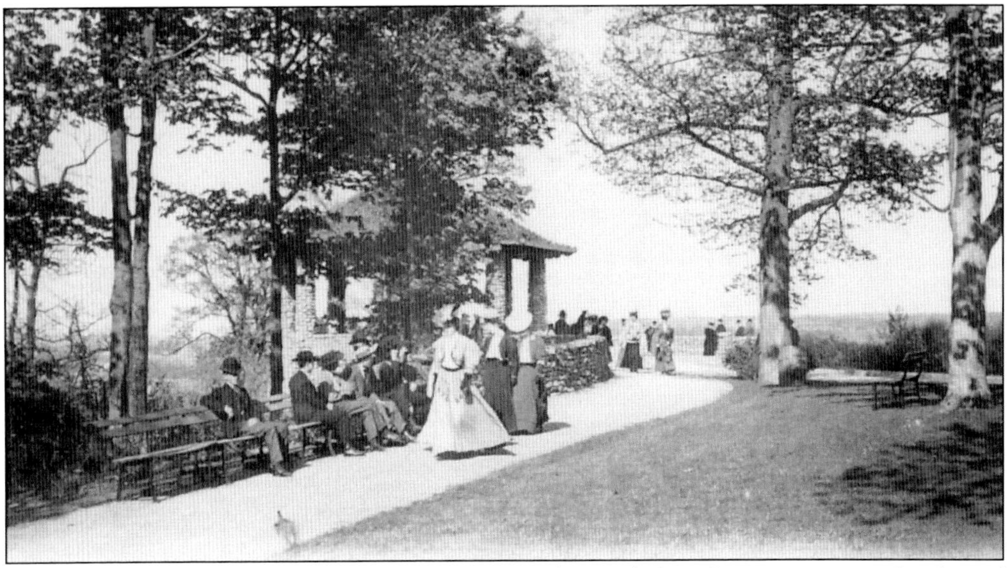

Thompson Park, Watertown. A popular spot to gather with friends or just sit in solitude and enjoy the panoramic vistas of the county, Thompson Park continues to be a place of enjoyment today as it did in the early 1900s.

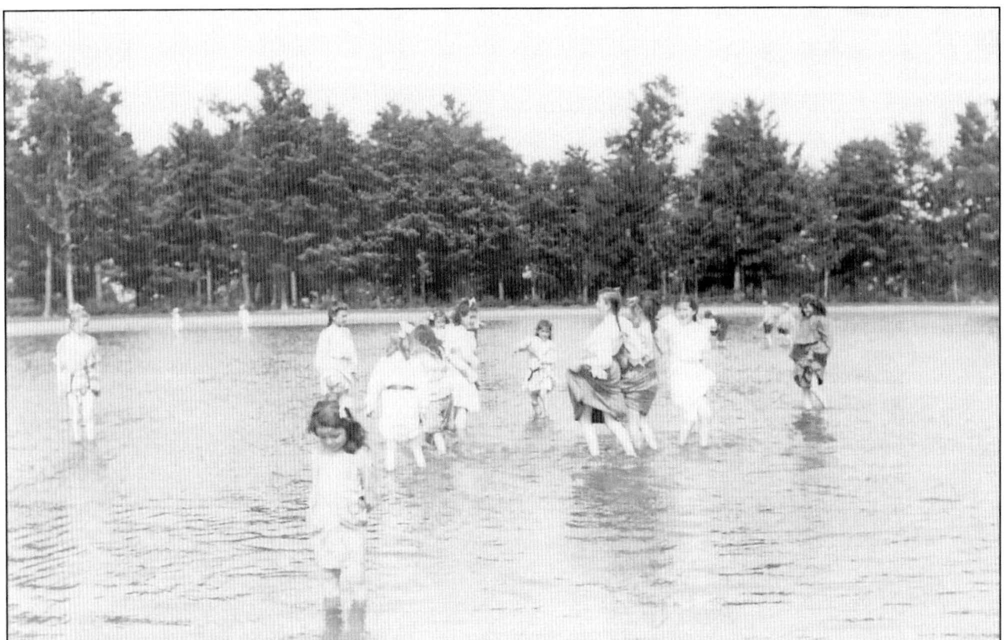

Thompson Park, Watertown. Children relax, play, and get their feet wet in the wading pool at the top of the park in this 1920s view.

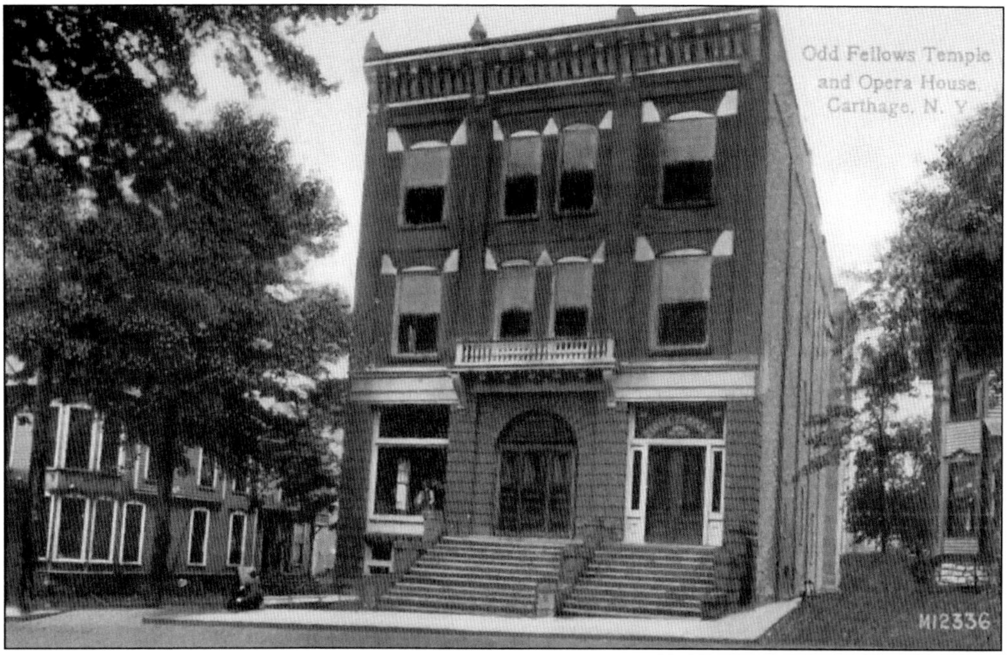

Odd Fellows Temple and Opera House, Carthage. The opera house shared its space with the meetings of the Odd Fellows of Carthage, a benevolent fraternal organization. This commanding three-story, brick structure dominated Carthage's downtown.

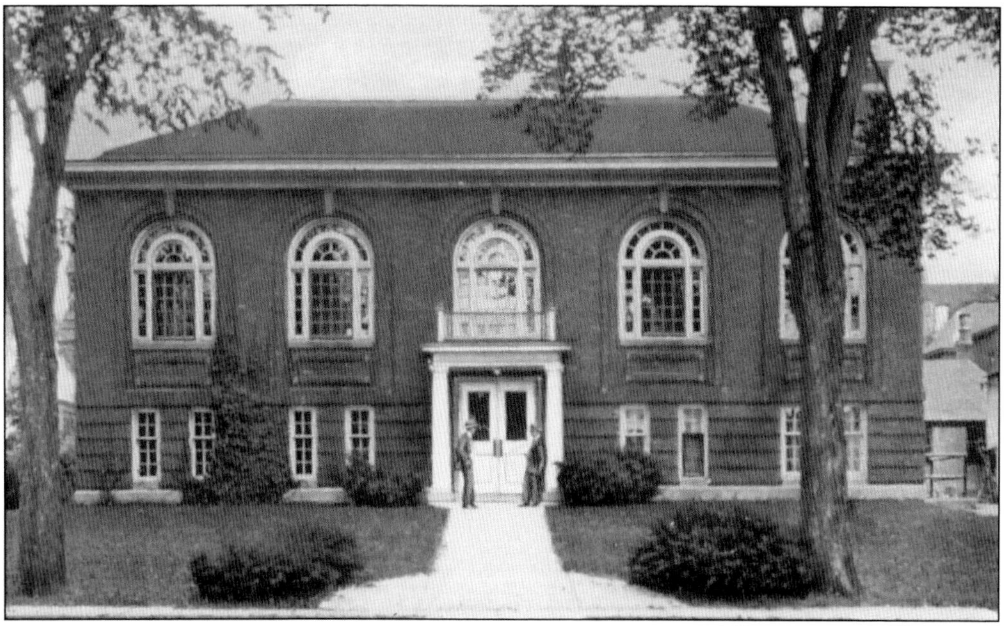

The public library, Carthage. The public library in Carthage, located on Budd Street, was built in 1916. The site was purchased for $2,600, and with the support of Nettie Hewitt, Ruth Strickland, and the rest of the Carthage Federation of Women's Club members, the cornerstone was placed. It was not until one year later that the first books were put on the shelves and a grand opening was scheduled.

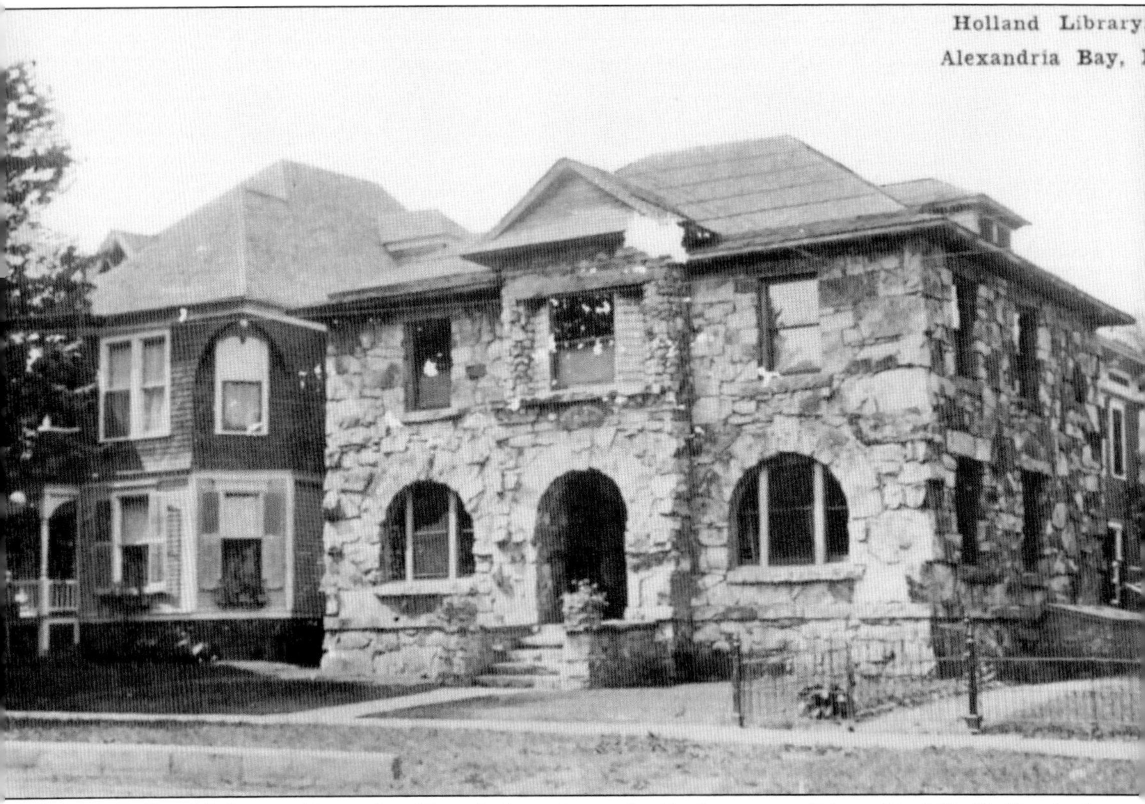

Holland Library, Alexandria Bay. Sailing down the St. Lawrence River, Dr. J.G. Holland, the editor of *Scribner's* magazine, was attracted to the area around Alexandria Bay and decided to build a summer home there. In addition to being a distinguished summer resident of Alexandria Bay, Holland enthusiastically donated a large sum of money to build a library for the town. Together with other prominent citizens' financial endorsements, the Young Men's Library Association was formed. Holland Library stood as a monument to Holland as well as the hard work of the citizens of Alexandria Bay.

Four

Trains and Trolleys

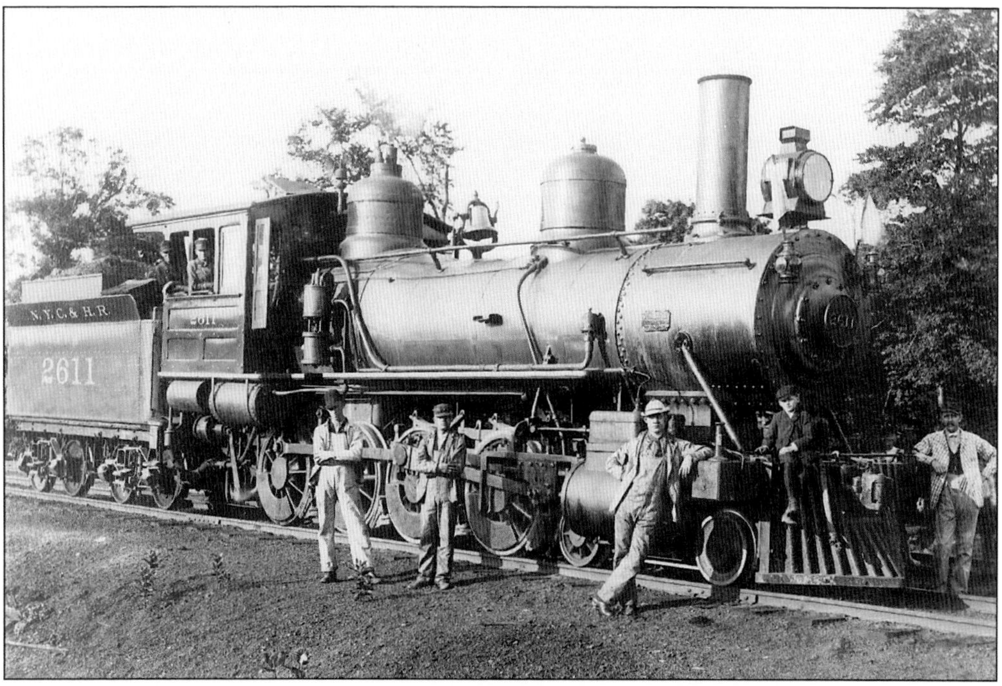

Locomotive for the New York Central and Hudson River Railroad. Taking a break before reaching their next destination, workers from the New York Central and Hudson River Railroad have time to pose for a photograph. The young boy situated on the grill is presumably a child of one of the workers.

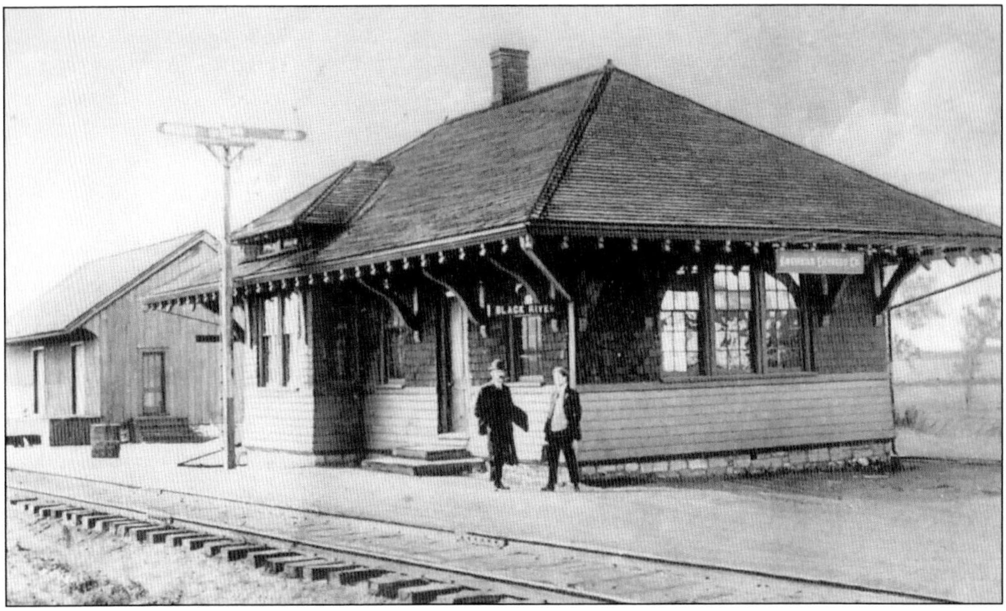

Black River Station. Black River Station was located on Middleton Road.

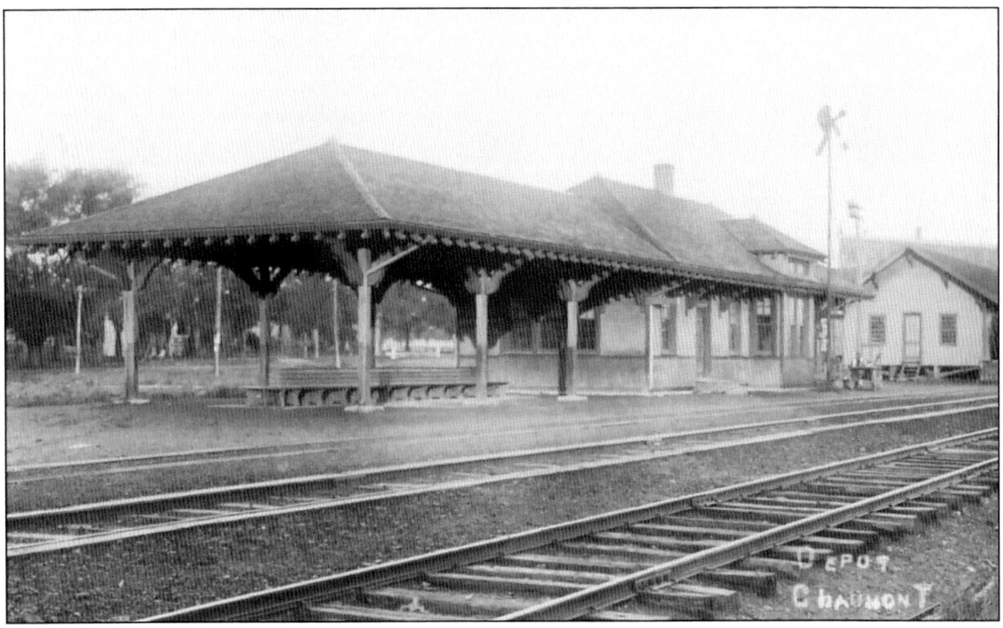

Chaumont Station. This station was located on Main Street.

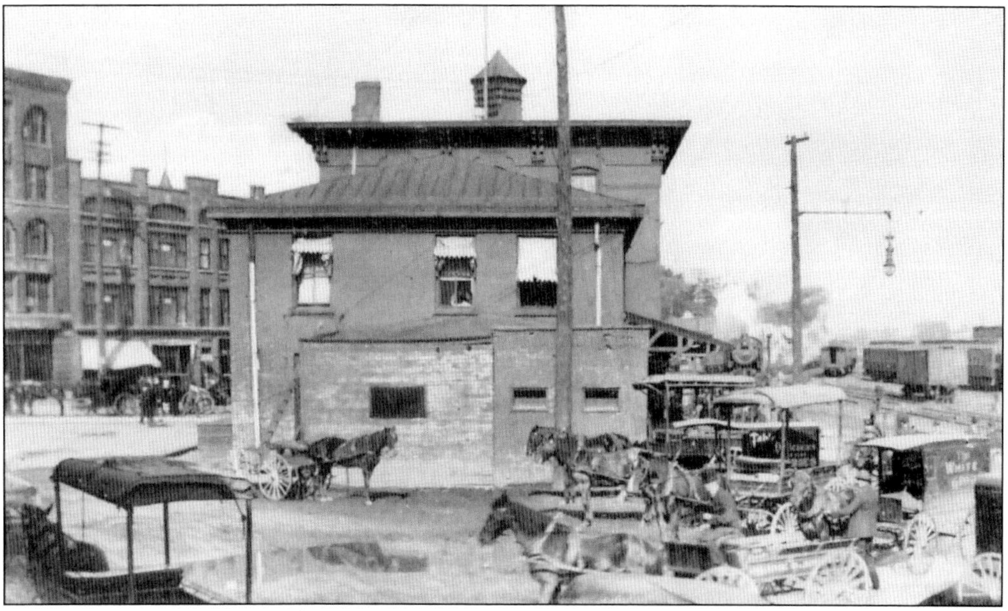

Watertown Station. The old Watertown Station was located on Factory Street.

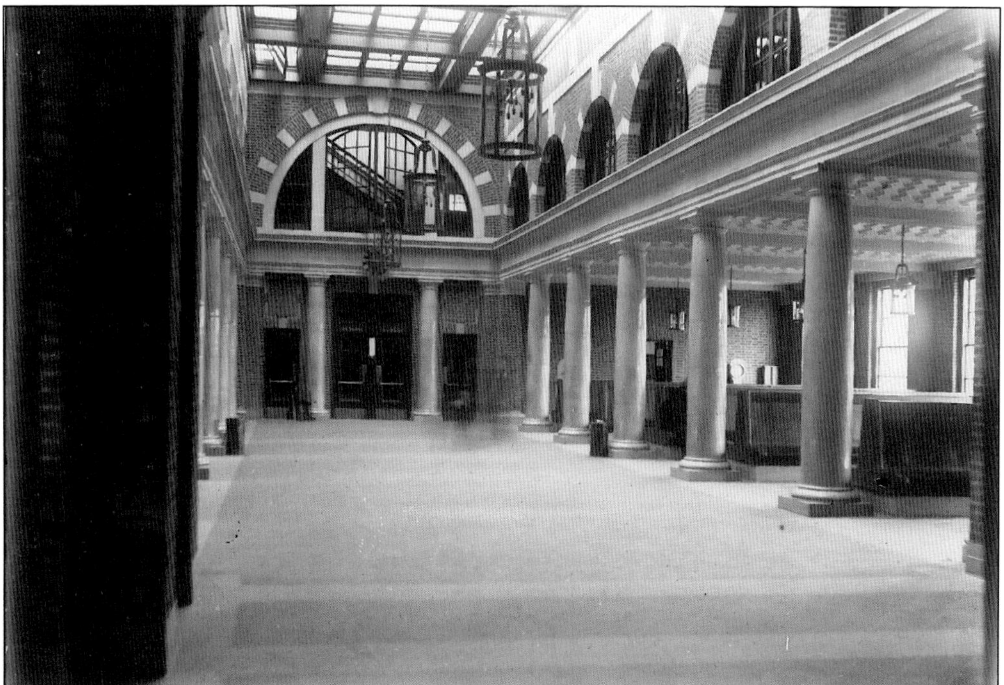

Watertown Train Station. The new Watertown Train Station, located just off Public Square and behind the Woodruff Hotel, was a grand structure that welcomed tourists and businessmen to the city. It was completed in 1910.

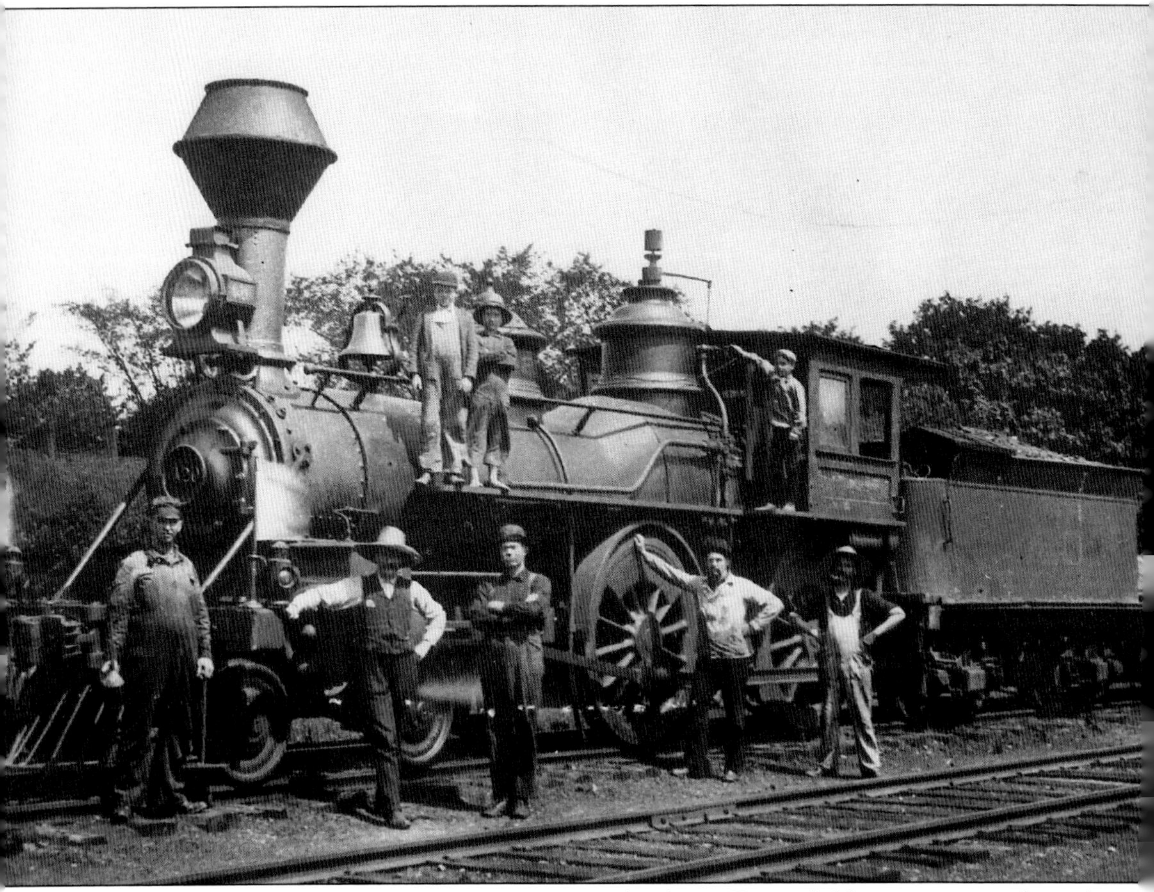

Locomotive of the Rome, Watertown & Ogdensburg. Even children participated in the excitement that the iron horse brought to the people of the North Country! It is certain that the three children perched atop the locomotive had a story to tell their parents that evening.

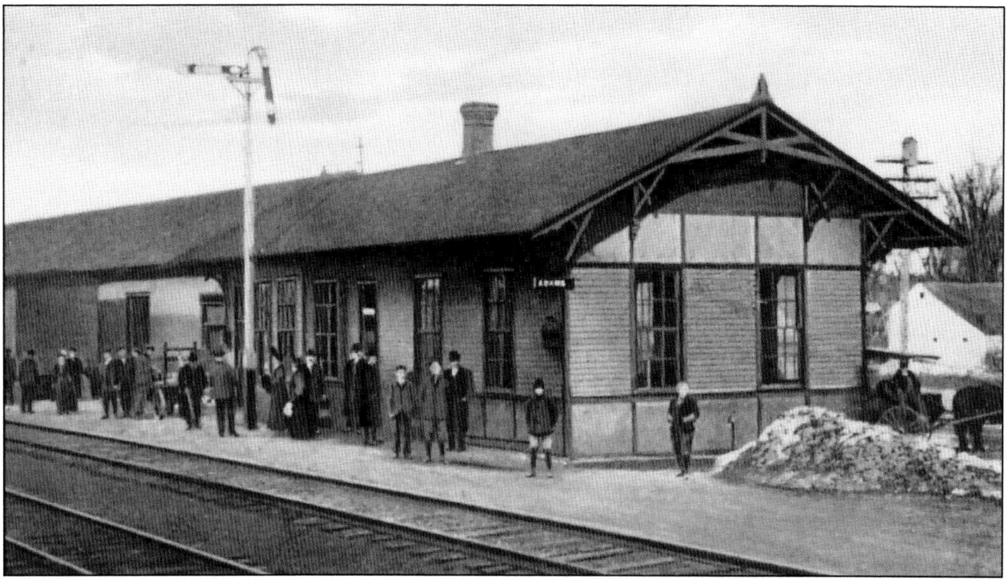

Adams Station. Adams Station was located on Railroad Street.

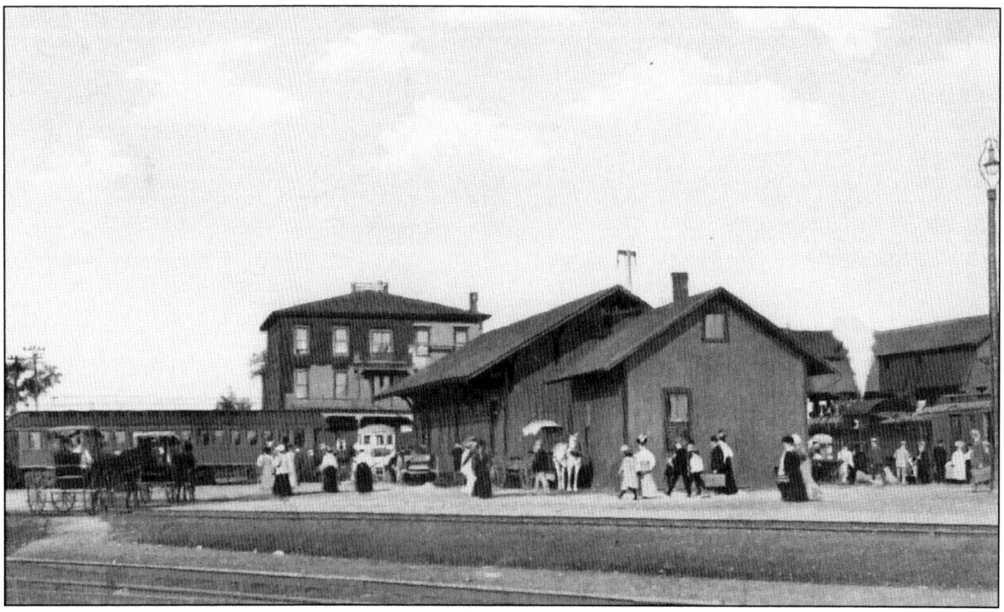

Philadelphia Station. Philadelphia Station was located on Railroad Street.

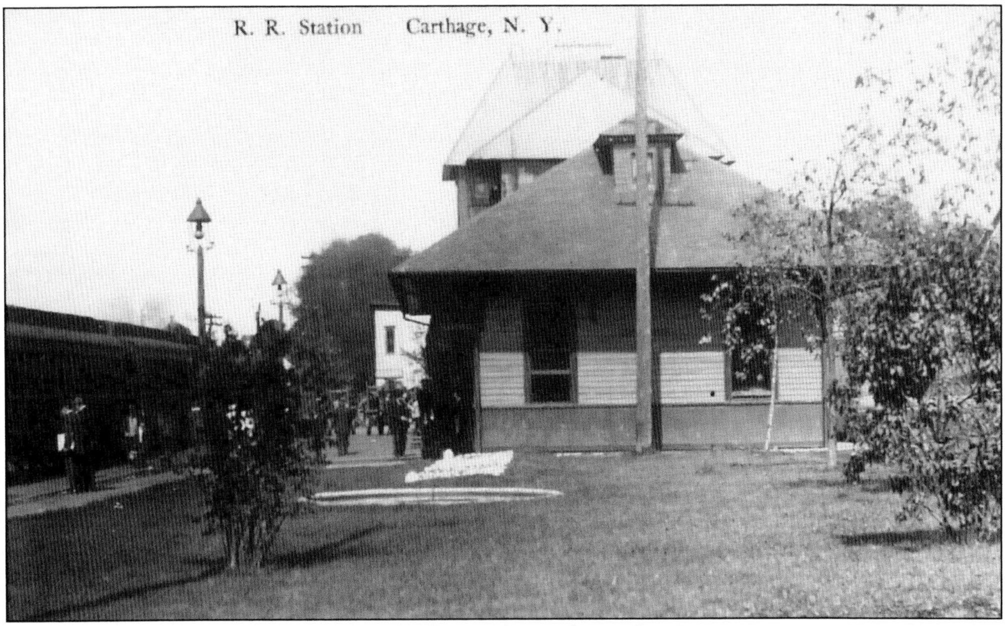

Carthage Station. Carthage Station was located on Alexandria Street.

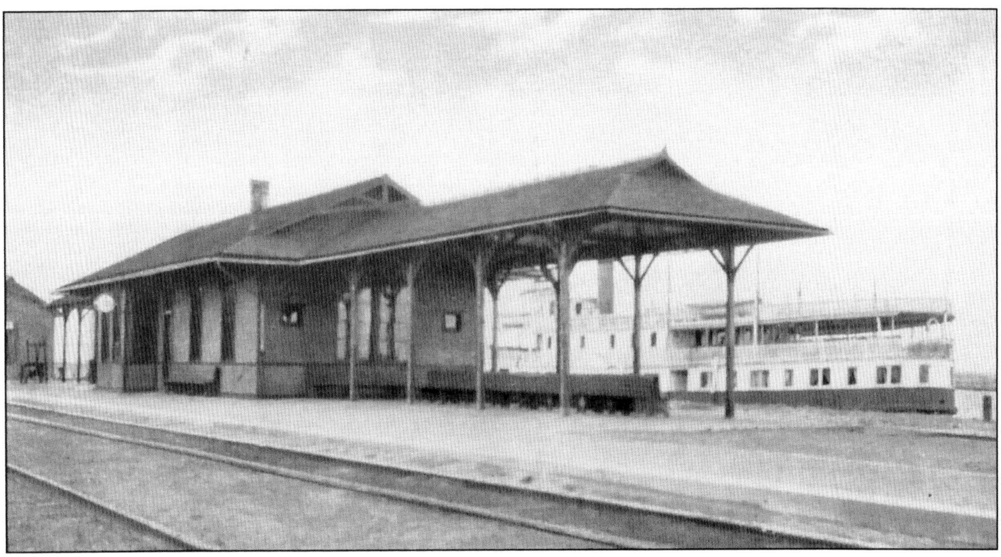

Cape Vincent Station. Cape Vincent Station was located on Broadway.

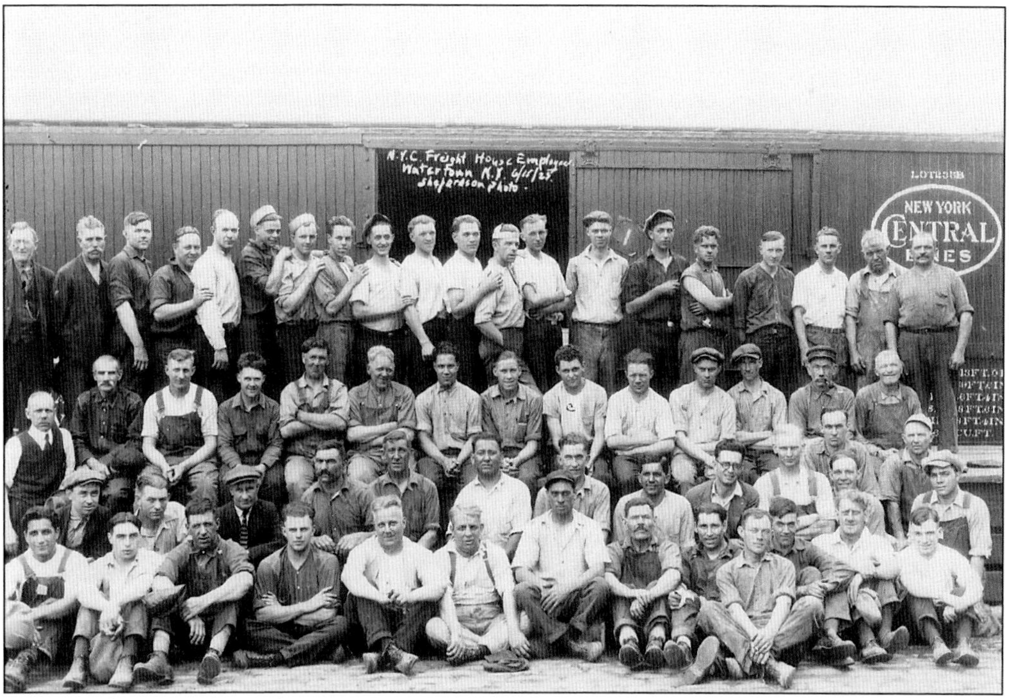

New York Central employees, *c.* 1925. It took a lot of manpower to keep the trains running. The individuals in this photograph all worked in the New York Central Freight House in Watertown.

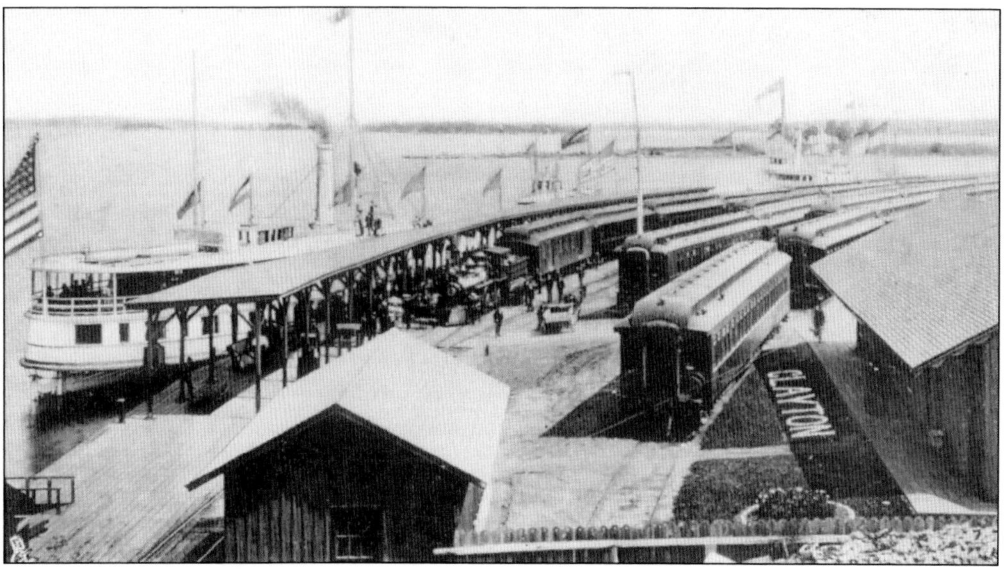

Clayton Station. Clayton Station was located on Water Street.

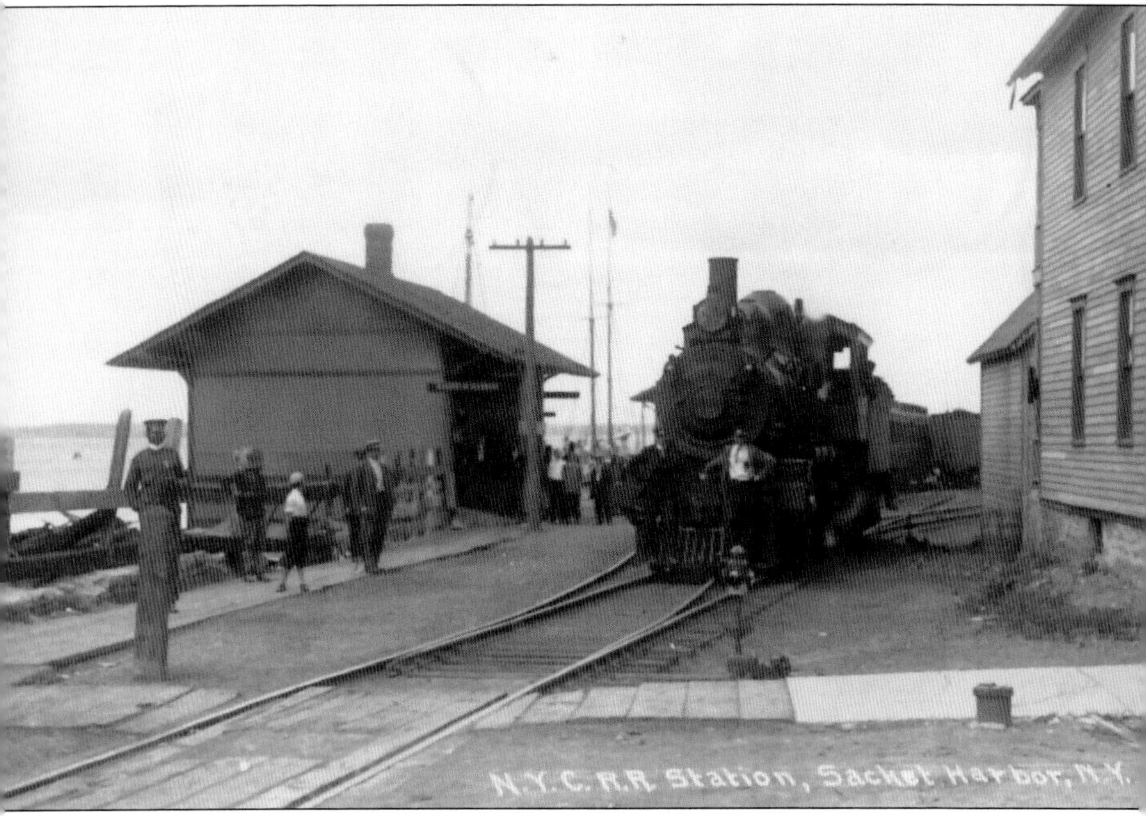

Sackets Harbor Station. Sackets Harbor Station was located on Main Street.

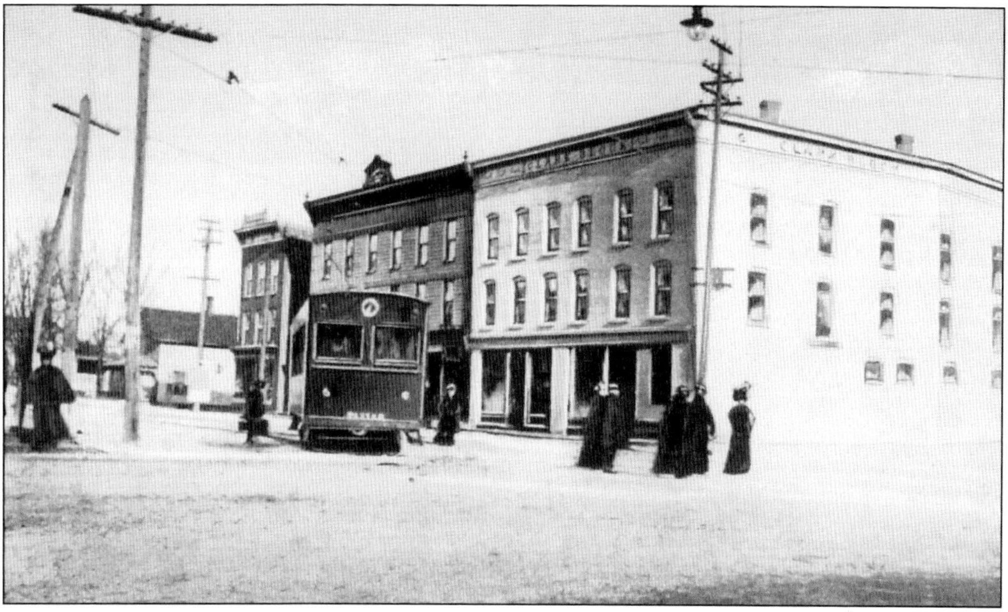

Dexter Trolley. Dexter Trolley was part of the Black River Traction Company. This trolley ran from Watertown to Dexter.

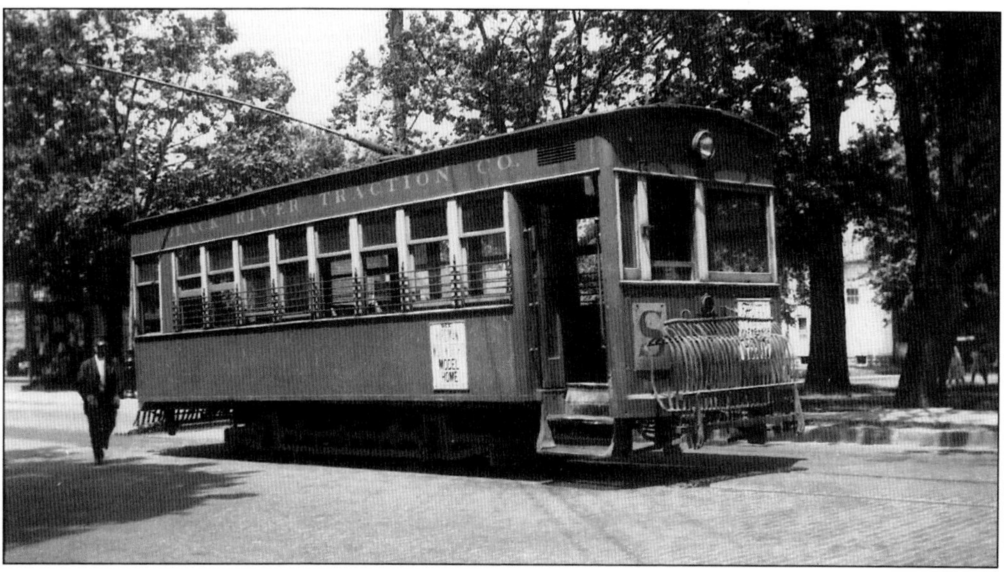

Trolley from Black River Traction Company. The trolley ran frequently bringing workers from Watertown, where they resided, into Dexter to work at the many paper mills along the Black River.

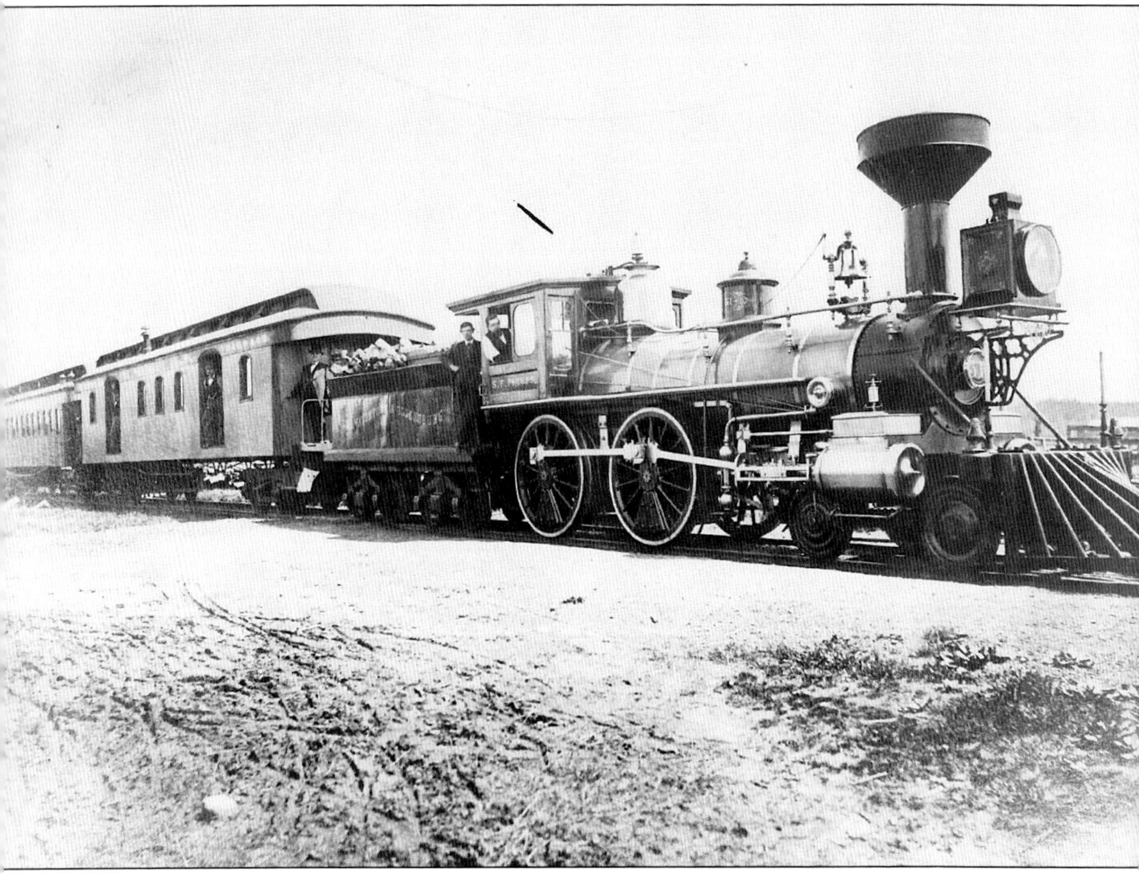

Train from the Rome, Watertown & Ogdensburg Railroad. All aboard! Wood-burning locomotives such as this one traveled at top speeds of 60 miles per hour, but 45 miles per hour was established as a more prudent speed.

Five

Thousand Islands

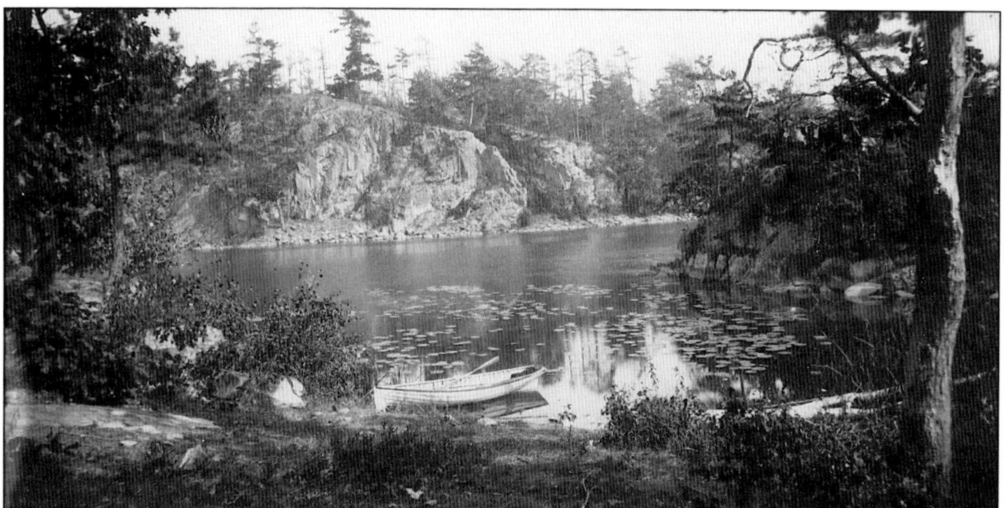

St. Lawrence skiff. A St. Lawrence skiff lies idle along the shoreline of Thousand Islands Park. The skiffs, finely-constructed vessels, were used by many to fish or just row through the islands.

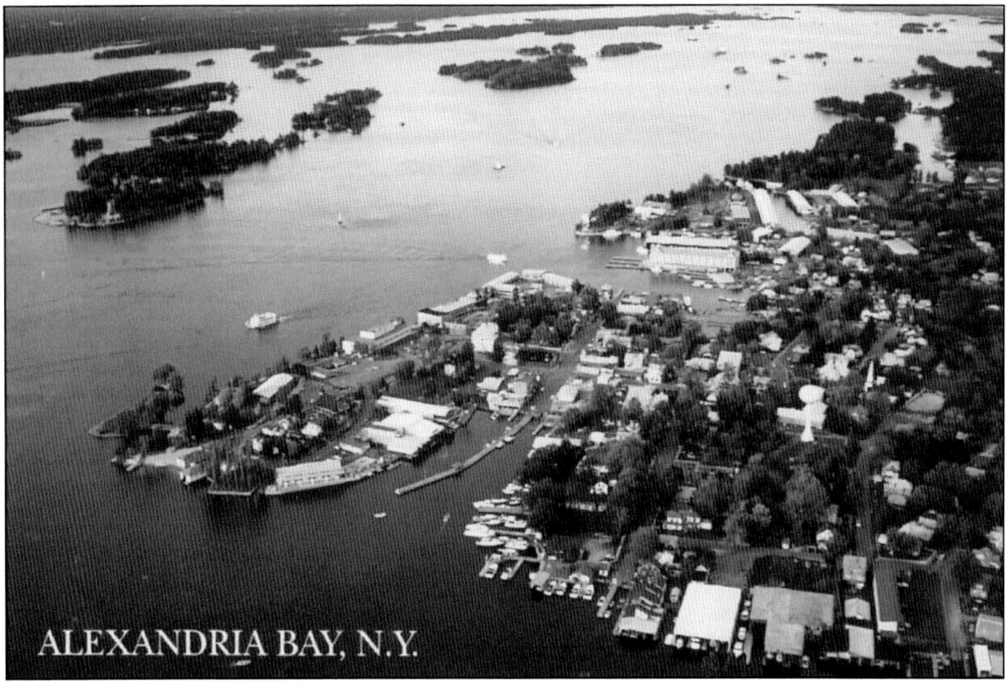

Aerial view of Alexandria Bay. Alexandria Bay has been considered a summer resort area for over a century. Even as early as 1898 it is said that the town's population doubled during the summer months.

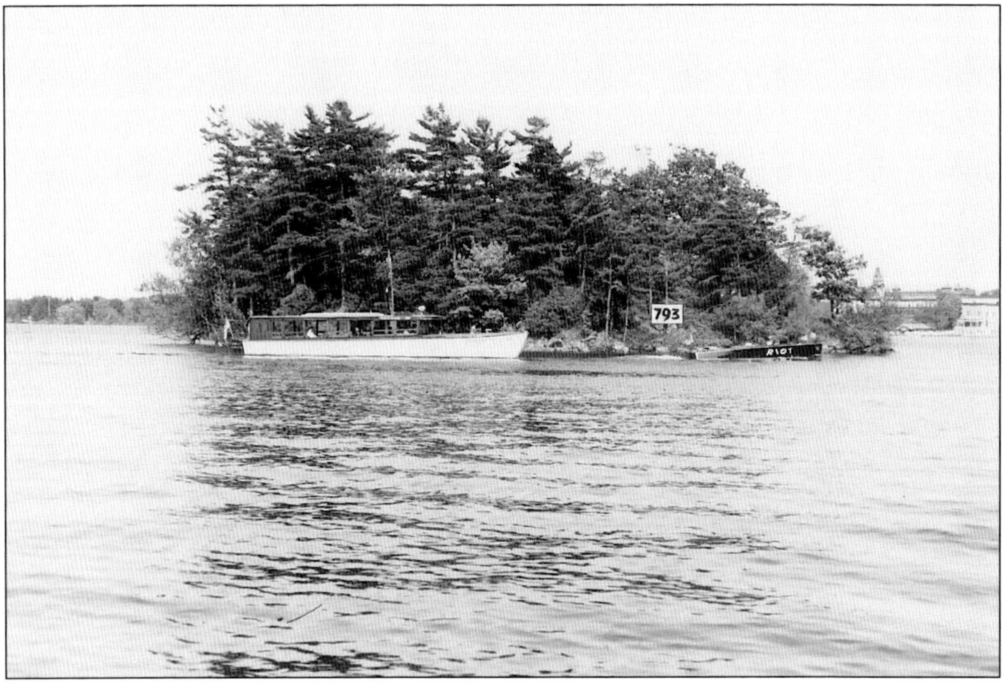

Tour boat. Tour boats soon became the most favorable way to view the glory of the Thousand Islands. This boat gradually makes its way around an island off the coast of Alexandria Bay. The Thousand Islands House lies graciously in the background.

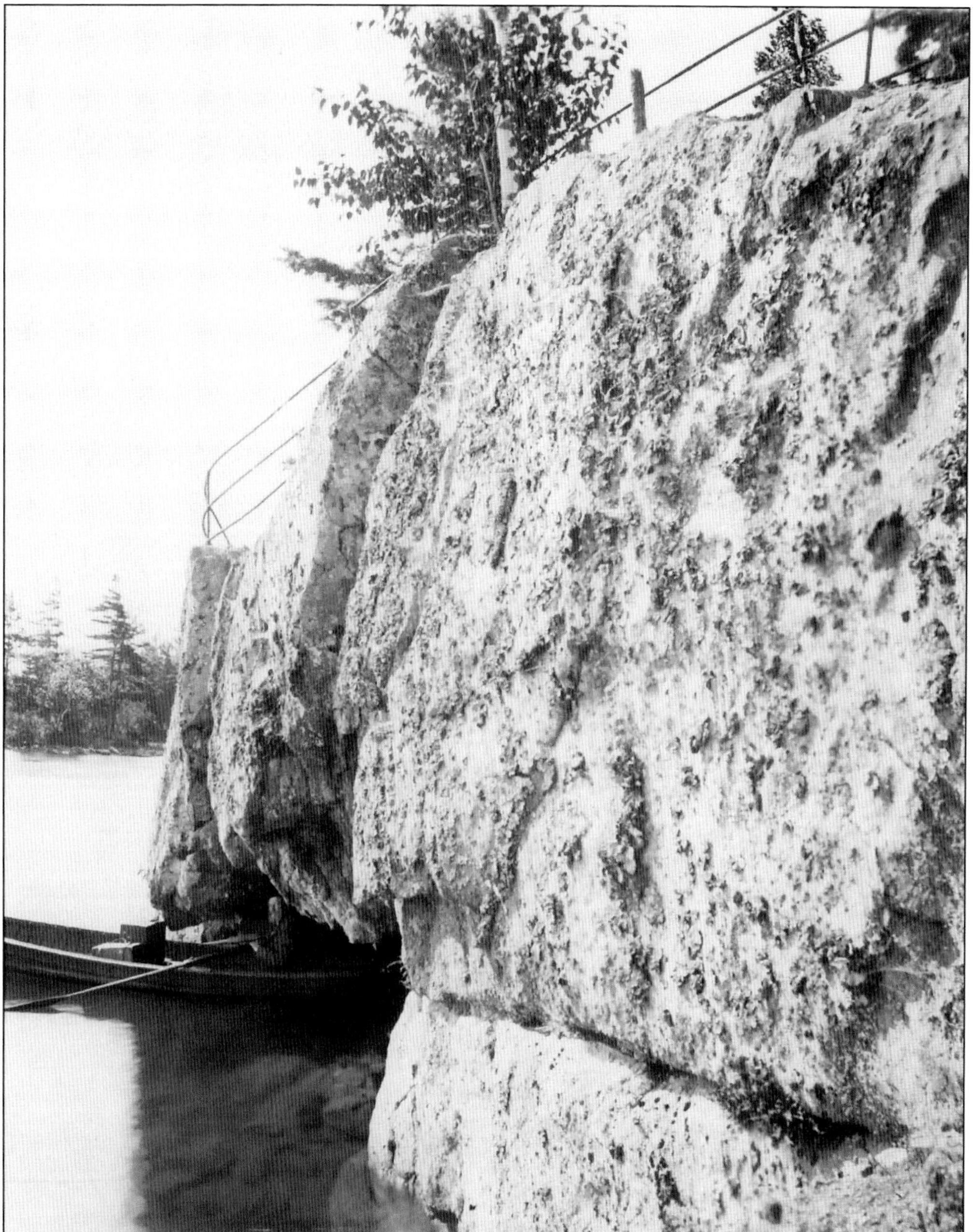

Devil's Oven. Located just above Alexandria Bay, Devil's Oven is said to have been the hideaway home of the pirate Bill Johnston in 1838 and 1839. Johnston was notorious throughout the islands for plundering and burning the ships and steamers that traversed the islands. At one point Johnston went into hiding at Devil's Oven. His daughter, Kate, was often seen rowing alone toward Devil's Oven to give her father provisions.

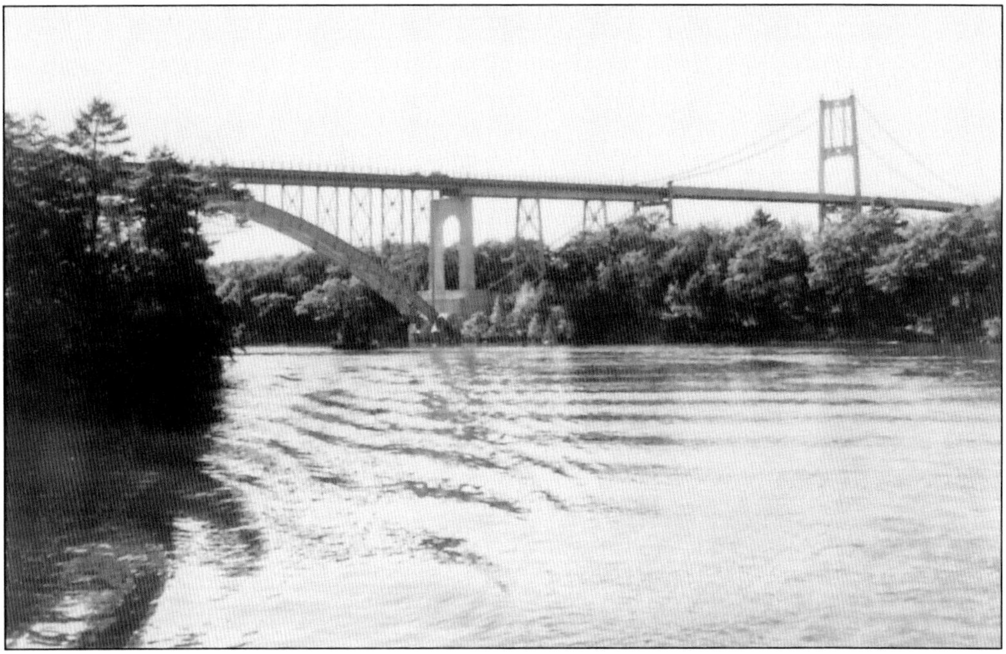

Lost Channel. The Lost Channel is located near the Canadian span of the Thousand Islands Bridge.

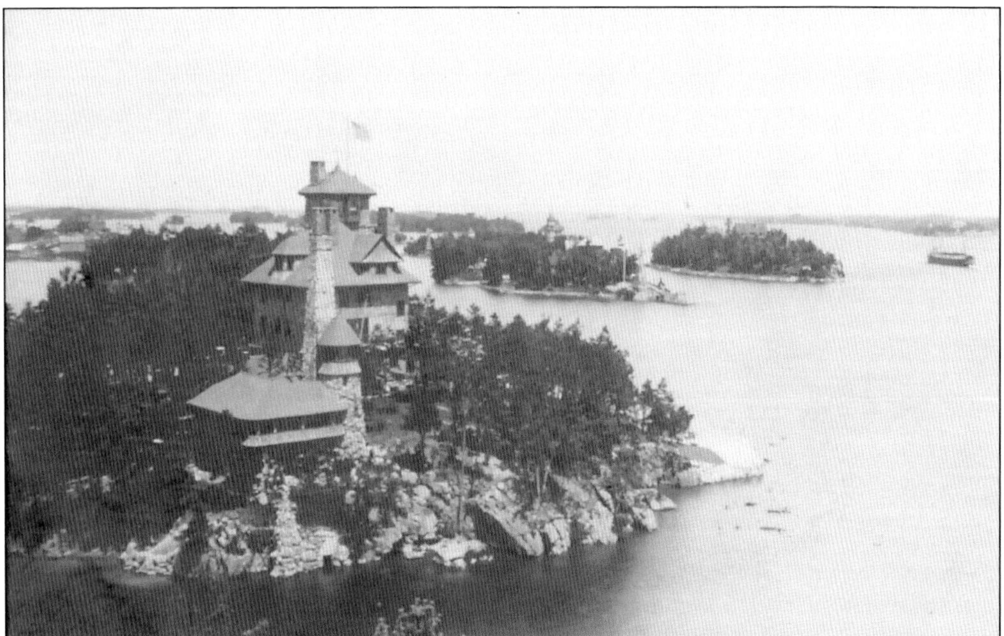

Castle Rest, the summer island home of George M. Pullman. This island typifies the prosperity of many island homes on the St. Lawrence River. George Pullman was best known for his invention of the Pullman sleeping car, a moving hotel that offered the comforts of a first-class hotel.

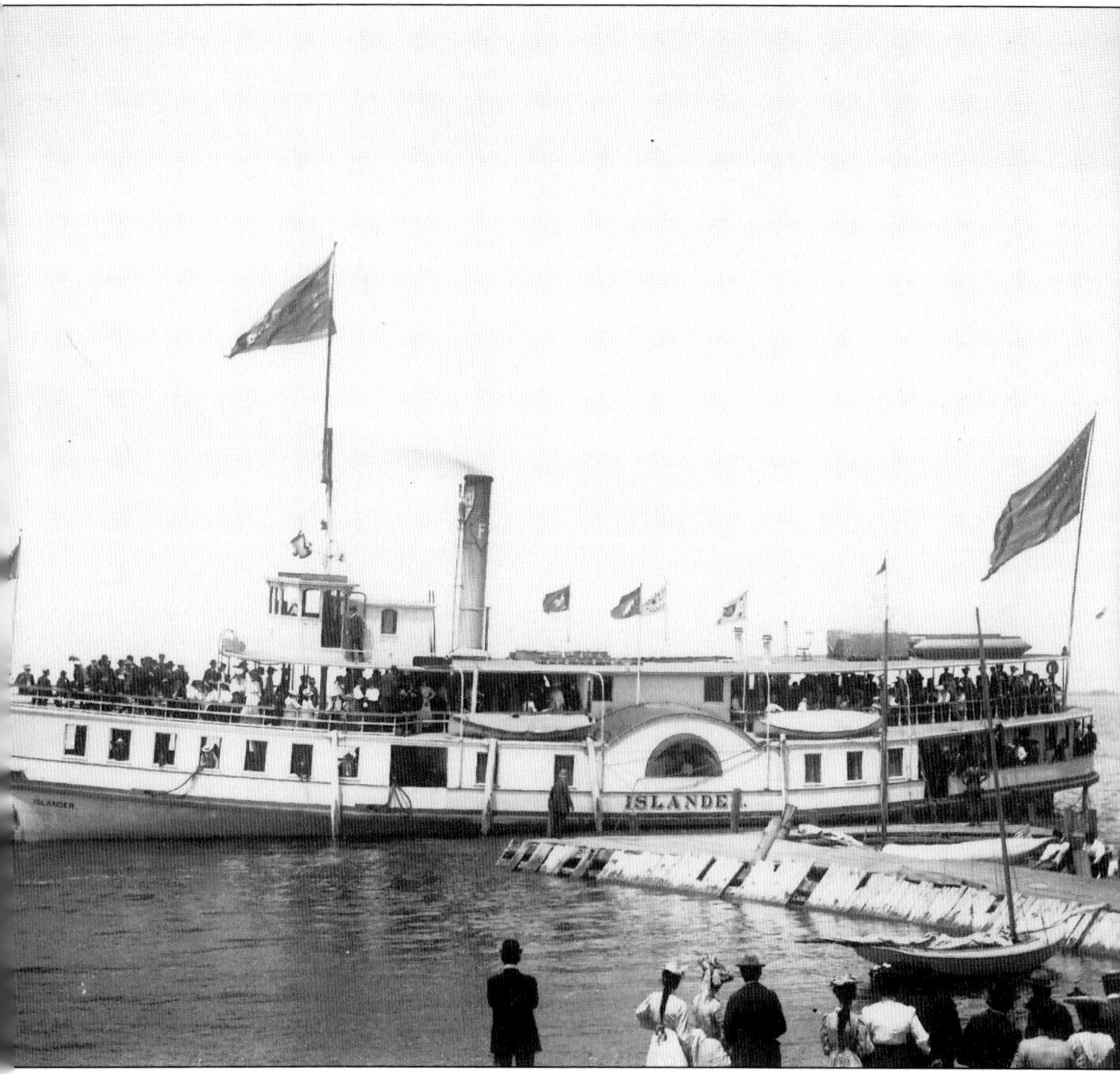

The *Islander*. Steamers were first launched on the St. Lawrence River in 1817. The boats soon became popular for their use as tour boats and transport to the various islands. Some of the ships even had sails and used them when the wind was favorable.

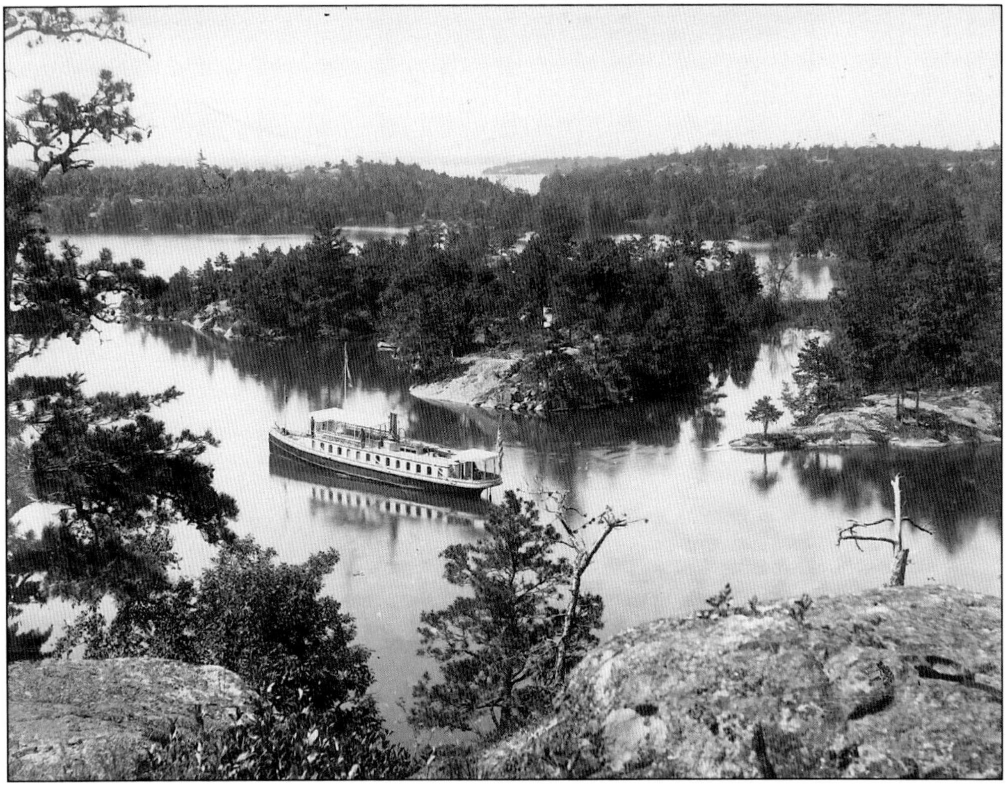

Steamer. The steamer *Magic* navigates its way through the scenic Lost Channel in the Thousand Islands.

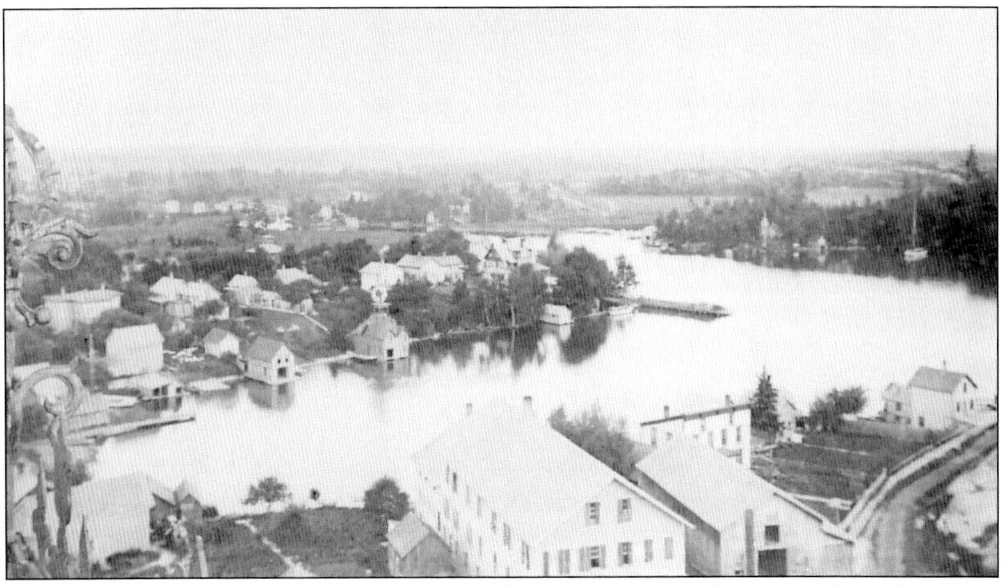

Alexandria Bay. Settlement of the town began because of its desirable port. Alexandria Bay is located directly on the shores of the St. Lawrence River. This made it a popular stopping point for any boater traveling up the St. Lawrence River or into Lake Ontario.

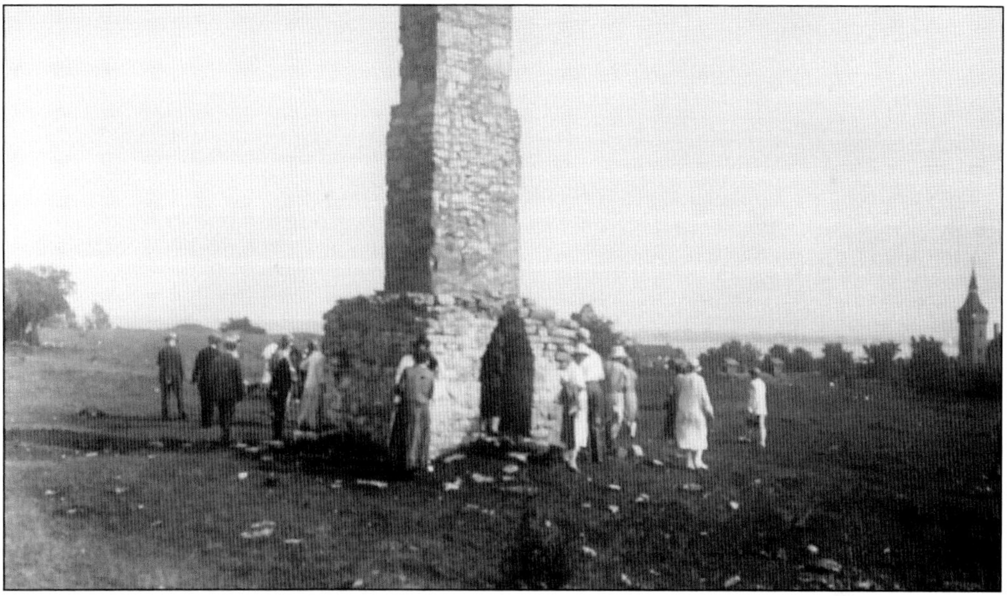

Carleton Island. Located off the coast of Cape Vincent, Carleton Island is historically significant for the role it played during the Revolutionary War. Carleton Island was an outpost for the British during the Revolution. A fort was built, Fort Haldimand, in 1777. Its location was considered advantageous for both an offensive and defensive operation.

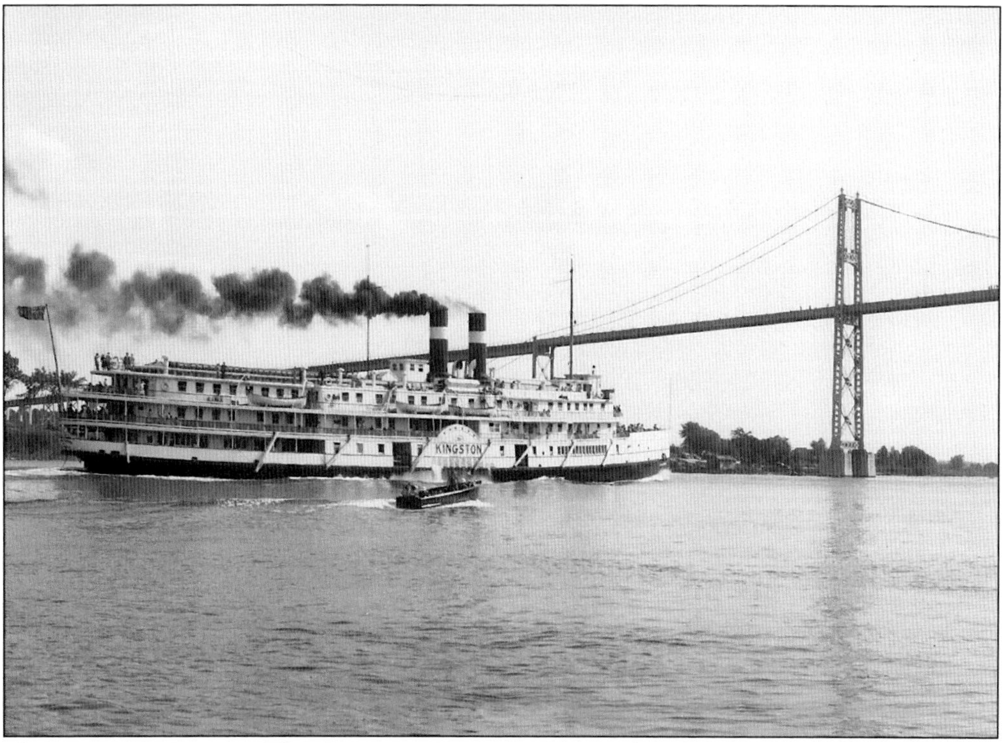

The Steamer *Kingston*. The Steamer *Kingston* passes under the Thousand Islands Bridge. This steamer, weighing 2,925 tons and stretching 288 feet in length, could provide sleeping accommodations for five hundred travelers. The boat was retired from service in 1949.

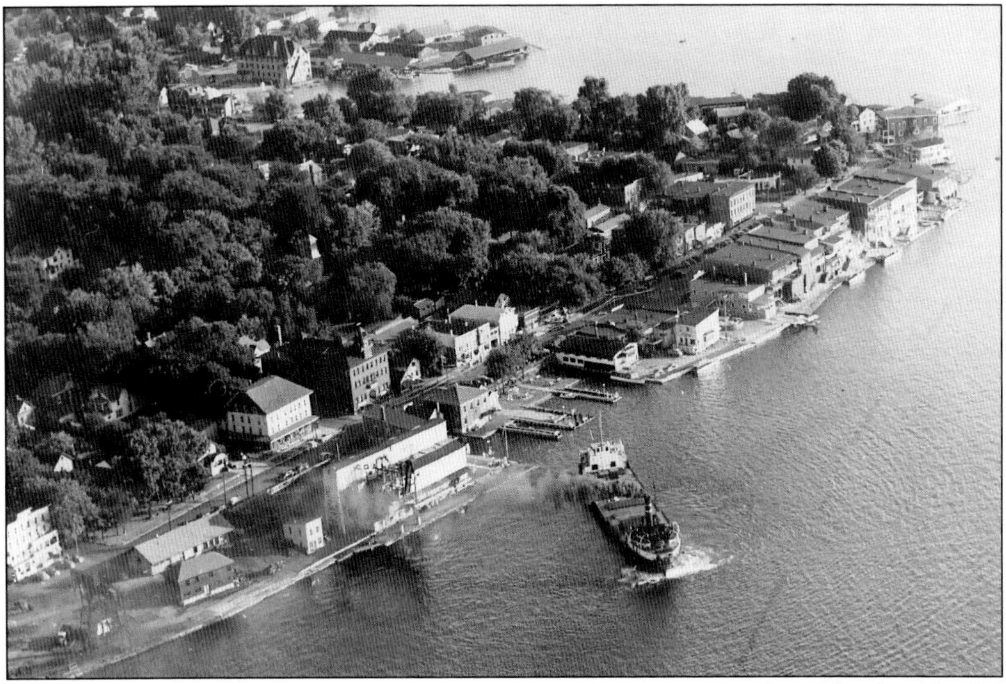

Clayton. Steamers carrying passengers to their summer-destination islands and freighters loaded with grain would depart from Clayton frequently. The train terminal was located directly on the wharf of the town, which made it convenient.

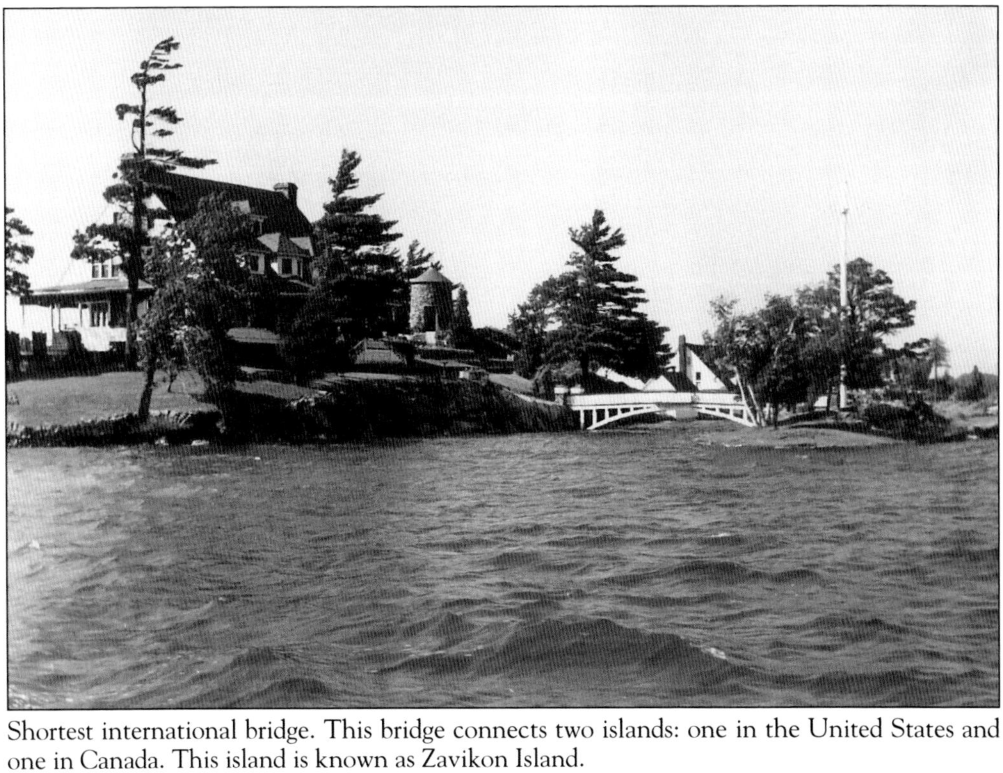

Shortest international bridge. This bridge connects two islands: one in the United States and one in Canada. This island is known as Zavikon Island.

Rock Island Lighthouse. Located offshore from Fisher's Landing and on the island for which it was named, Rock Island Lighthouse is one of the many lighthouses within the Thousand Islands that warns boaters of the rocky shoals.

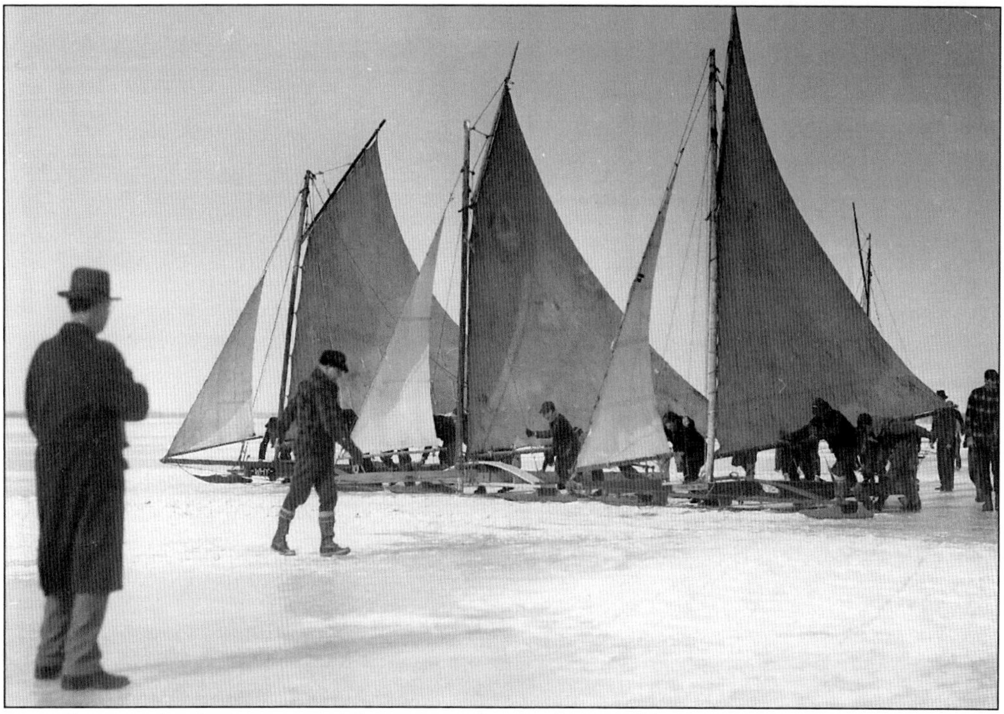

Ice sailing on the St. Lawrence. The most ardent sailors could not give up the sport during the North Country's long winters. Sailing across the frozen St. Lawrence River became a popular, albeit chilly, sport! (Photo courtesy of David Lane.)

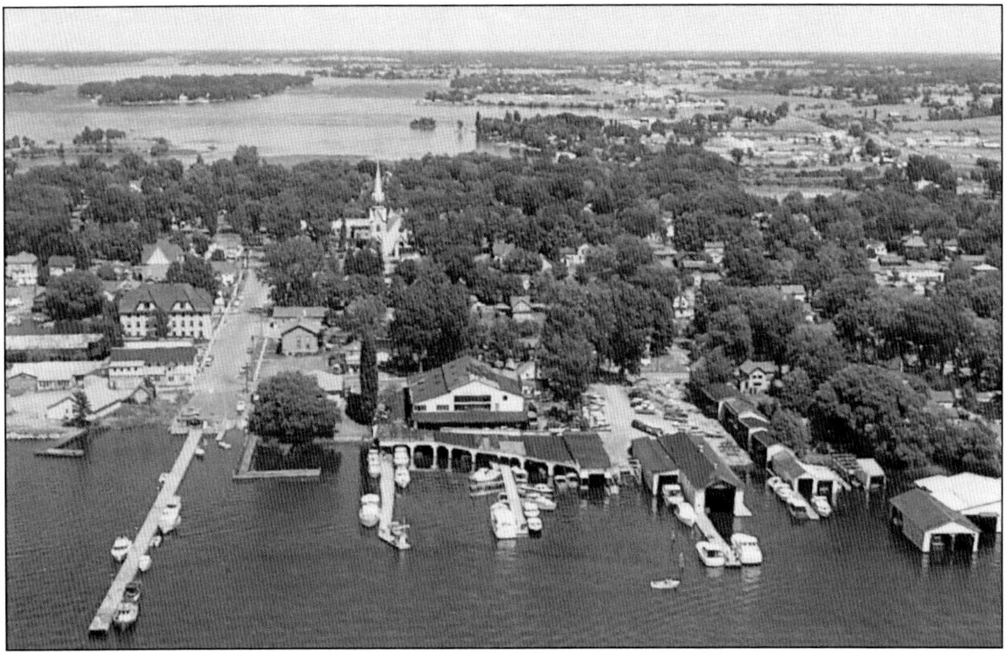

Clayton. Incorporated in 1872, Clayton continues to be a thriving community for both seasonal residents and those staying throughout the year.

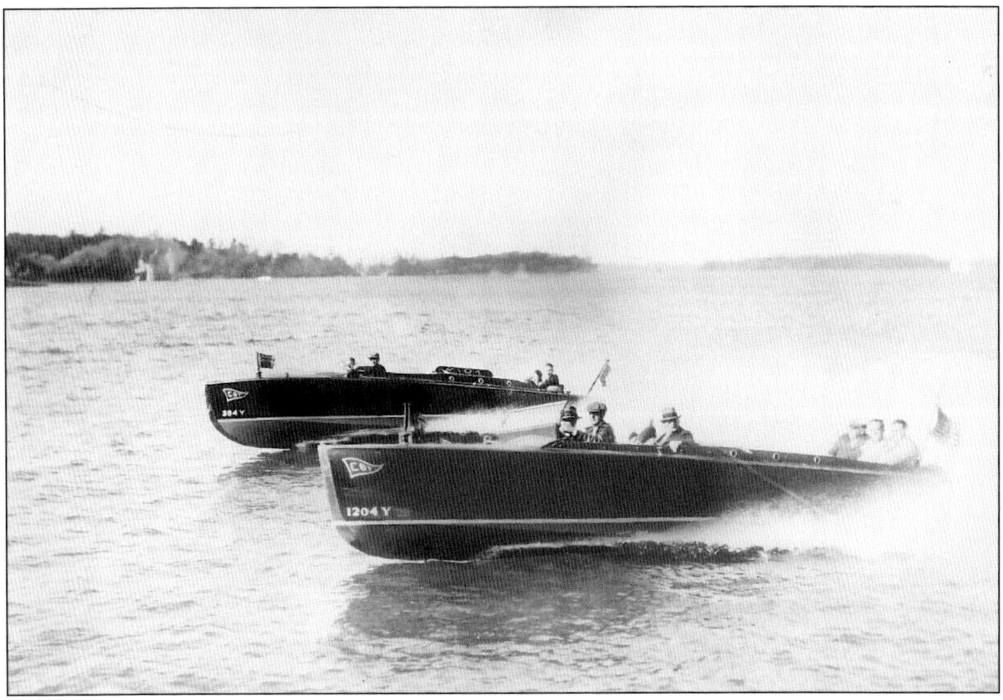

Recreation on the St. Lawrence. Those who owned homes on the islands would often have wooden runabouts to get them to the mainland for supplies. The boat pictured in the foreground is a 1927 Chris Craft.

Six

Lake Ontario

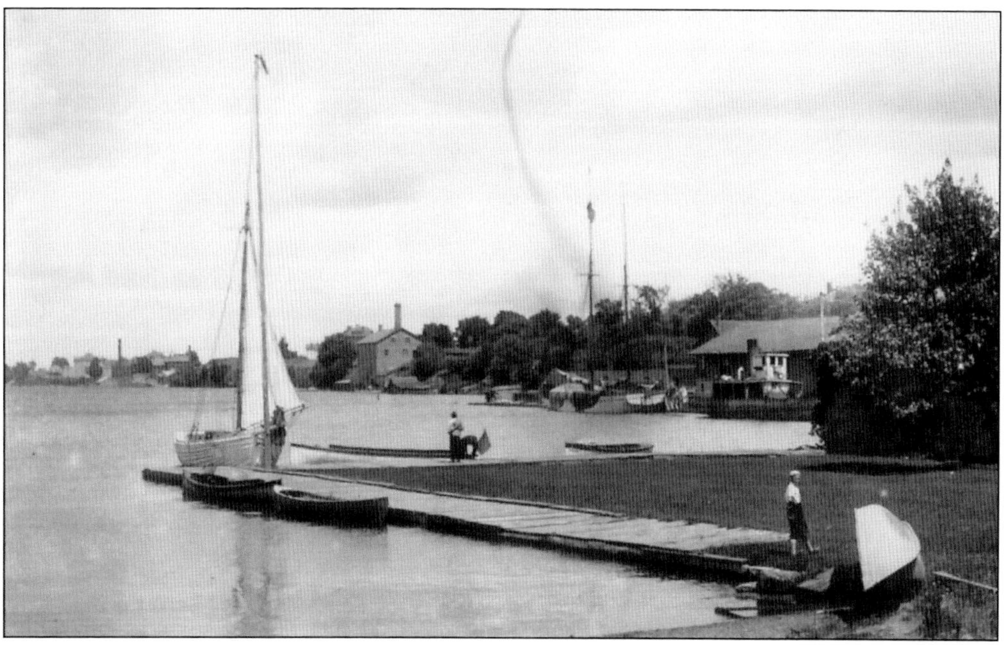

Sackets Harbor, c. 1900. Sackets Harbor is the oldest incorporated village in the county. The village is situated on the shores of the Black River Bay. Sackets Harbor was instrumental and best known for its role in the War of 1812.

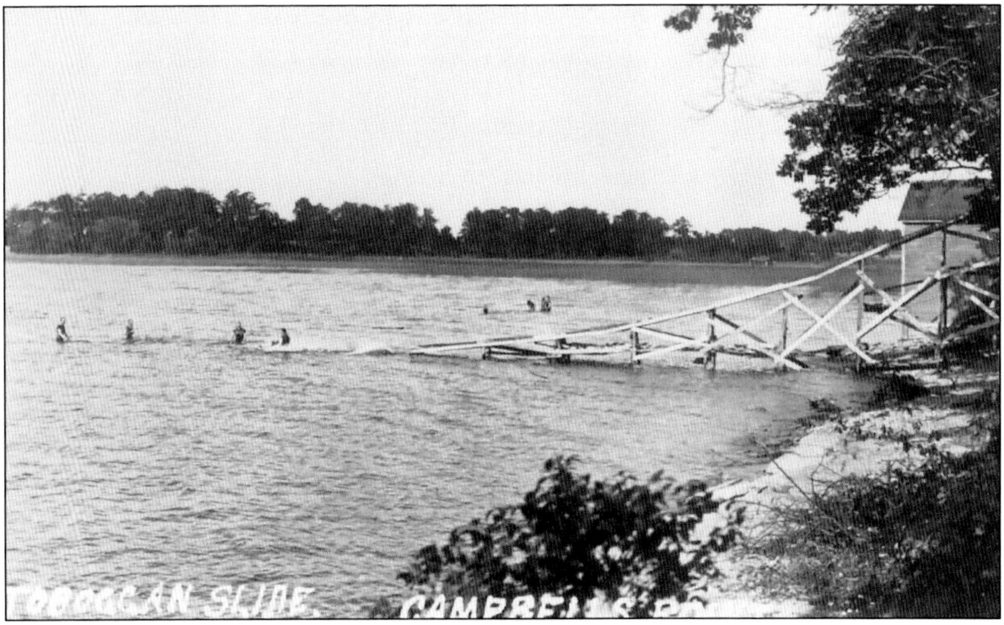

Campbell's Point, *c.* 1910. A toboggan slide greets summer visitors and those seeking recreation at Campbell's Point.

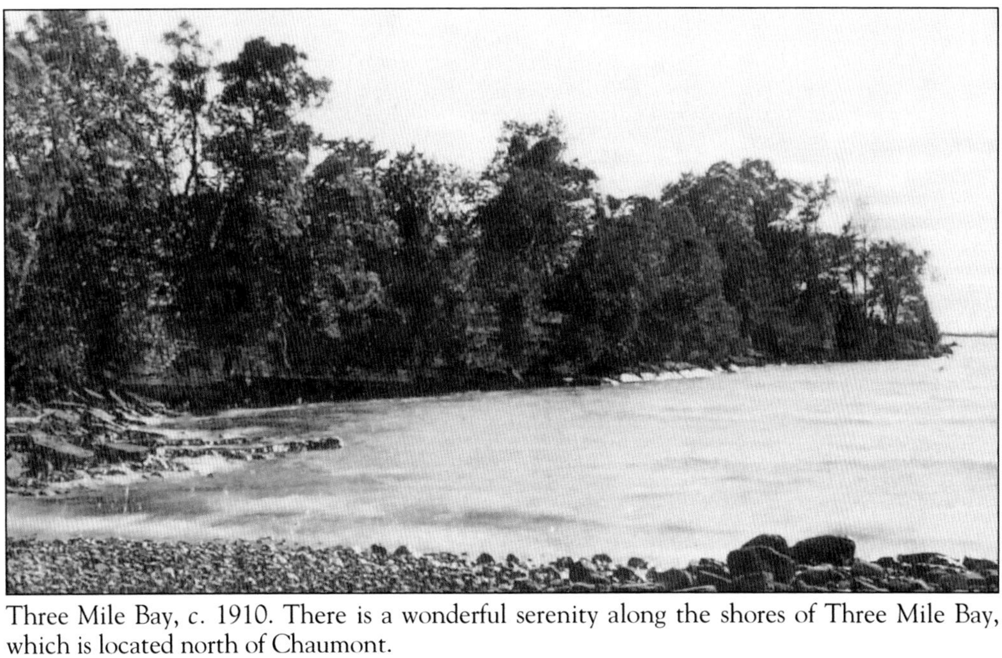

Three Mile Bay, *c.* 1910. There is a wonderful serenity along the shores of Three Mile Bay, which is located north of Chaumont.

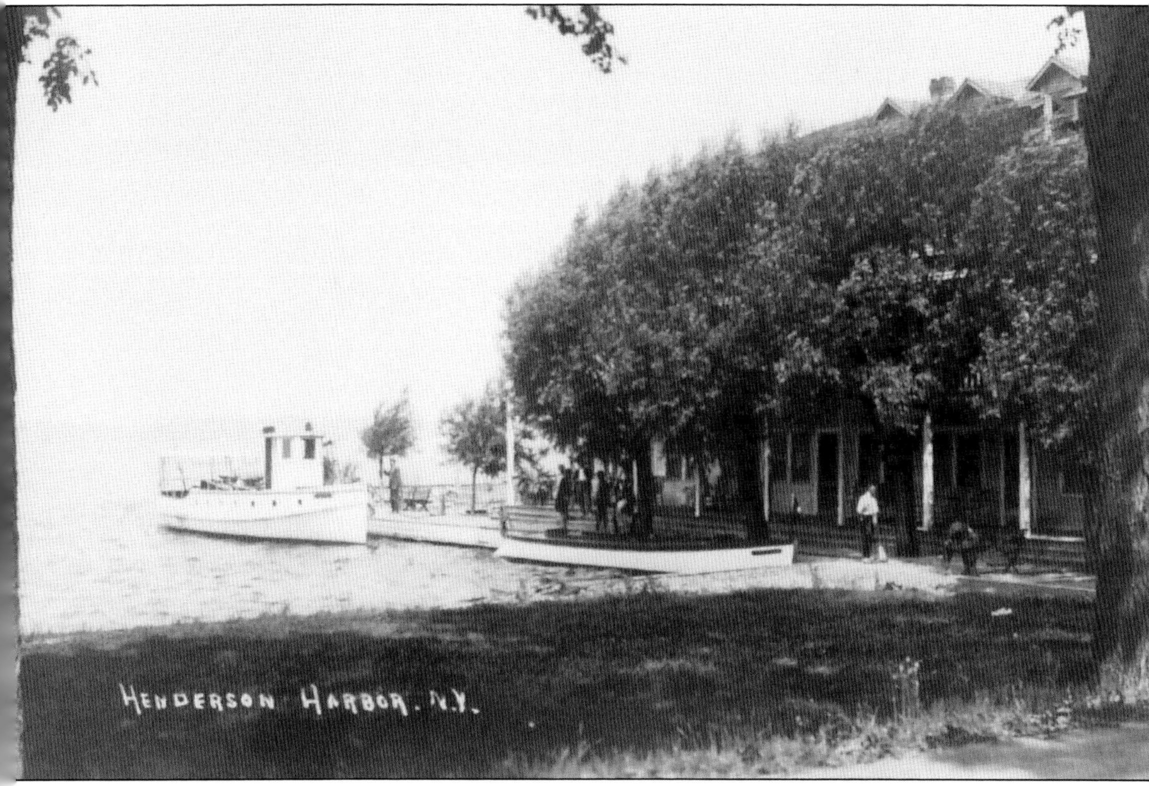

Henderson Harbor, c. 1910. Henderson Harbor was a portage route used by the Iroquois Indians in the 1500s. They would carry their canoes across the land between Stony Creek and Lake Ontario. Henderson later became a popular place for settlement by the New England settlers. By 1807, the town consisted of 128 legal voters.

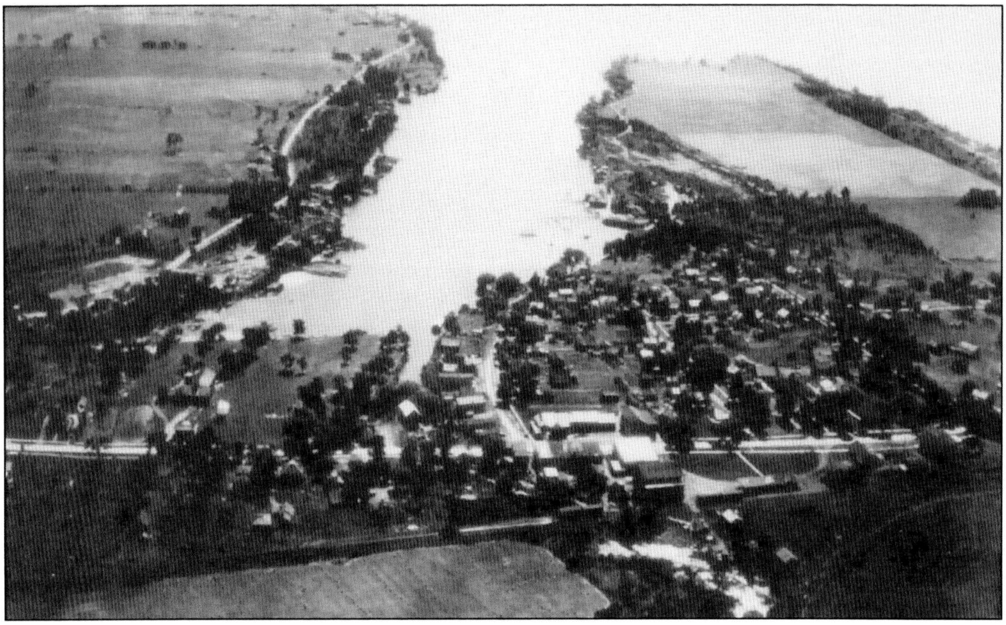

Chaumont, *c*. 1905. Chaumont was founded in 1802 and named for the French émigré James LeRay de Chaumont. Chaumont Bay was noted as one of the best fishing grounds in the state, and its product provided occupations and comfort to hundreds of families.

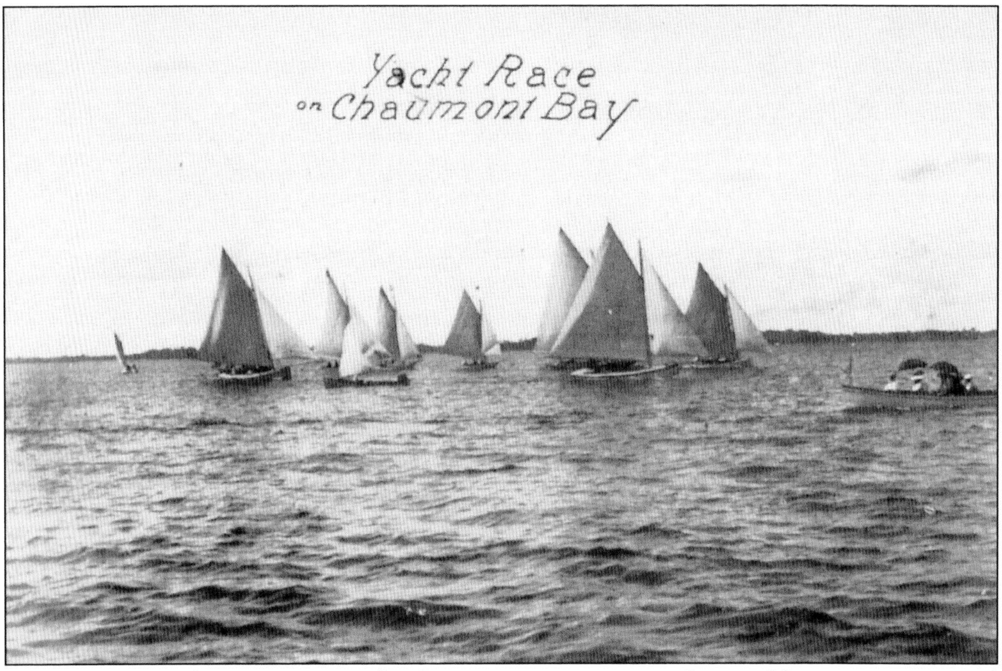

Yacht Race on Chaumont Bay. Lake Ontario was a serene and peaceful environment until the yacht races were scheduled and took place. The competition was fierce and everyone had their sights set on the finish line. However, after the race was completed and the sun had set, everyone would join together in the Crescent Yacht Club House for dinner, entertainment, and socializing.

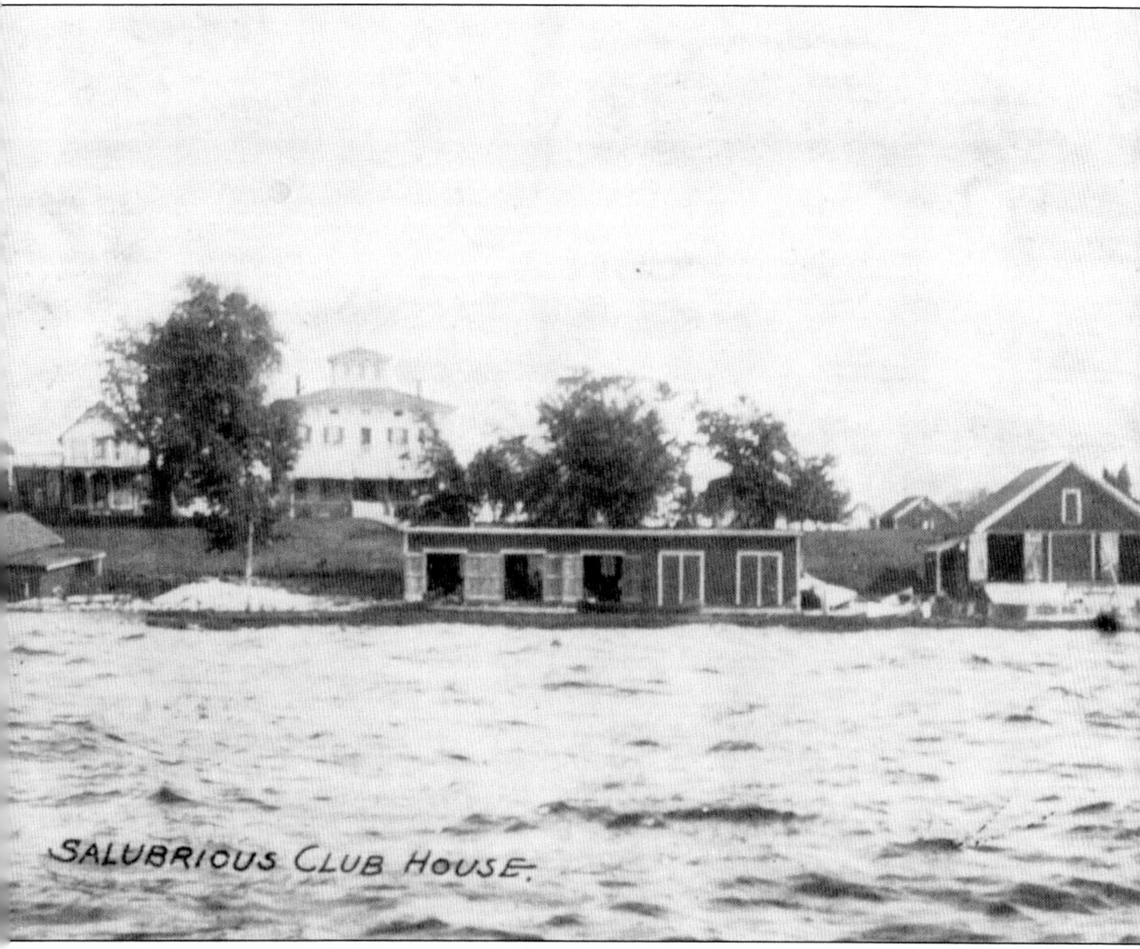

Chaumont, *c.* 1907. Point Salubrious, located in Chaumont, is celebrated as the scene of the first public protest by a group of women. It is said that the women involved disagreed with the placement of a road being constructed to surround the point. As fast as the men constructed the new road, the women were there to fill it back up with brush and trees until the men gave up in despair. This picture shows Point Salubrious and the clubhouse in its quieter days.

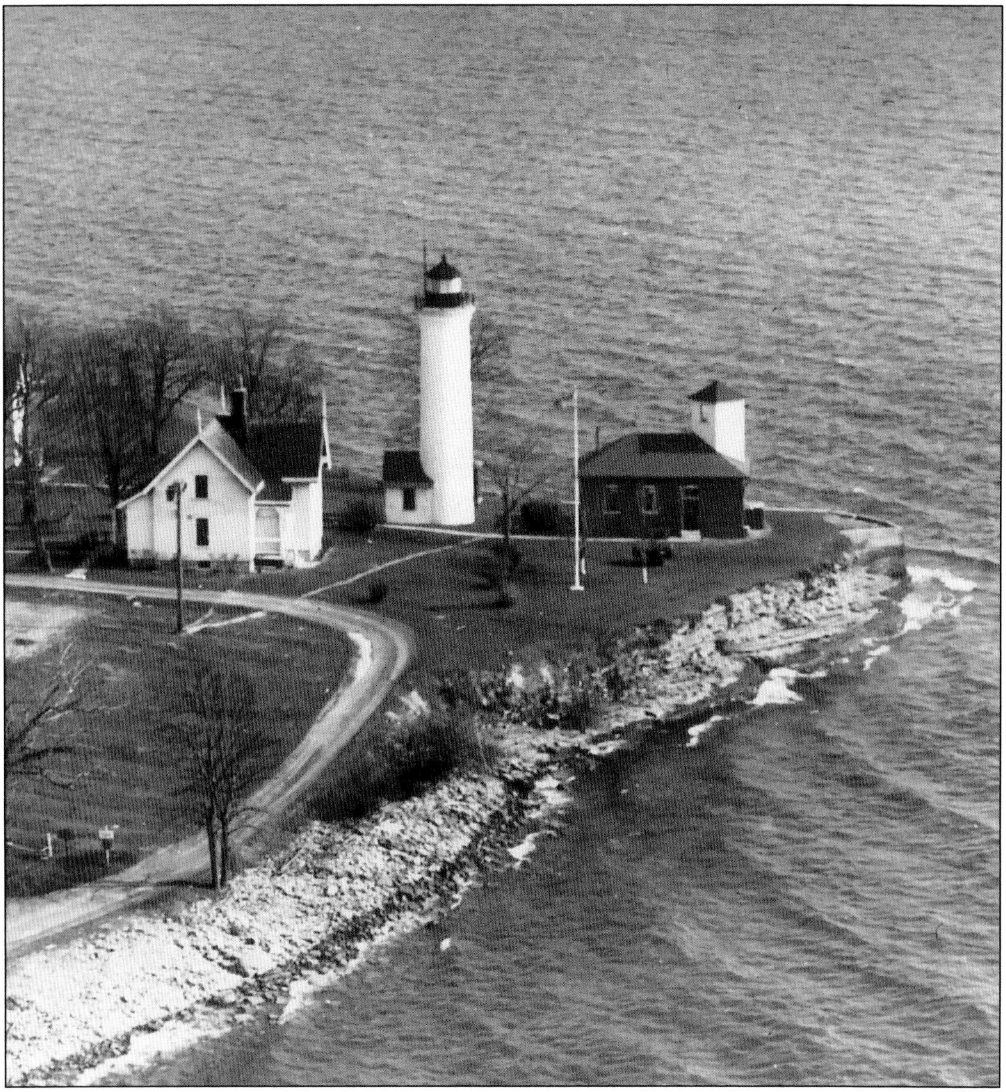

Cape Vincent, *c.* 1930. The Tibbett's Point Lighthouse is a stone structure connected to a round brick tower that is 67 feet high. The lighthouse was built in 1827 and continues to mark the point where Lake Ontario and the St. Lawrence River converge.

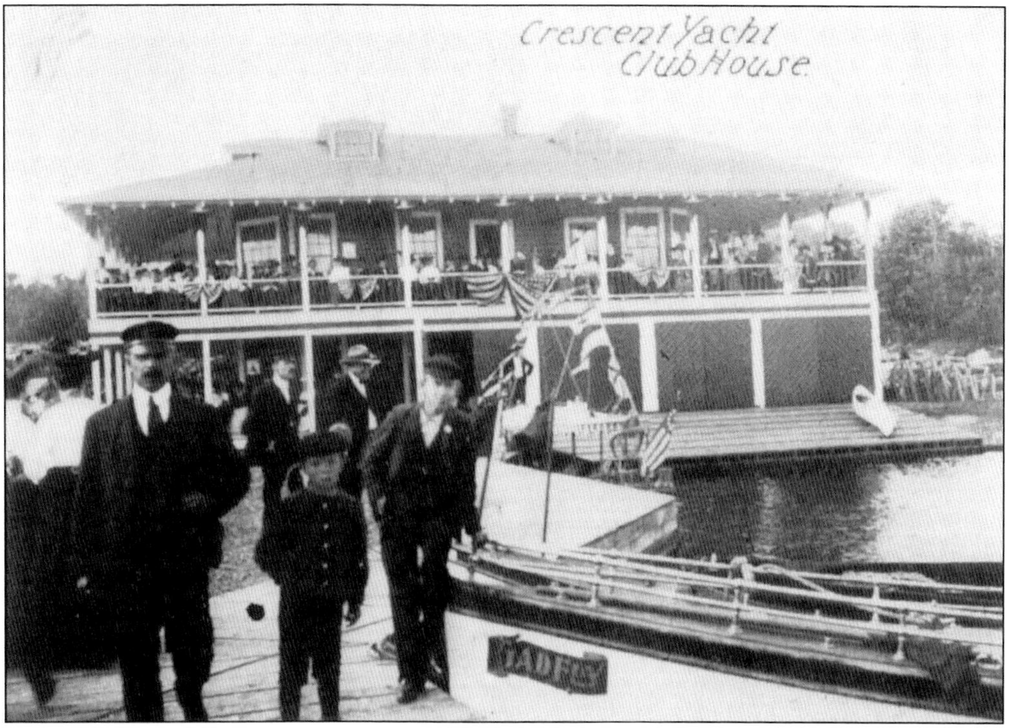

Crescent Yacht Clubhouse. Crescent Yacht Club was established in 1901 at Sackets Harbor. On Labor Day, 1904, the clubhouse was formally opened in Chaumont. The club expanded during the Roaring Twenties. The yacht club was well known throughout Lake Ontario as a club possessing skilled and talented sailors.

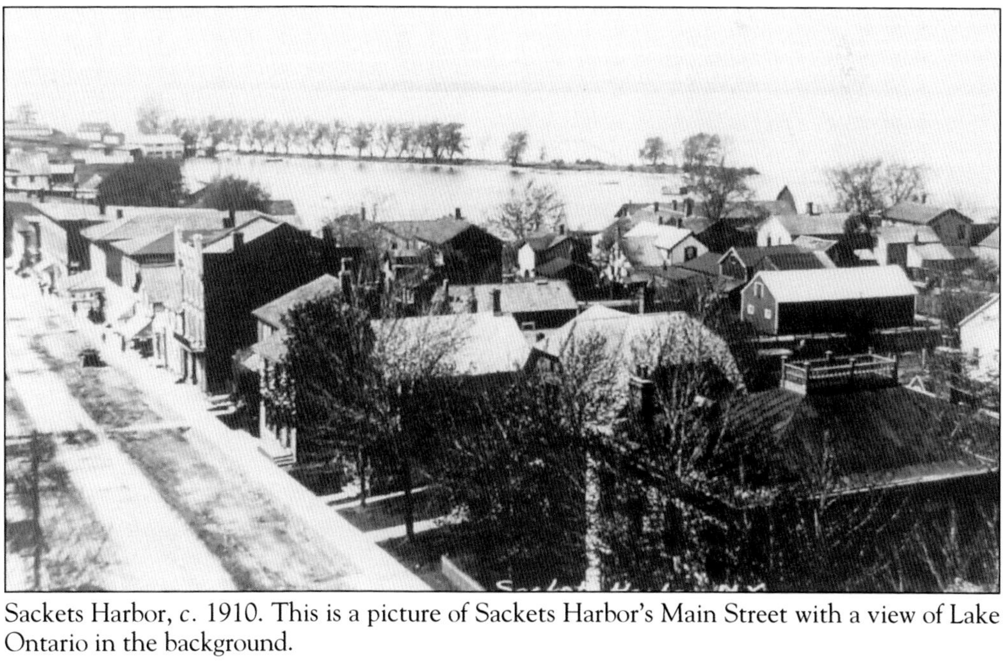

Sackets Harbor, *c*. 1910. This is a picture of Sackets Harbor's Main Street with a view of Lake Ontario in the background.

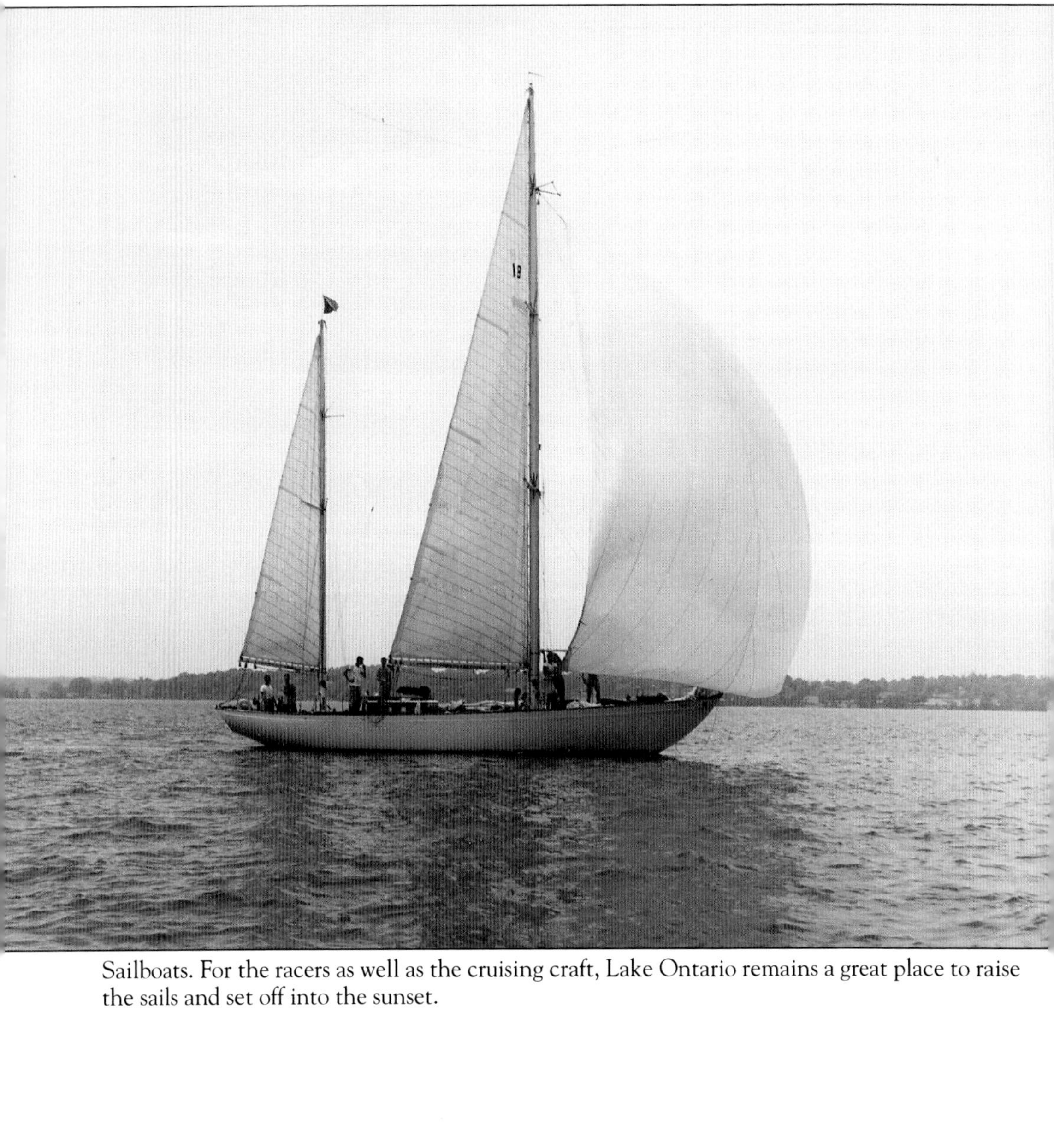

Sailboats. For the racers as well as the cruising craft, Lake Ontario remains a great place to raise the sails and set off into the sunset.

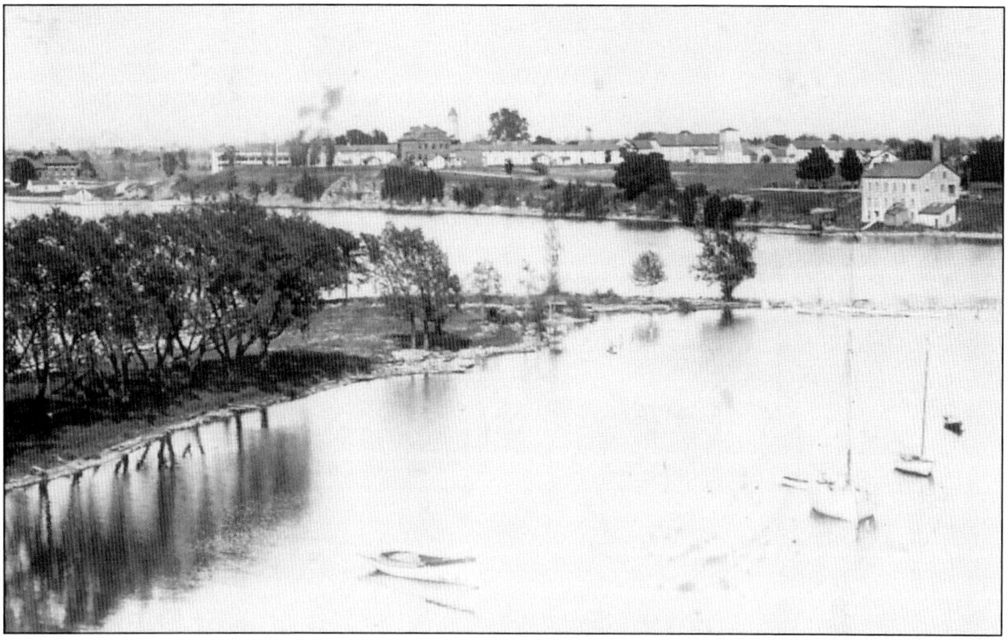

Sackets Harbor, c. 1900. Madison Barracks, a military camp, can be seen in the background of this photograph. Madison Barracks was erected shortly after the War of 1812 when it was realized how important the area was for fortifying the nation's borders.

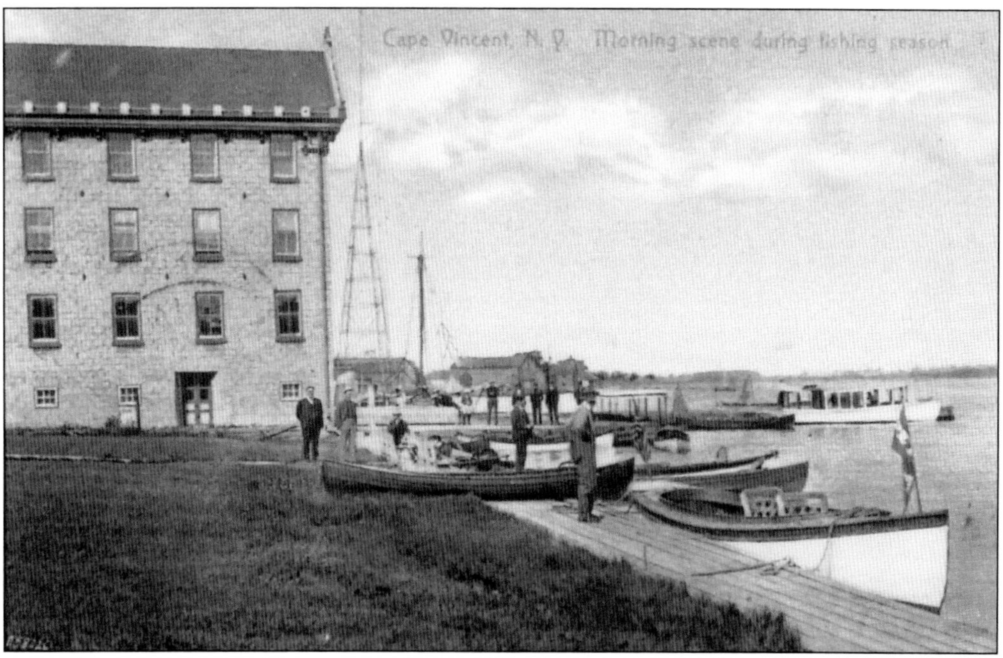

Cape Vincent, c. 1908. This is an early morning scene during the fishing season. The United States Fish Hatchery is located in the left of the picture.

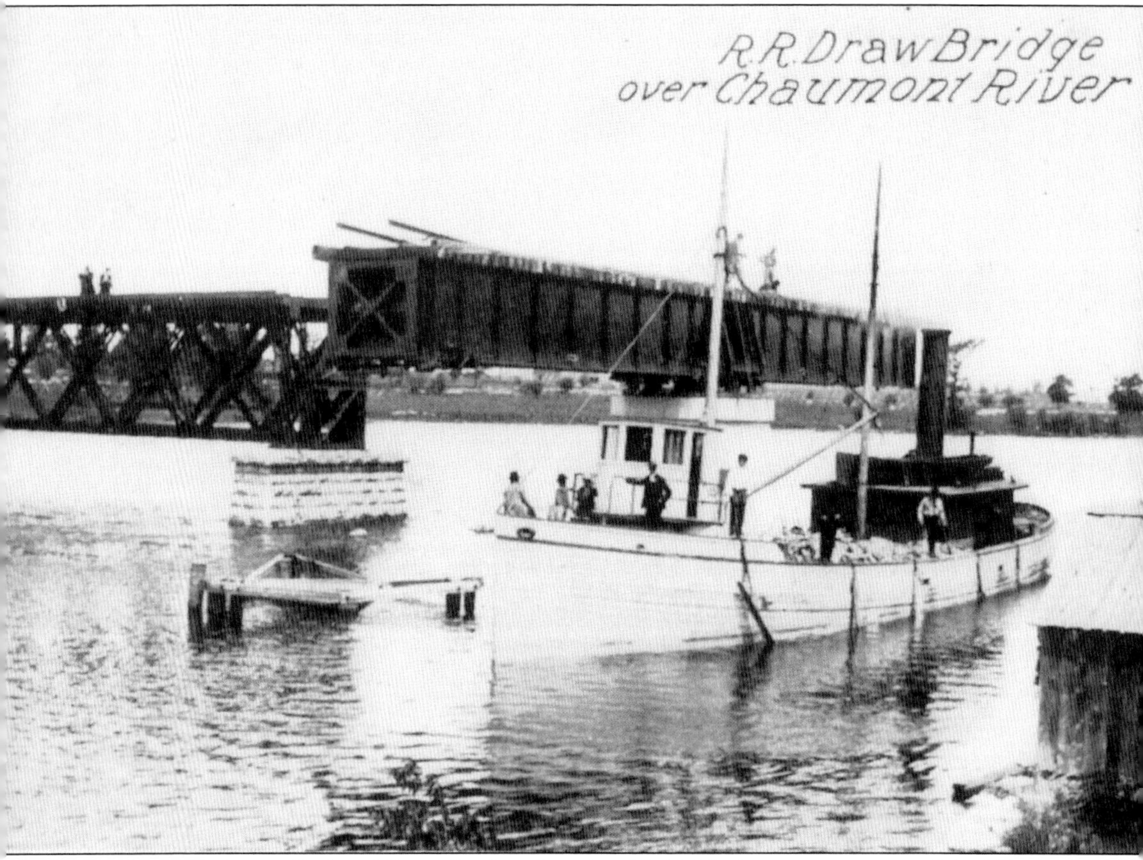

Chaumont River Railroad Draw Bridge. On May 13, 1836, the incorporation of the Watertown and Cape Vincent Railroad Company was enacted. It was not until 1851 that the tracks were completed to Chaumont. The following year, in 1852, a bridge was built and the railroad track completed to Cape Vincent. The completion of the bridge was important for the railroad as well as for fishermen entering Chaumont River from Lake Ontario.

Seven

Schools

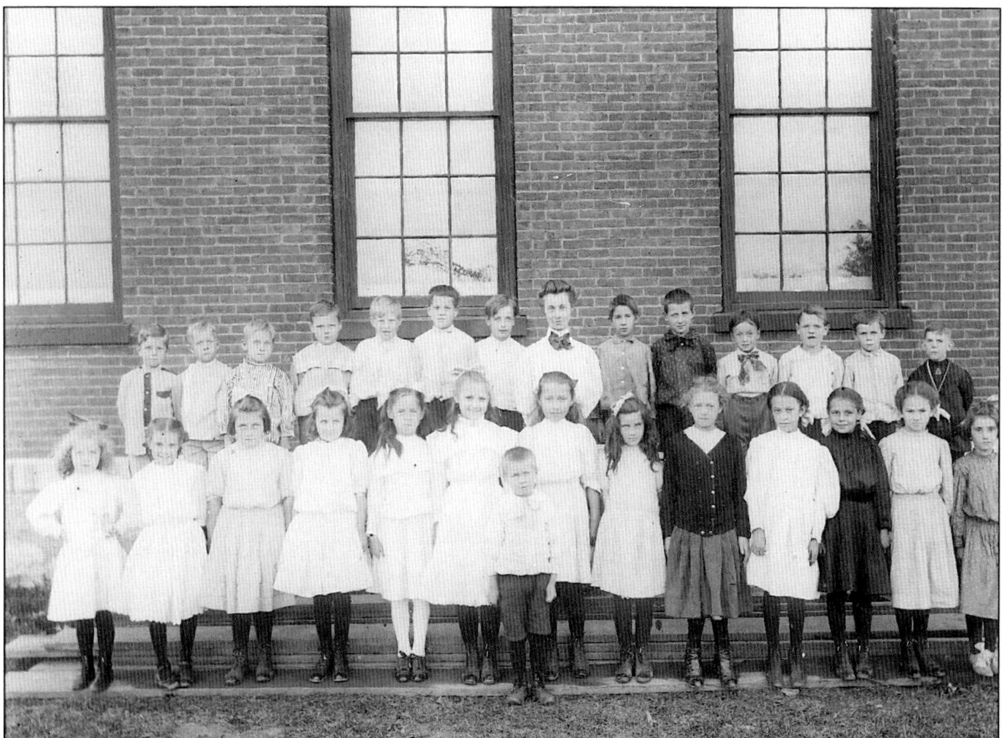

Pearl Street School, Watertown. The second grade class of Pearl Street School poses in front of the school for a photograph in 1909.

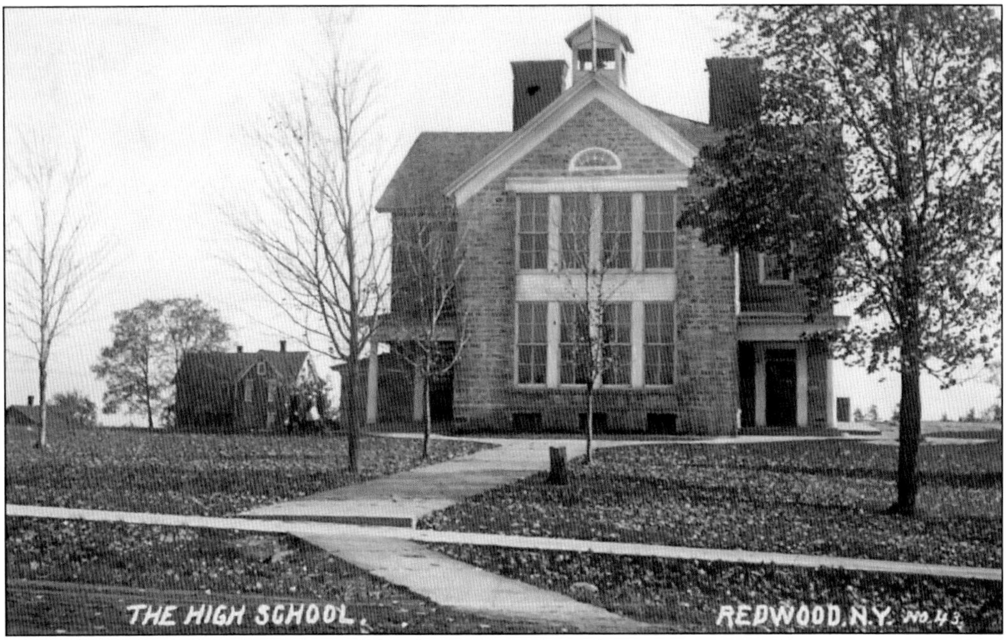

Redwood High School. The graded school of Redwood continued to advance its curriculum each year in an attempt to place the school in the regent's caliber. The school was built in 1859 and remained an institution throughout the nineteenth century.

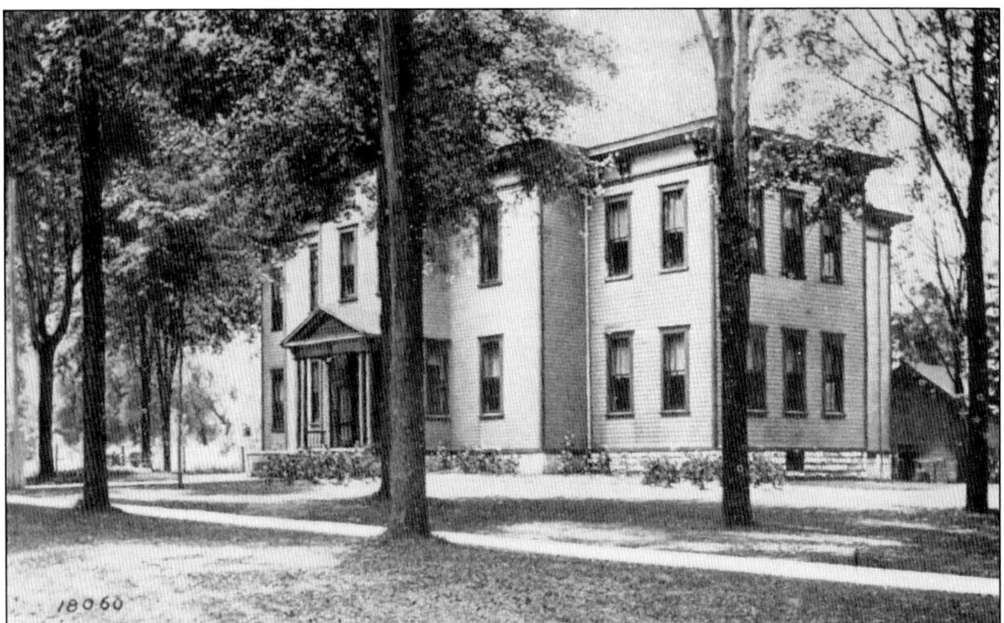

Cape Vincent. Cape Vincent High School was erected in 1879. By 1898, the high school had 289 pupils.

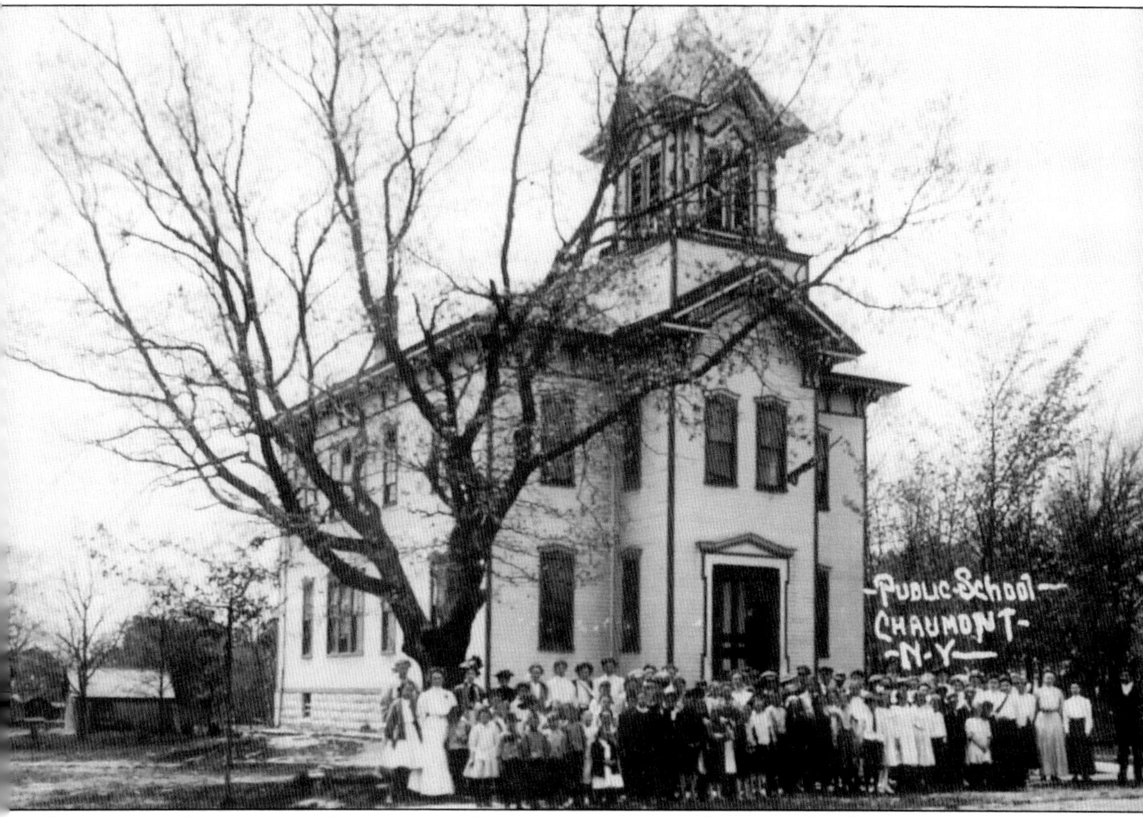

Chaumont Public School. Erected in 1880, this school was built for the local community that had, until this time, sent its children to Brownville for an education.

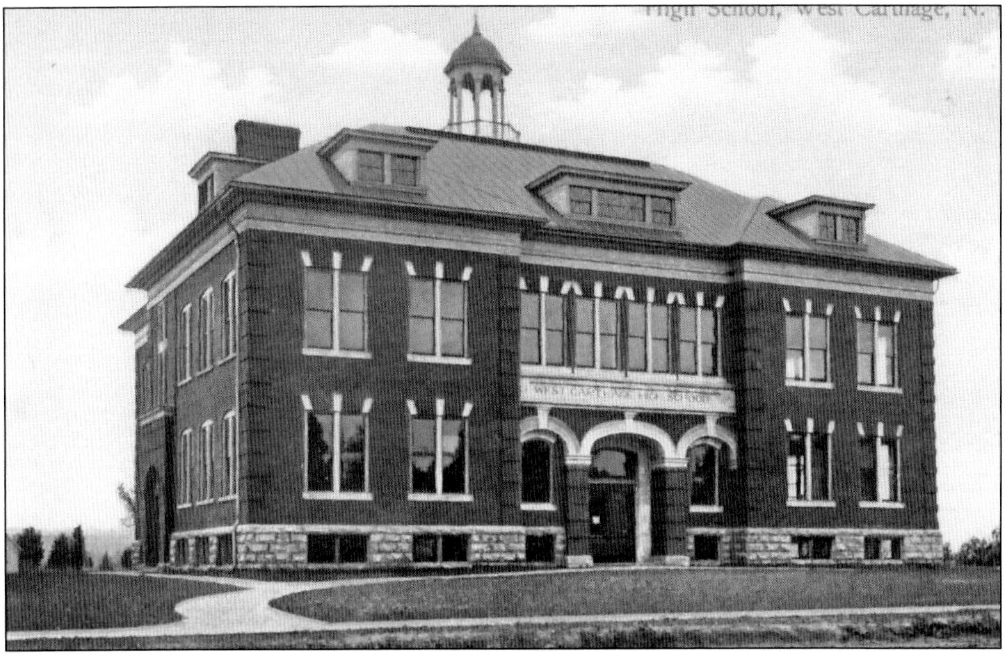

West Carthage High School. Built in 1905, the school was considered one of the most complete and substantial structures of its kind in this part of the state.

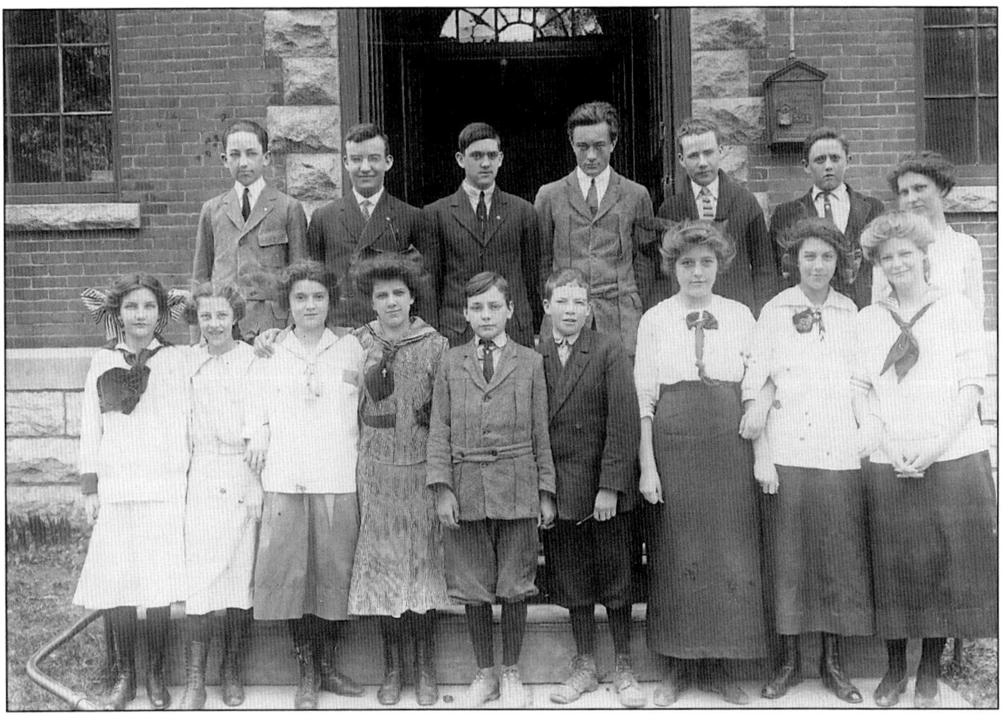

Mullin Street School. In 1918, a class of high school students poses for this picture.

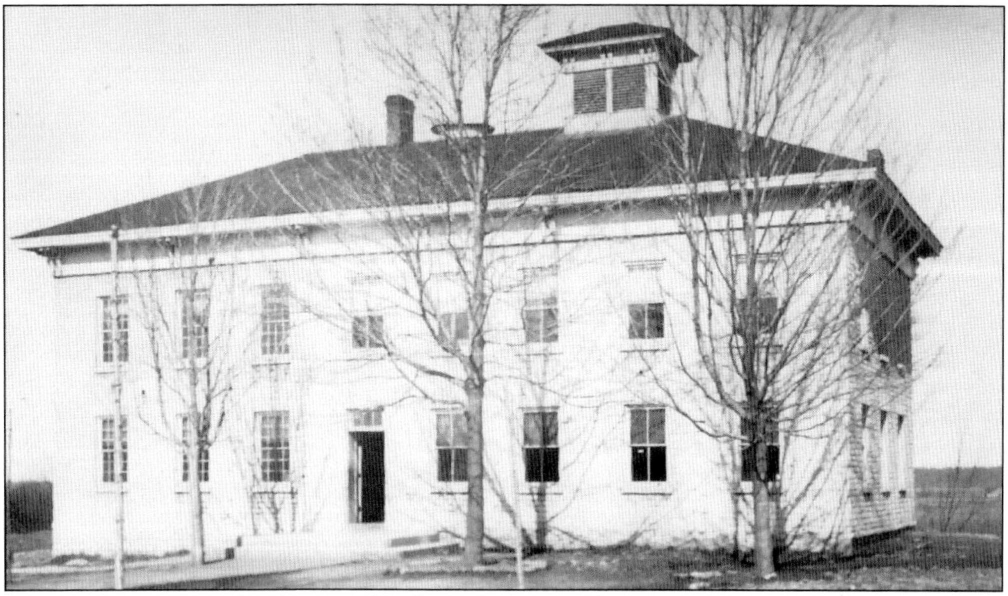

LaFargeville Public School. This school stood strong with eighty pupils in 1898, while attempts to build other educational institutions within the town struggled for support.

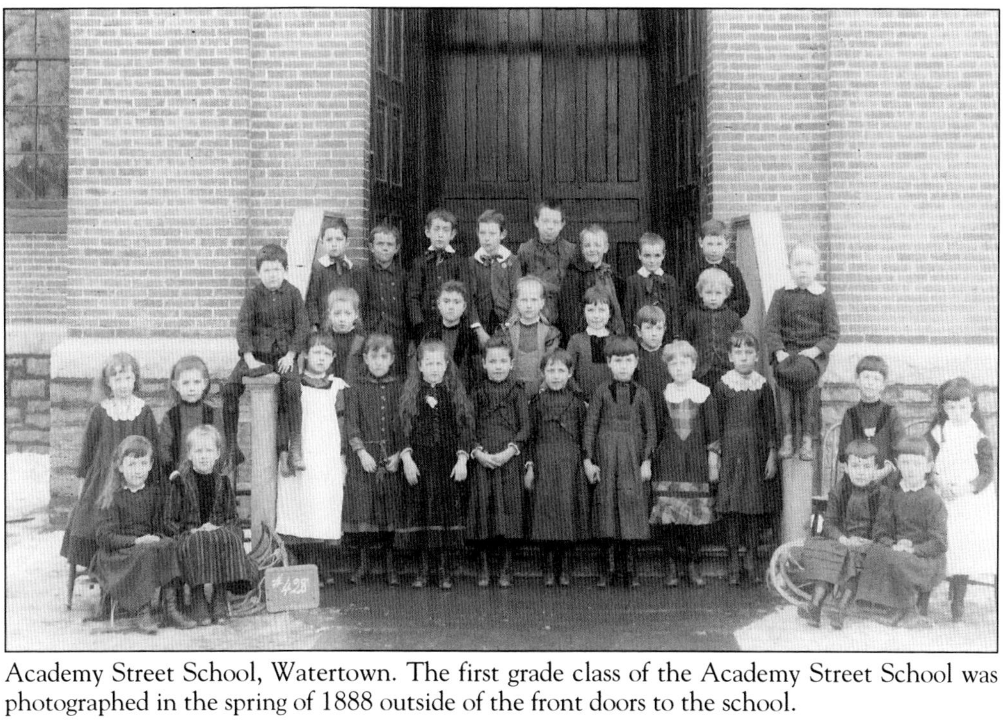

Academy Street School, Watertown. The first grade class of the Academy Street School was photographed in the spring of 1888 outside of the front doors to the school.

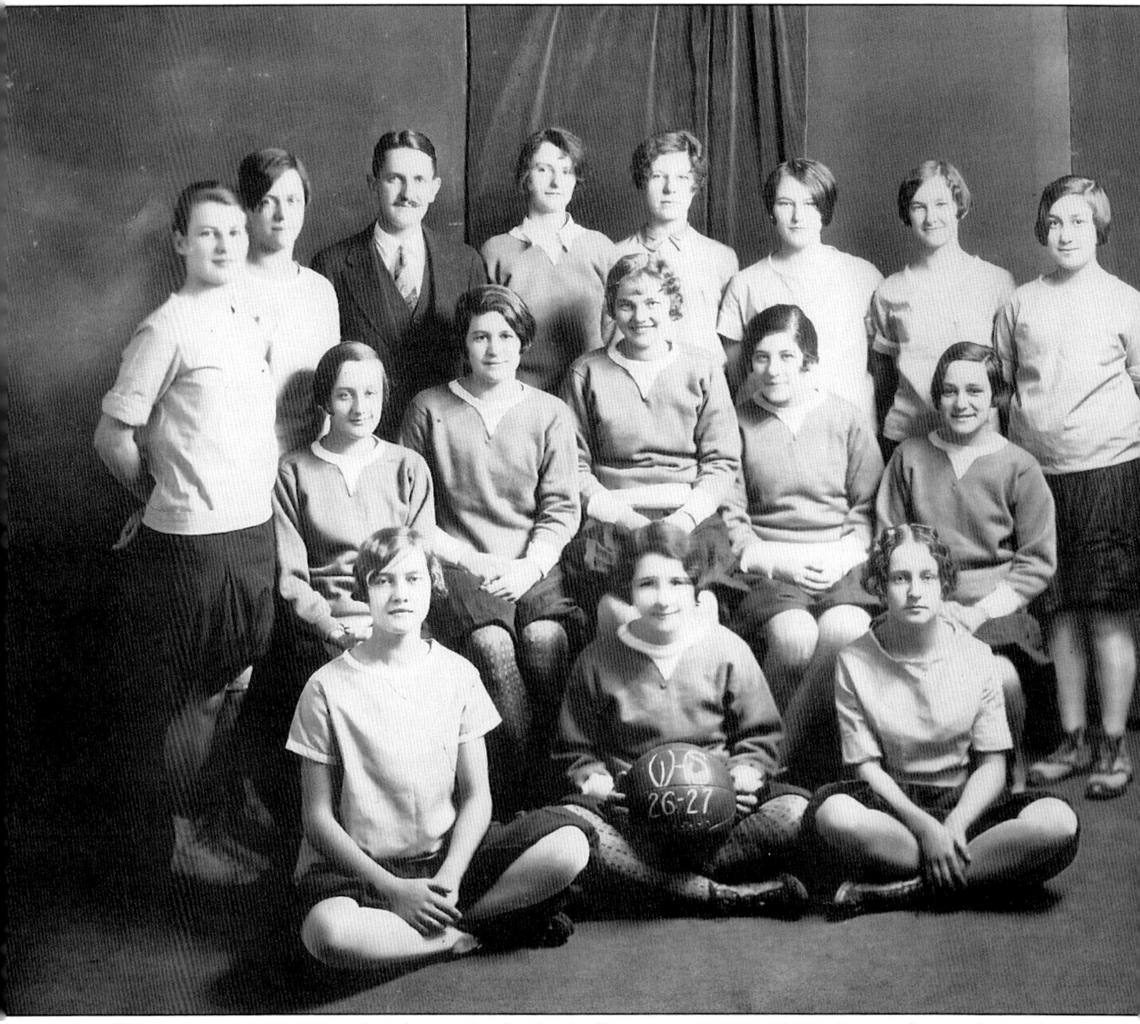

Watertown High School girls varsity basketball team in 1926–1927. Sports have always been a very important extracurricular activity for the schools of Jefferson County.

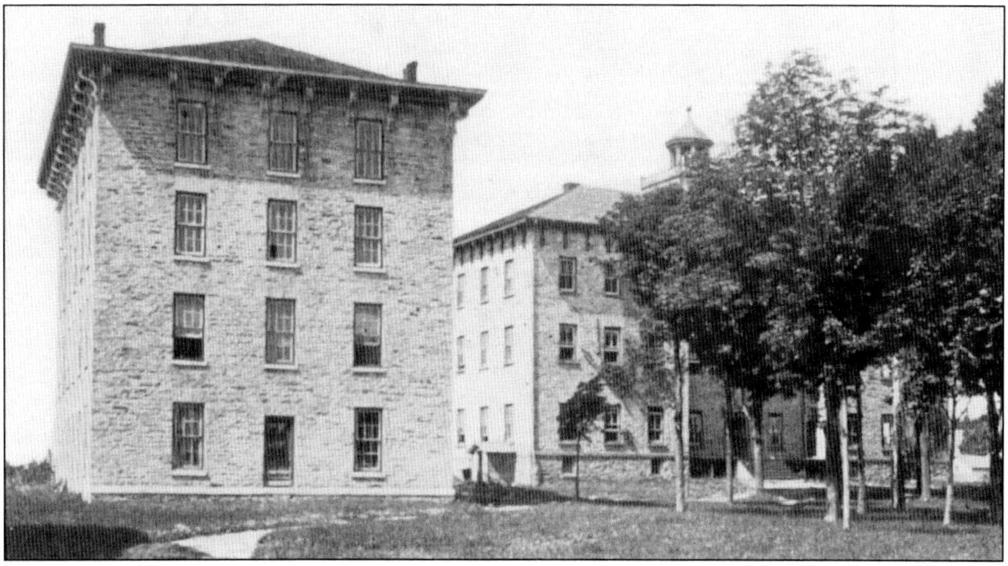

Antwerp High School. In 1870 this four-story stone structure was constructed as a boarding and ladies school. It later became popularly known as the Antwerp High School.

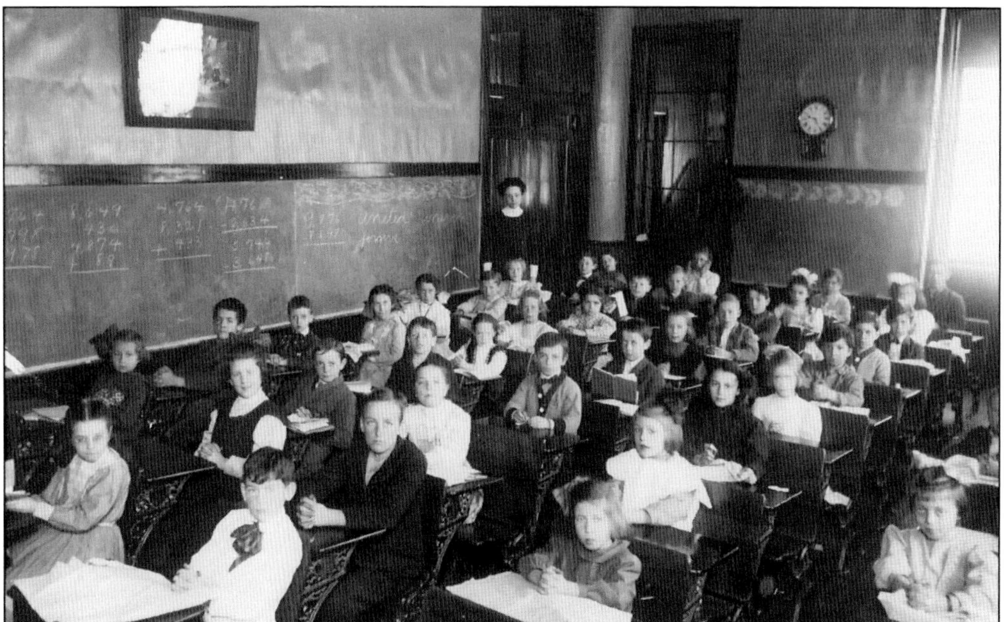

Hamilton Street School, Watertown. A group of very serious third-graders and their teacher Mrs. Williams is shown inside their classroom at the Hamilton Street School in Watertown.

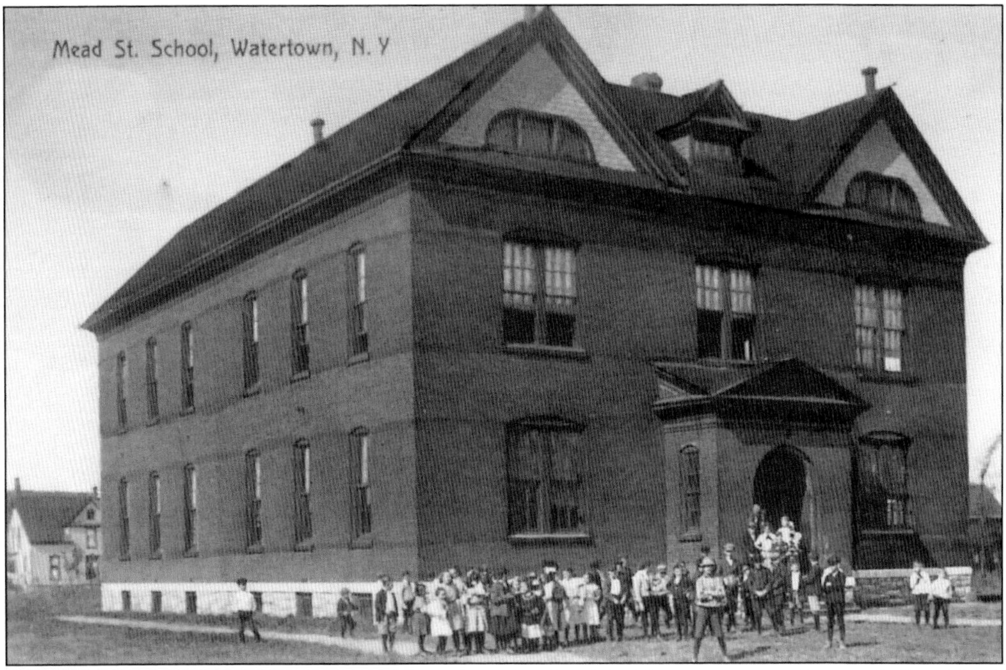

Mead Street School, Watertown. A group of schoolchildren pose in front of the Mead Street School. By 1898 the City of Watertown had twenty-nine hundred students enrolled in its schools. This was quite substantial considering the population of the city was only twenty thousand.

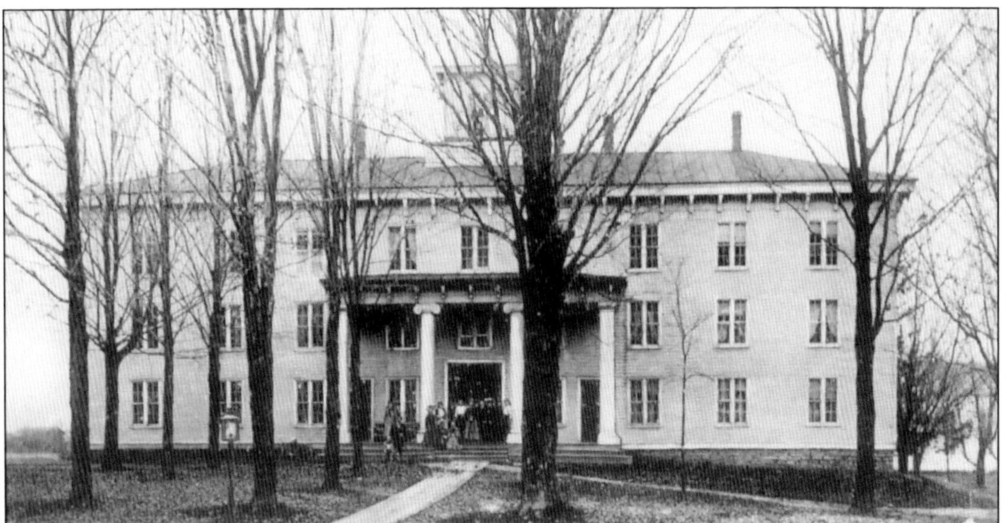

Belleville Union Academy. Opened in 1829, the school fell victim to bankruptcy in 1837. In 1840 the academy was again opened for the school year. By 1856, under the guidance of Principal J. Dunbar Houghton, the school reached a point of excellence never before attained.

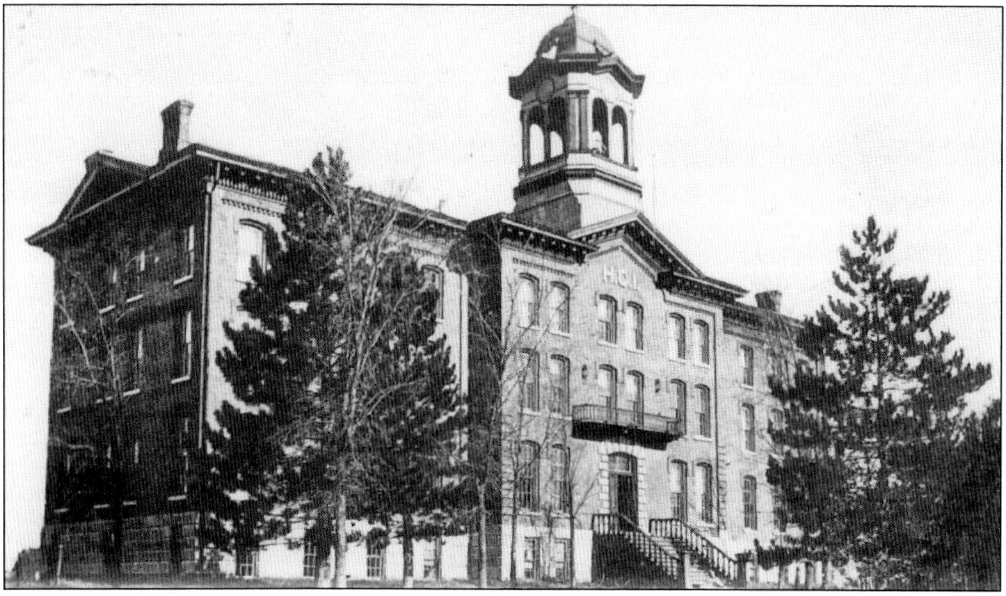

Adams Collegiate Institute. Established in 1855, the school changed its name to the Hungerford Collegiate Institute in 1864. The school was named after General Solon D. Hungerford, who gave a substantial endowment to the school. The building burned down in 1884.

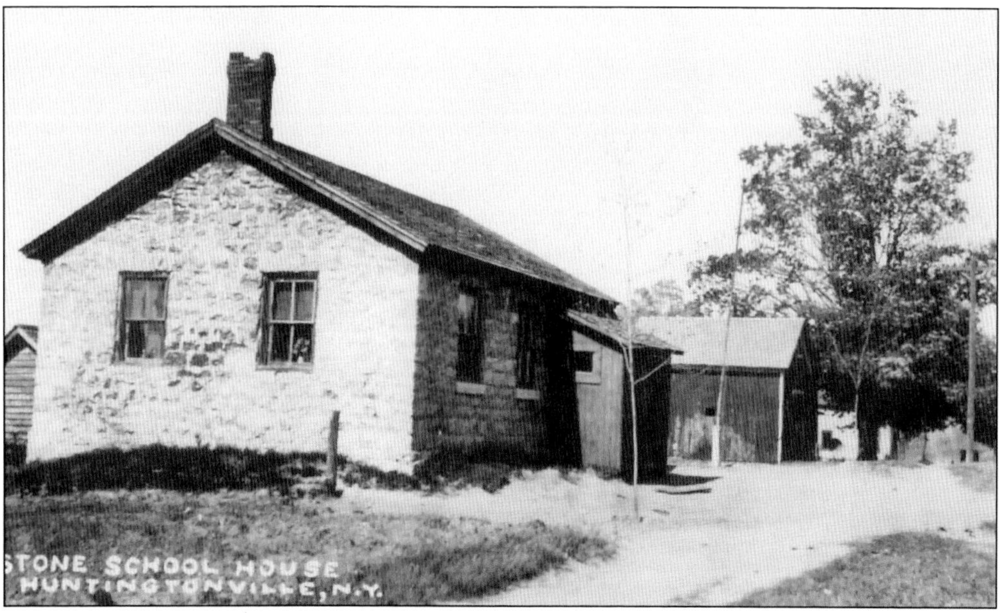

Huntingtonville. East of Watertown, along Huntington Street but within the city limits, lies a little community called Huntingtonville. Today, there is little evidence that this community has a separate identity. The Stone School House, as it was named in this picture, served all schoolchildren in what was once a distant and remote location.

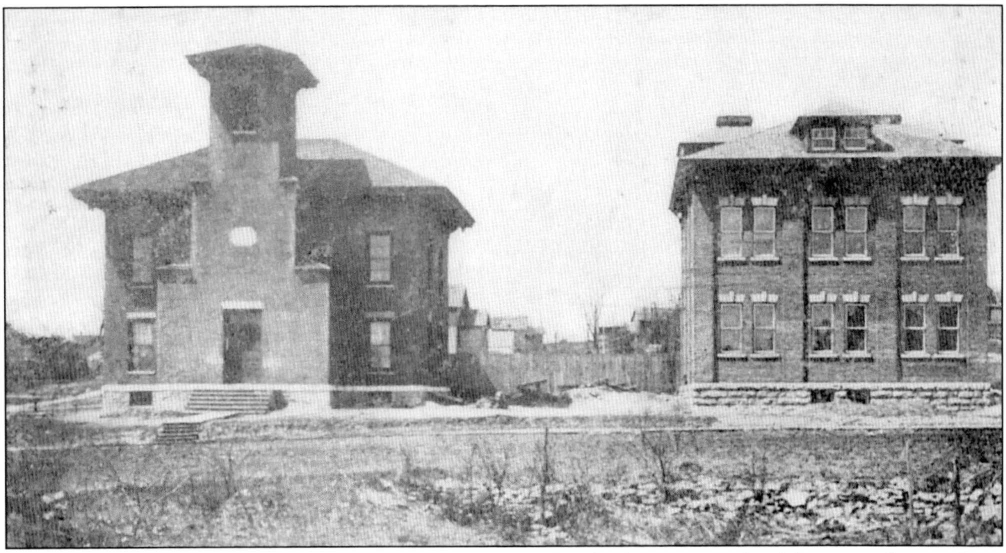

Old and new school buildings, Dexter. Dexter schools drew considerable attendance from outside the district. The school in Dexter was one of the best and most liberally supported schools in this part of the country. Dexter had operated a school since the town's incorporation in 1855. In 1894 the new schoolhouse was built.

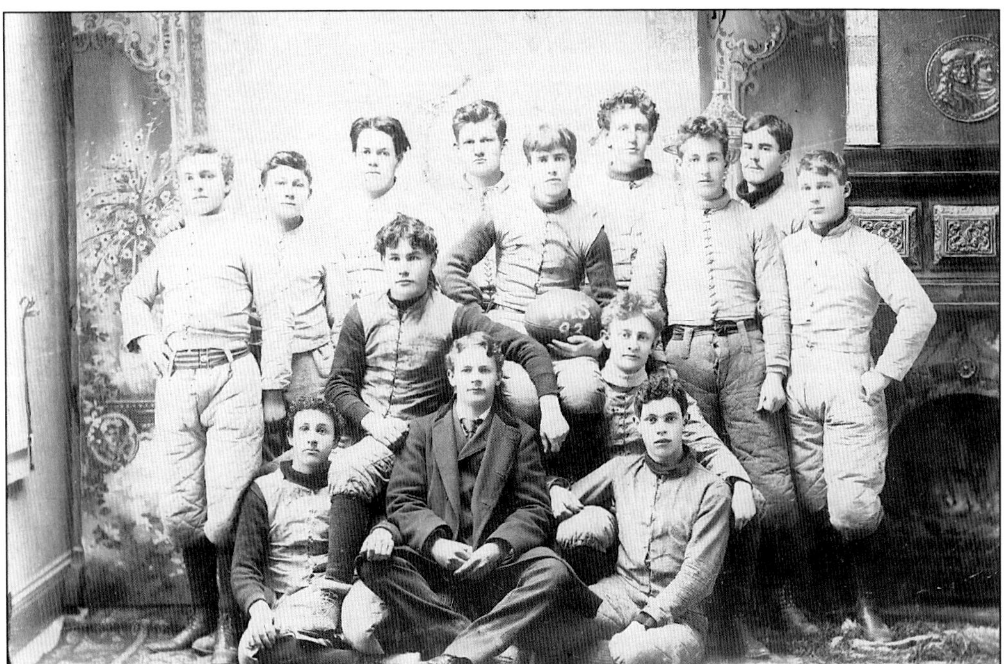

Watertown High School football team of 1893. During that year, the school's football team won the championship.

Eight

Churches

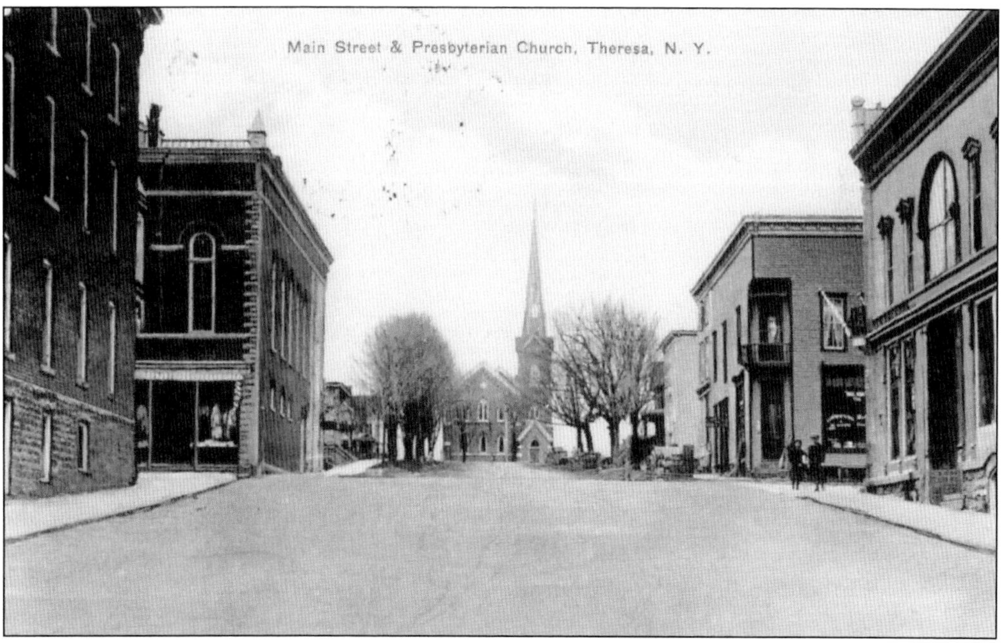

Presbyterian church, Theresa. Commonly known as the Flower Memorial Church, this church was built in 1879 with the generous funding of Governor Roswell P. Flower and his brother, Anson. The church was a tribute of love to their parents, Nathan and Mary Flower. The Presbyterian church was organized in Theresa in 1825, and its first edifice was dedicated in 1838.

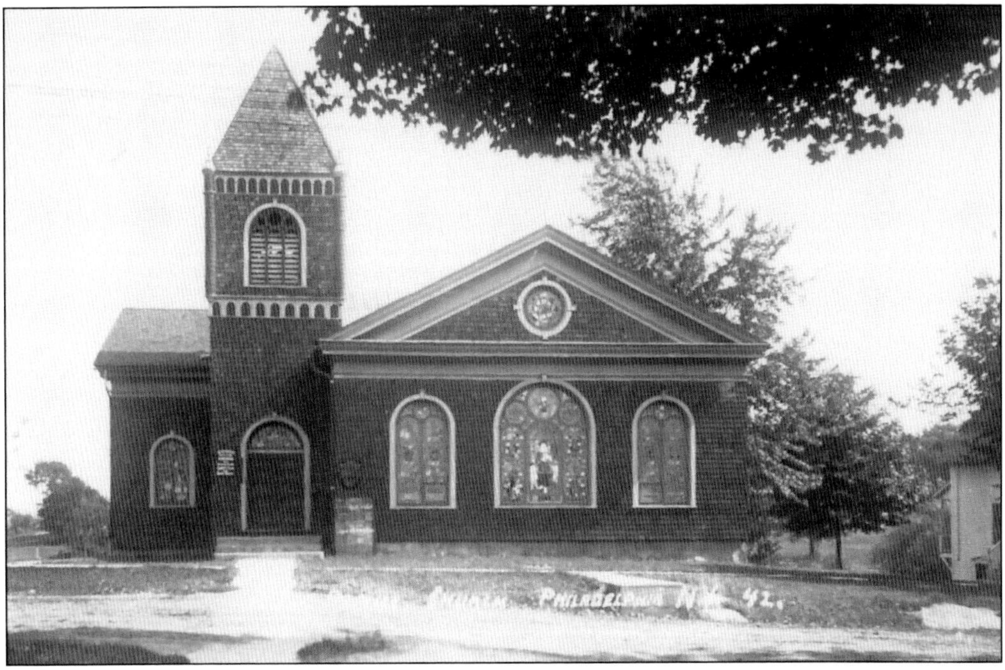

Baptist church, Philadelphia. Organized in 1840, it was not until 1841, in union with the Congregational church, that a house of worship was built on Main Street. The building became the sole property of the Baptist church in 1868.

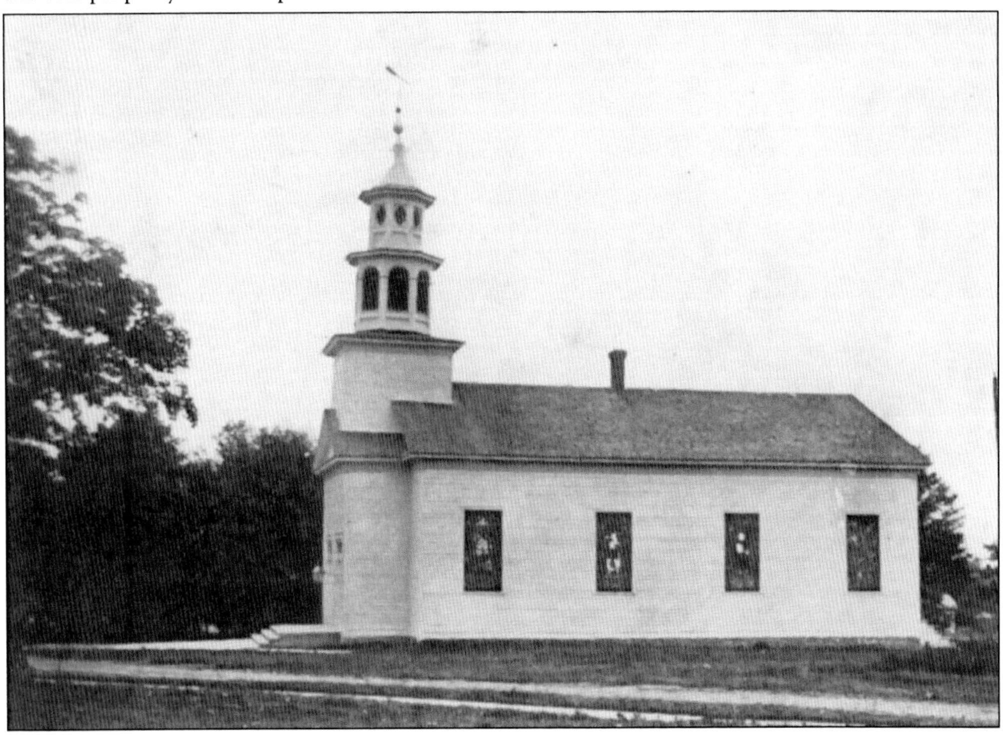

First Universalist Church, Henderson. Formed January 13, 1823, the church was not erected until sixteen years later in 1839.

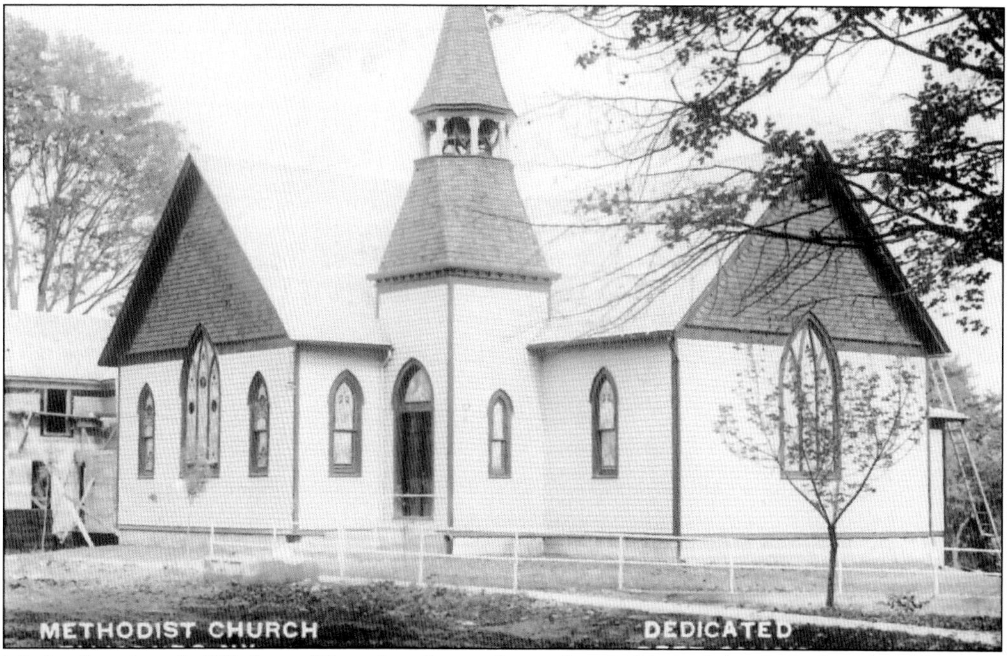

Methodist church, Ellisburg. This church was formed in 1832, and the first church edifice was built in 1833. Lyman Ellis, the founder of Ellisburg, was a trustee of the church. The church pictured was built in 1912 after a fire had destroyed the original structure the previous fall.

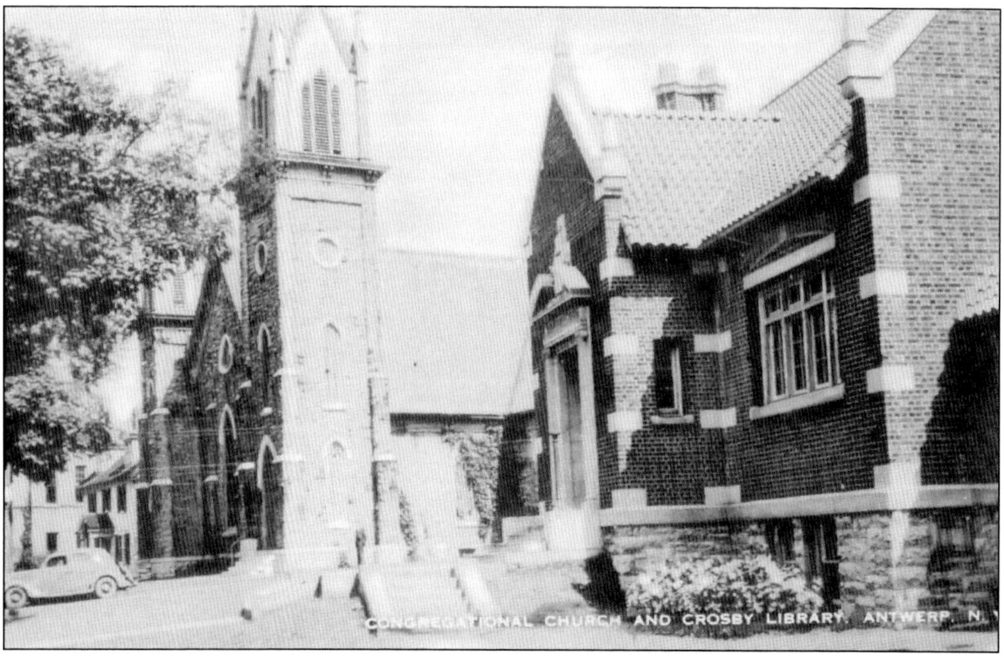

Congregational church, Antwerp. Formed in July 1819, the Congregational church is the oldest church organization in the town of Antwerp. Started as a Presbyterian church in 1854, its members voted to adopt the Congregational form of government. The building is made of limestone mined from the town's quarries.

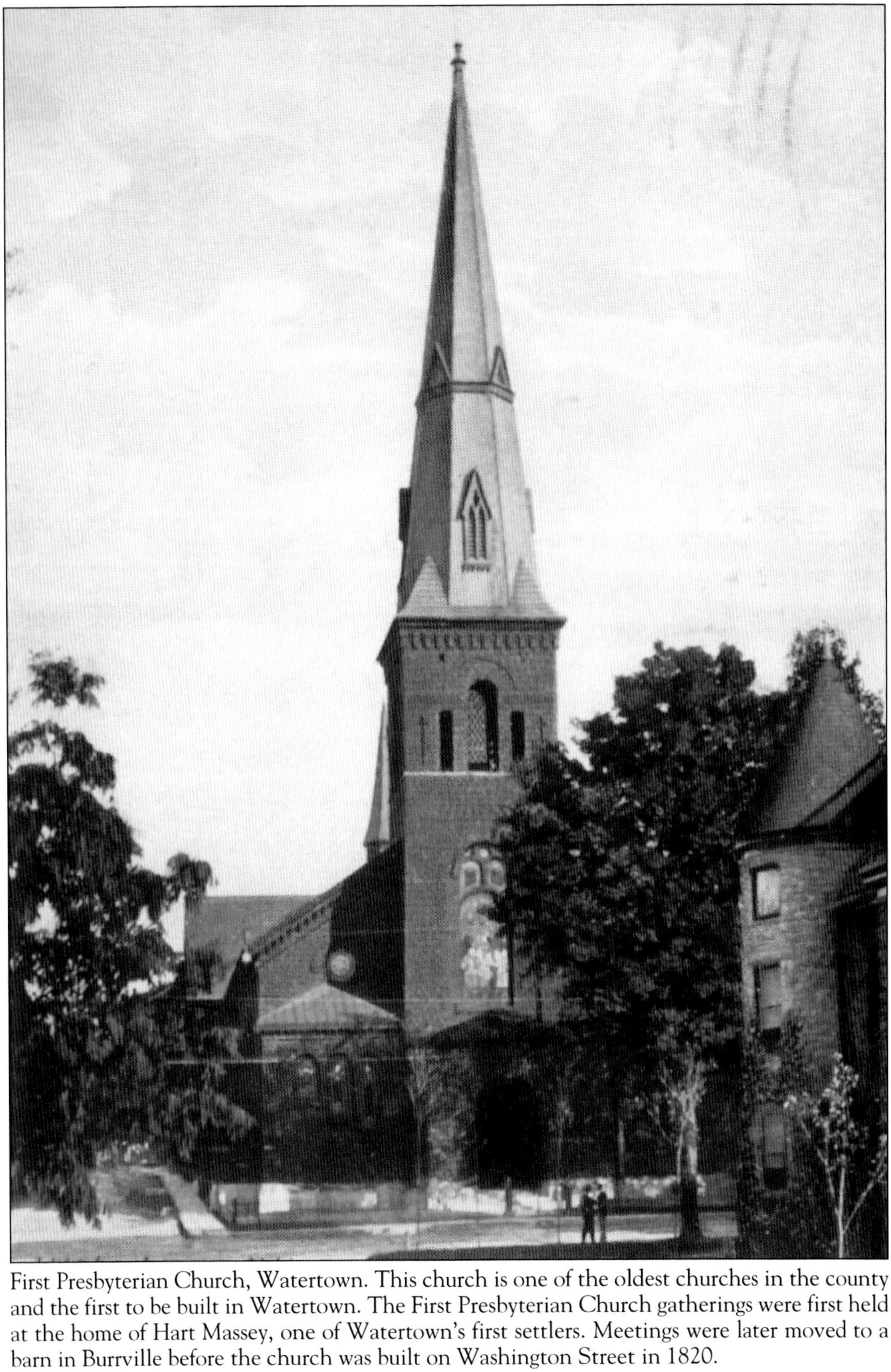

First Presbyterian Church, Watertown. This church is one of the oldest churches in the county and the first to be built in Watertown. The First Presbyterian Church gatherings were first held at the home of Hart Massey, one of Watertown's first settlers. Meetings were later moved to a barn in Burrville before the church was built on Washington Street in 1820.

Methodist church, Depauville. The Methodist church was the first church in Depauville. Its edifice was built in 1825.

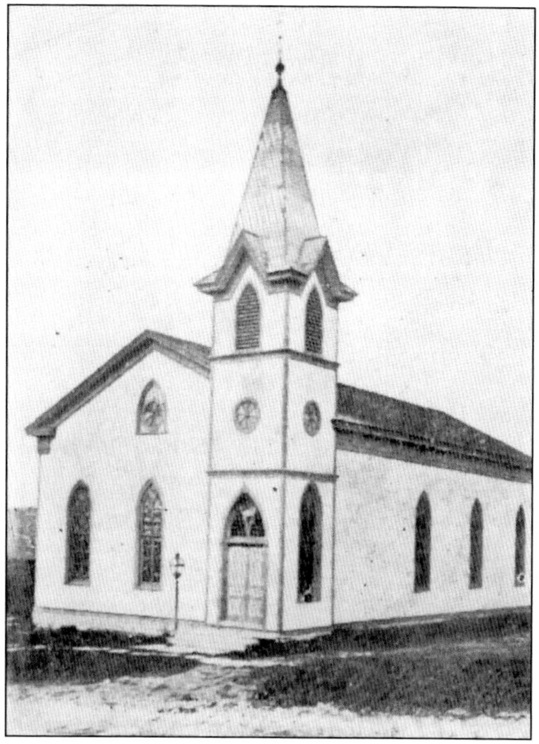

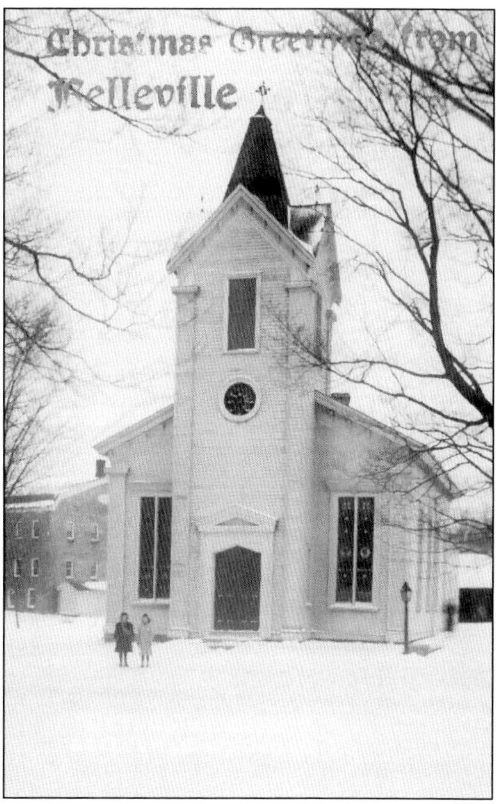

Methodist church, Belleville. The Belleville Methodist Episcopal Church was formed in 1841. This church also became the home of the Presbyterian and Catholic faiths for a short time.

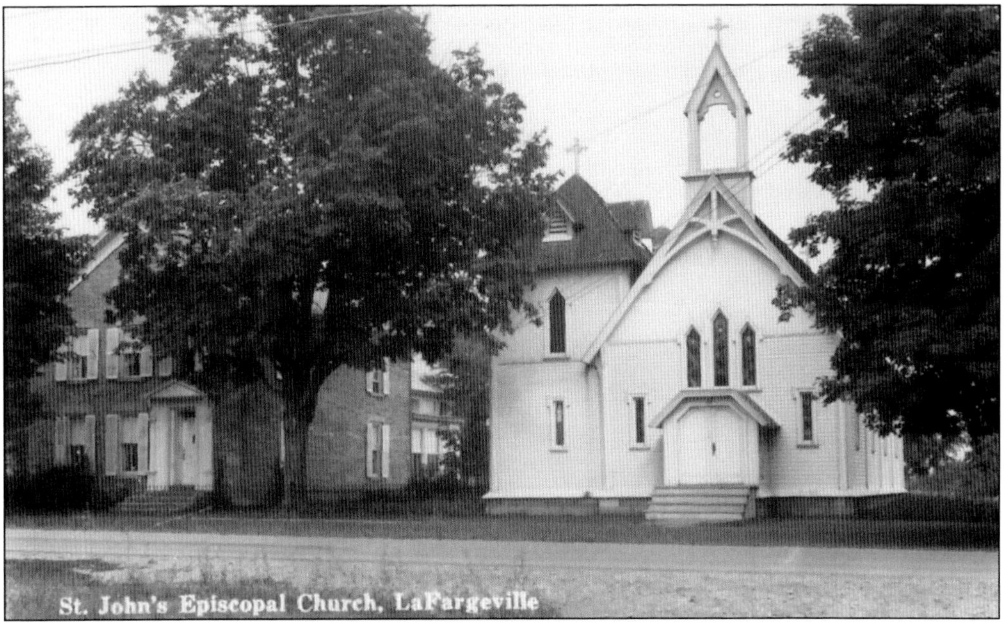

St. John's Episcopal Church, LaFargeville. The church, built in 1846, was considered a small but neat edifice sufficient for the needs of the congregation. Services were generally performed by priests from Watertown.

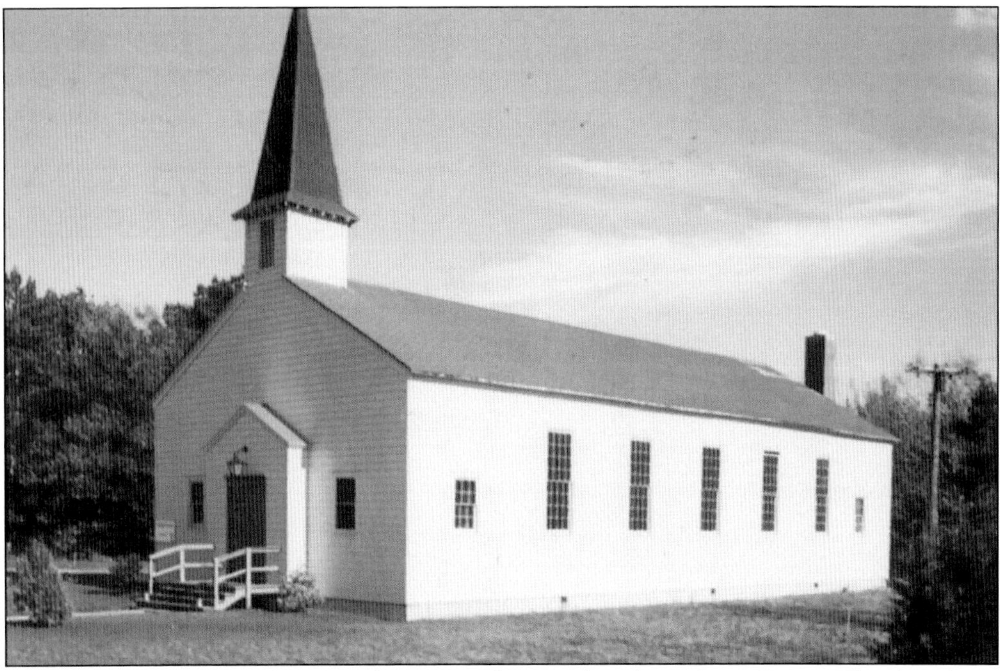

Chapel at Camp Drum. This chapel was one of seven chapels on Camp Drum. The chapel was there to give spiritual guidance to those in the military.

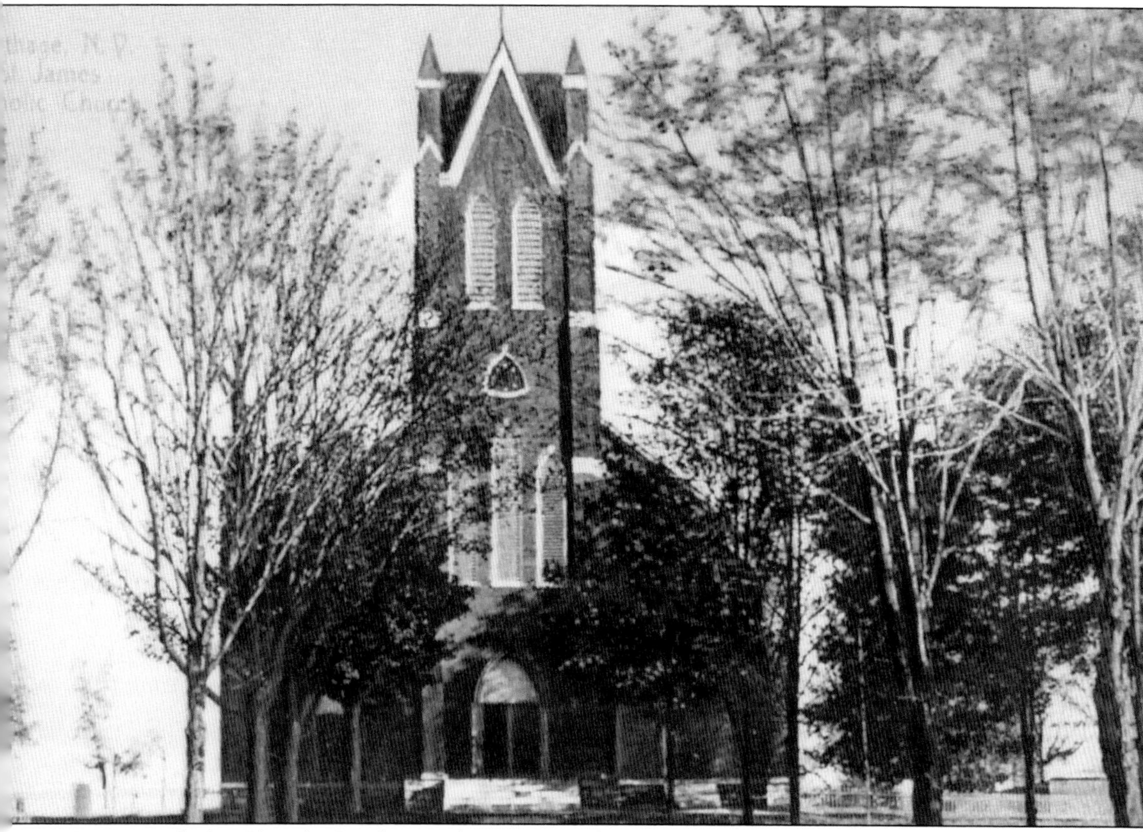

St. James Catholic Church, Carthage. The great Carthage fire of 1888 destroyed many buildings in West Carthage and Carthage. Amazingly, St. James Catholic Church was left untouched. The church was founded in 1819 and is the oldest church in Carthage. The grounds were donated by Vincent LeRay de Chaumont, a French aristocrat who settled in the North Country with his father.

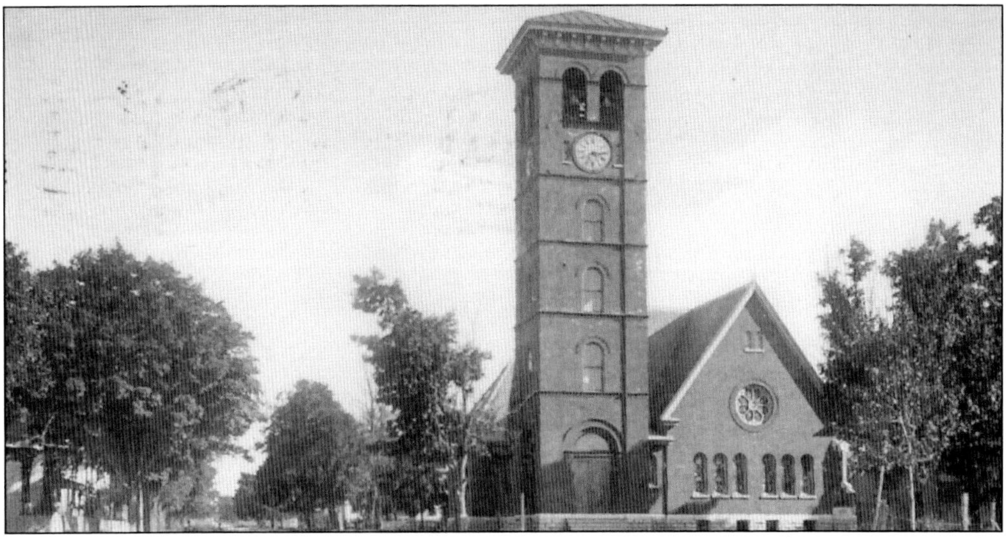

Presbyterian church, Sackets Harbor. Erected in 1816 on West Washington Street, the Presbyterian church is one of the oldest churches in the village. In 1843 a fire destroyed the church, and it was rebuilt on its present site of Main and East Broad Streets. The church pictured was built in 1900 and is not only the home of the church, but shares its space with the Hay Memorial Library.

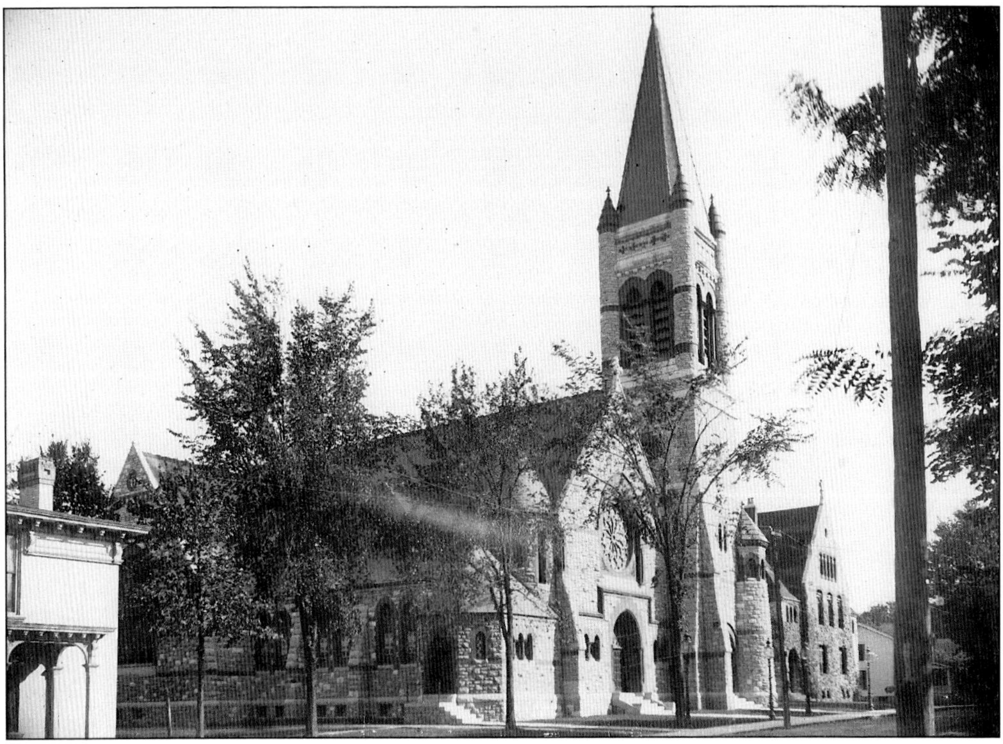

Trinity Church, Watertown. The first services for Trinity Church date back to 1812. They were held in a schoolhouse in the southeast corner of Public Square. By 1831 a lot on Court Street was purchased and a church was built. The church burned down in 1849. In 1888 the Sherman Street site was chosen and another church for Trinity was erected in 1890.

Catholic church, Brownville. Built on what was once known as Paddy Hill, because of the Irish attending the church, the Catholic church in Brownville was organized and its edifice built in 1870.

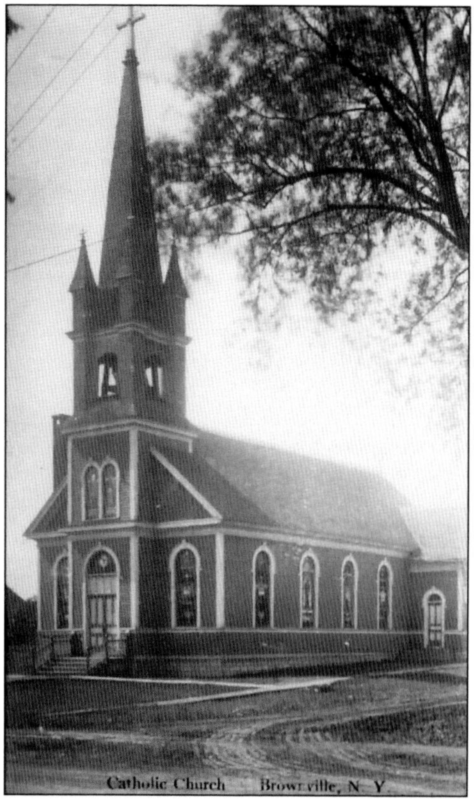

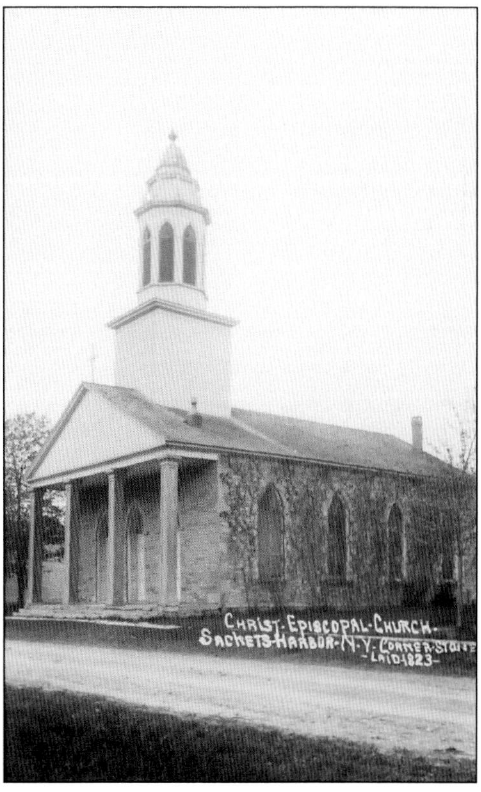

Christ Episcopal Church, Sackets Harbor. The church was organized in 1821. In 1823 the edifice was started, but it was not completed until nine years later in 1832.

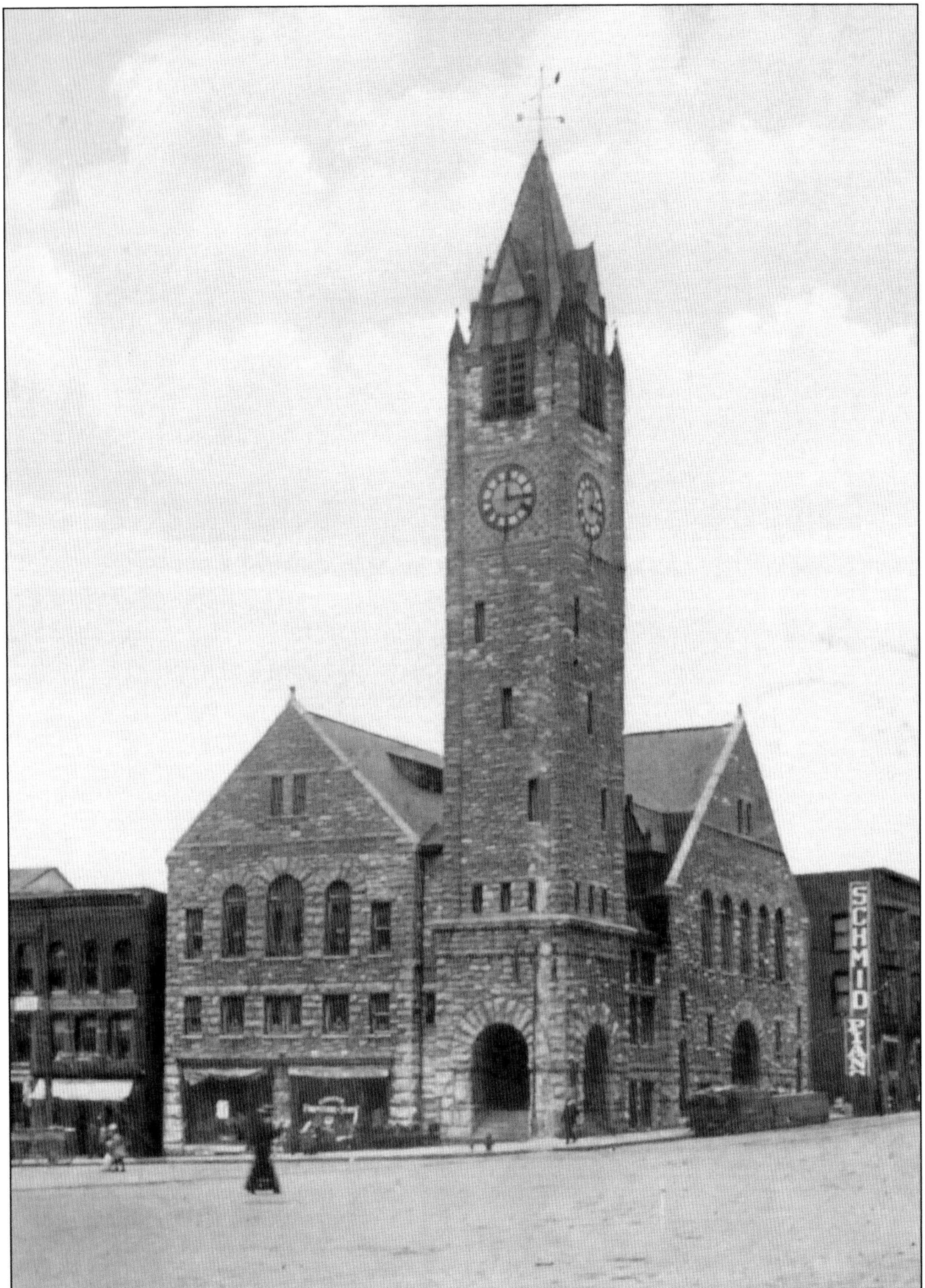

First Baptist Church, Watertown. The Baptist church of Watertown had its origins in 1823 but was not legally organized until 1827. In 1837 the church was built fronting Public Square and is a landmark in the city of Watertown. The church has been destroyed by fire twice—in 1838 and 1846. The church was rebuilt both times, always increasing in size.

Nine

Hotels and Taverns

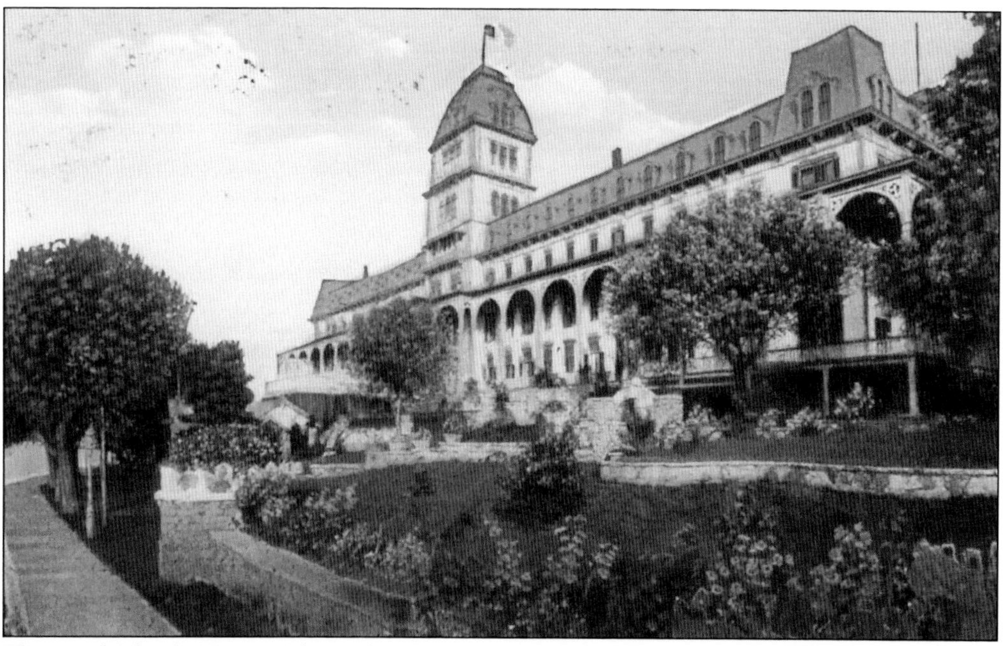

Thousand Islands House, Alexandria Bay, *c.* 1920. The Thousand Islands House occupied a commanding site above the upper wharf of Alexandria Bay. It was built in 1872 and had the capacity for three hundred guests.

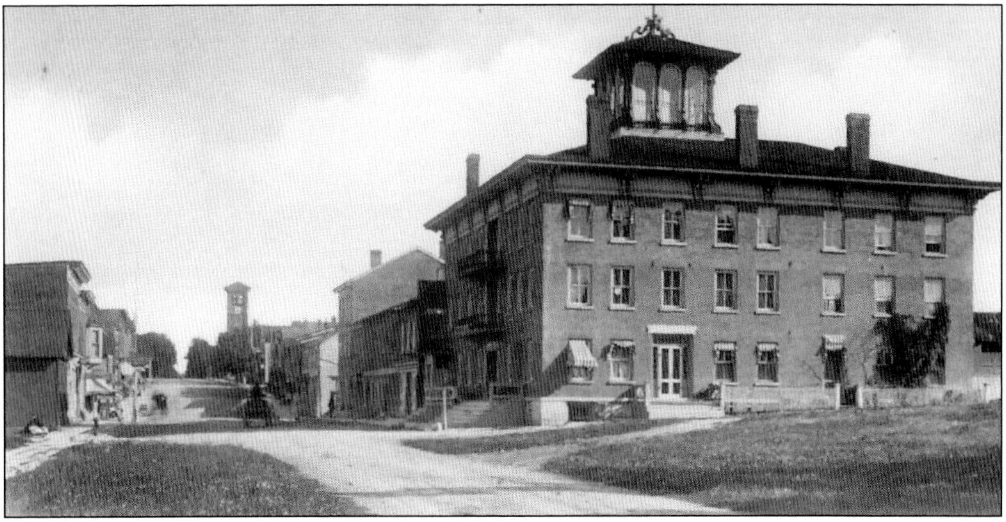

Everleigh House, Sackets Harbor, *c.* 1900. Built by Ambrose H. Dodge in 1843, the Everleigh House was opened to the public one year later.

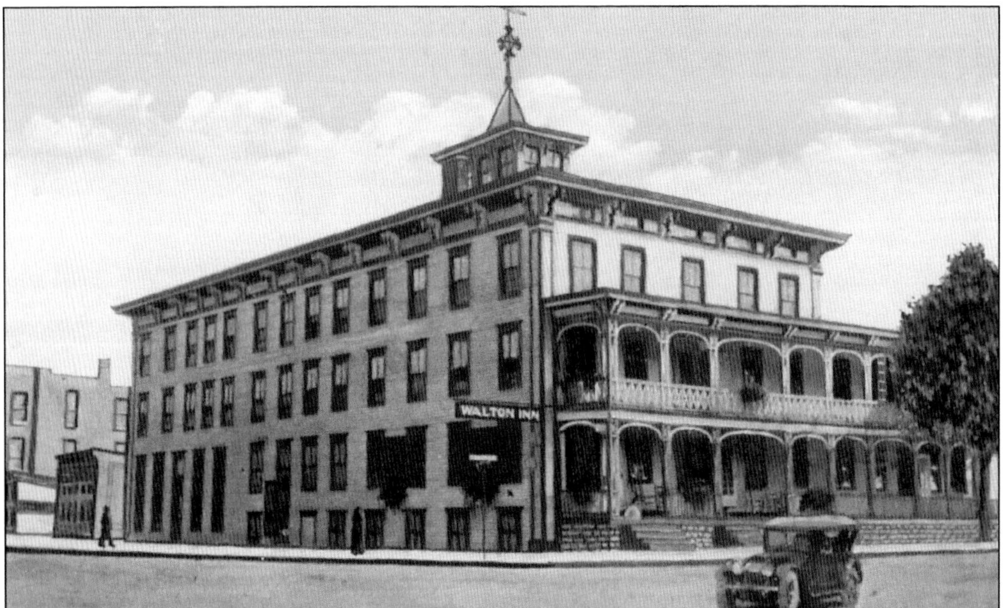

Walton Inn, Clayton, *c.* 1915. As more visitors discovered the beauty of the Thousand Islands in the late 1800s, it became necessary to enlarge small existing hotels in order to accommodate the increasing number of guests. The Walton Inn is one example.

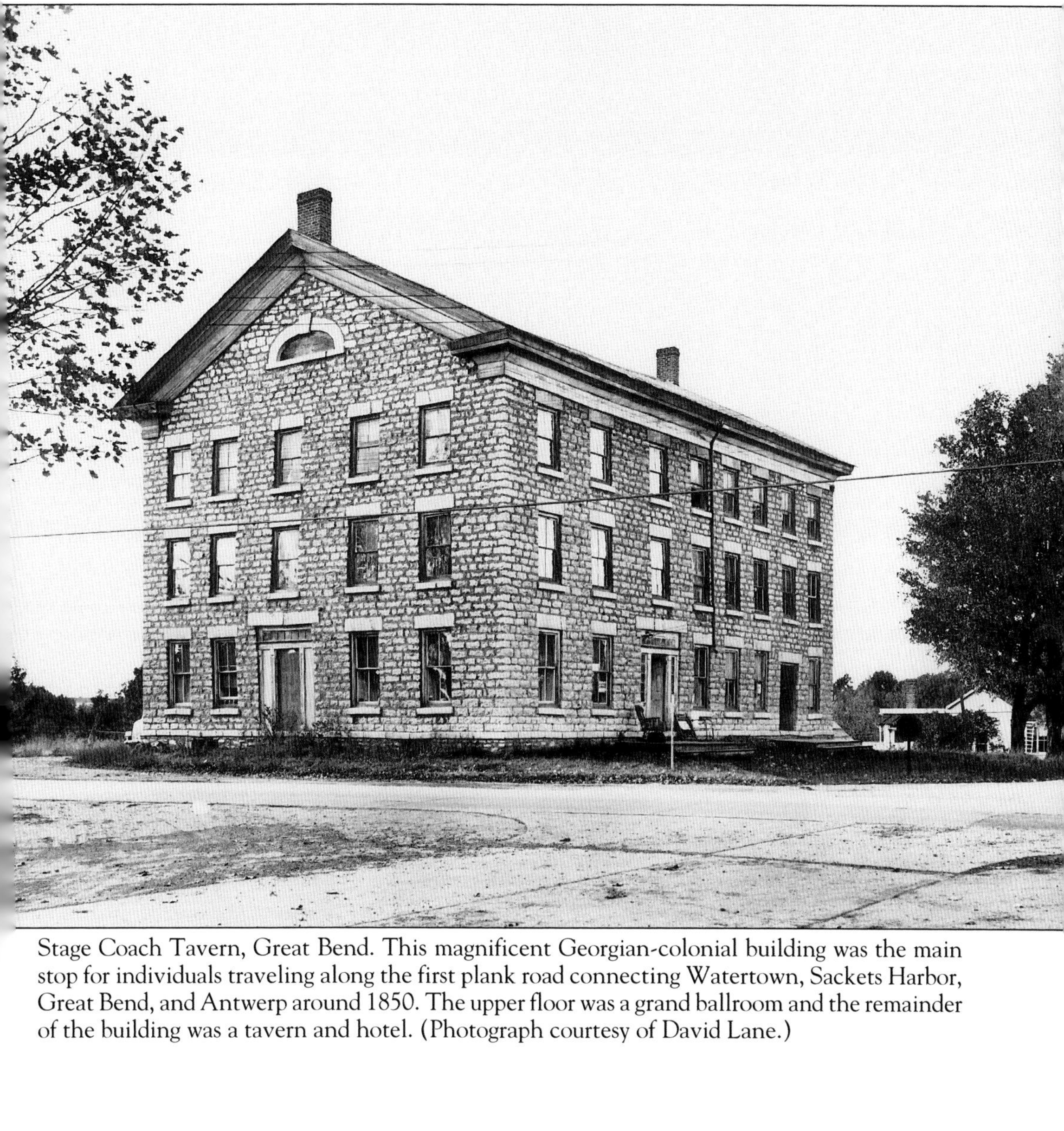

Stage Coach Tavern, Great Bend. This magnificent Georgian-colonial building was the main stop for individuals traveling along the first plank road connecting Watertown, Sackets Harbor, Great Bend, and Antwerp around 1850. The upper floor was a grand ballroom and the remainder of the building was a tavern and hotel. (Photograph courtesy of David Lane.)

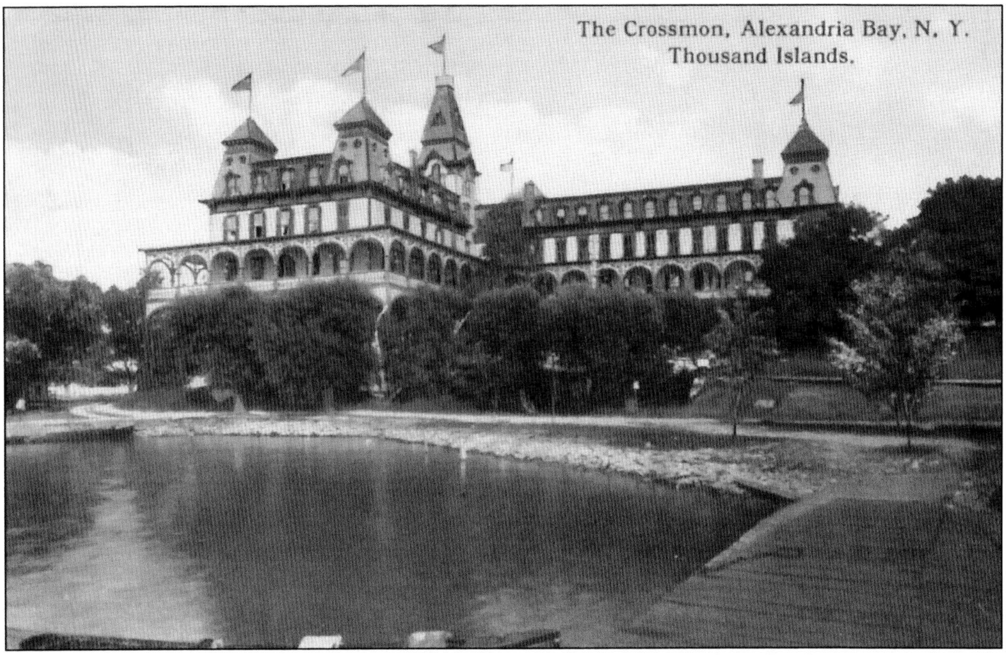

The Crossmon House, Alexandria Bay, *c.* 1920. Built in 1872 by Charles Crossmon, the Crossmon House entertained many eminent men of the nation. It was considered the largest hotel on the river and perhaps the most popular.

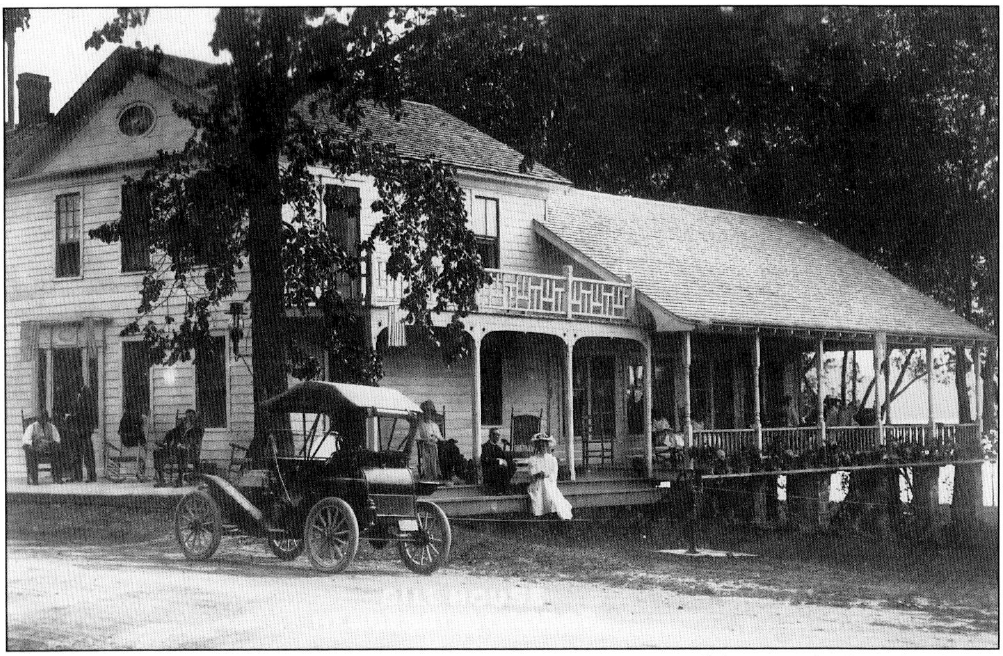

Gill House, Henderson Harbor, *c.* 1910. The Gill House was a small but popular boardinghouse located on beautiful Henderson Harbor, and it remains a favorite summer restaurant and inn.

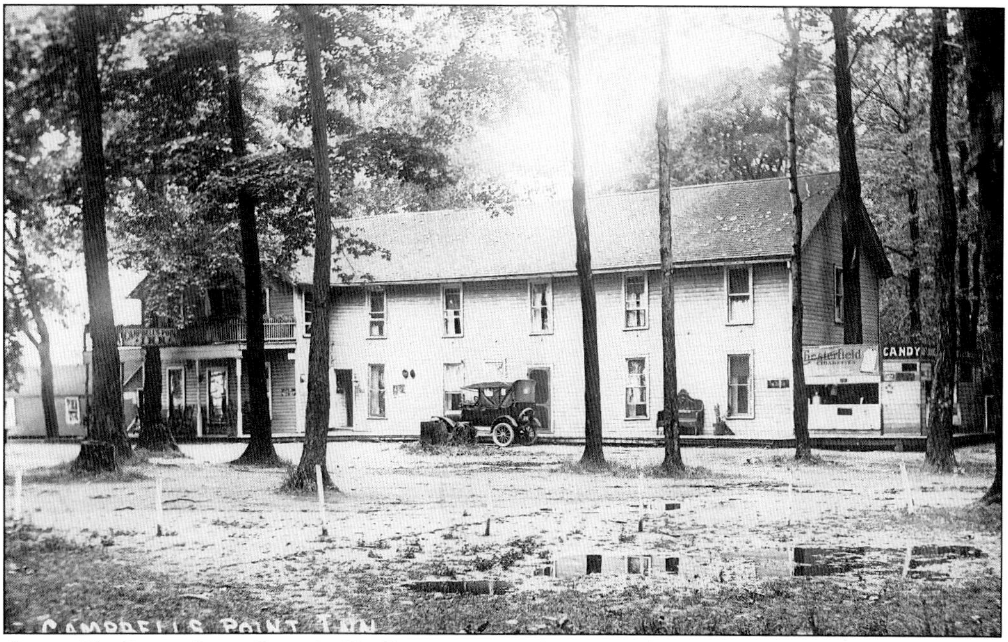

Campell's Point Inn, Campbell's Point, c. 1910. Located just south of Sackets Harbor, Campbell's Point is a private cottage community today.

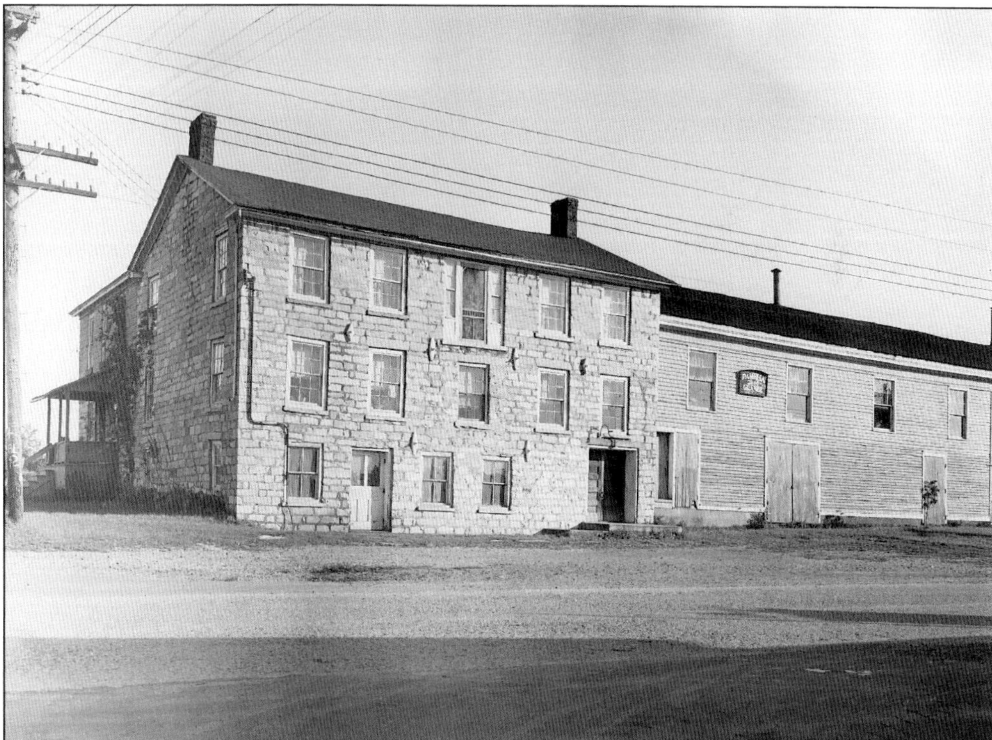

Four Corners Stagecoach Tavern and Hotel, Pamelia. Built in 1825, this historic structure, located at the Pamelia Four Corners, was a frequent overnight stop for visitors entering Jefferson County. (Photo courtesy of David Lane.)

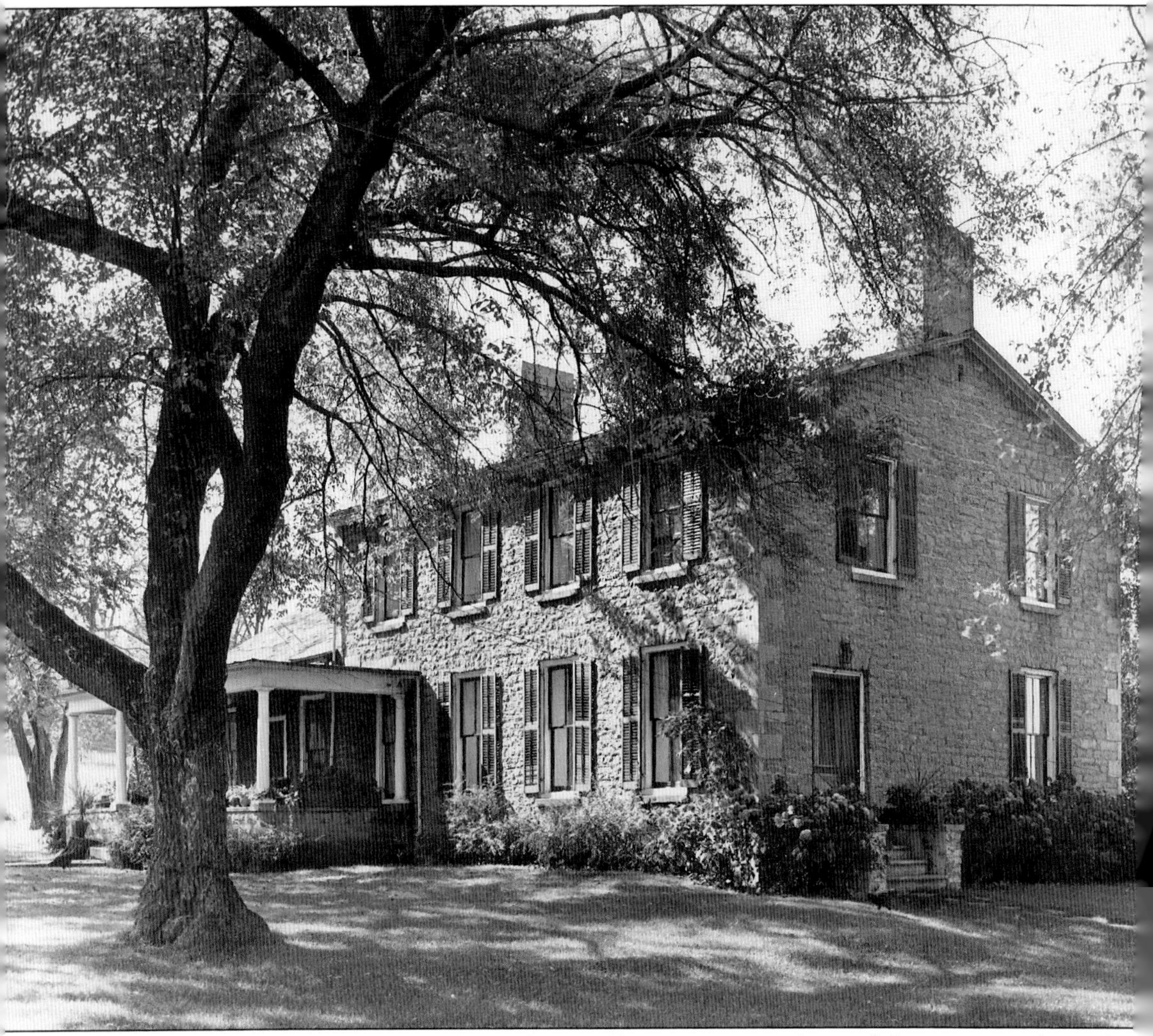

Talcott Falls Tavern, Talcott Falls. Talcott Falls Tavern reminds us of the romantic days of stagecoaches stopping at the inviting taverns for rest and nourishment. This outstanding tavern was built by Major Daniel Talcott, who insisted that a whiskey bottle be cemented at the very peak of its front gable. This was symbolic that the tavern never was without liquid cheer for its guests. (Photo courtesy of David Lane.)

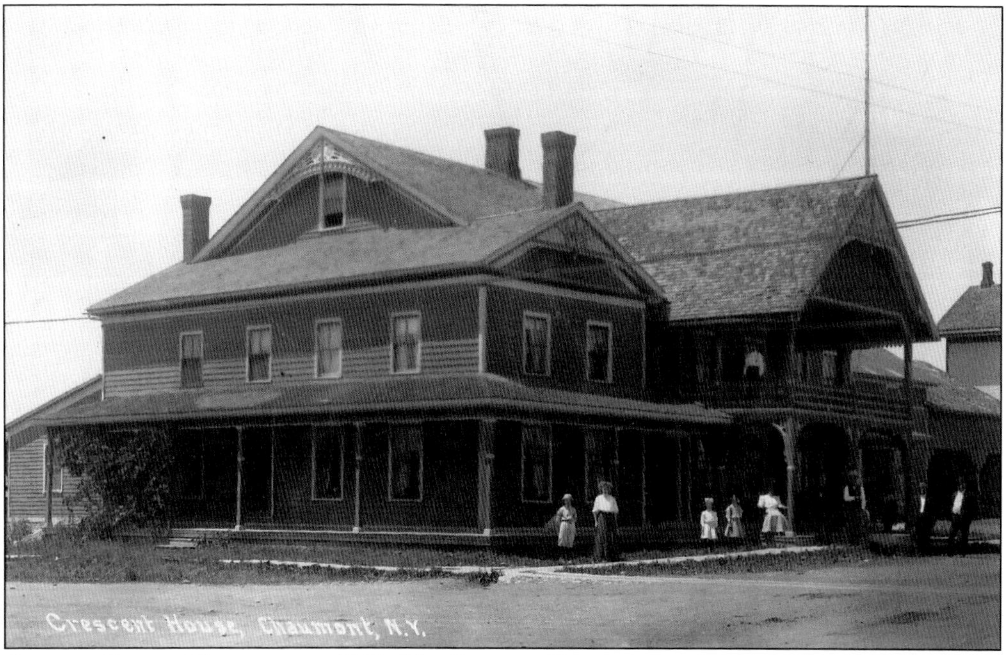

Crescent House, Chaumont, *c.* 1909. The Crescent House, located in the village of Chaumont, was frequented by visitors to the Chaumont Bay area.

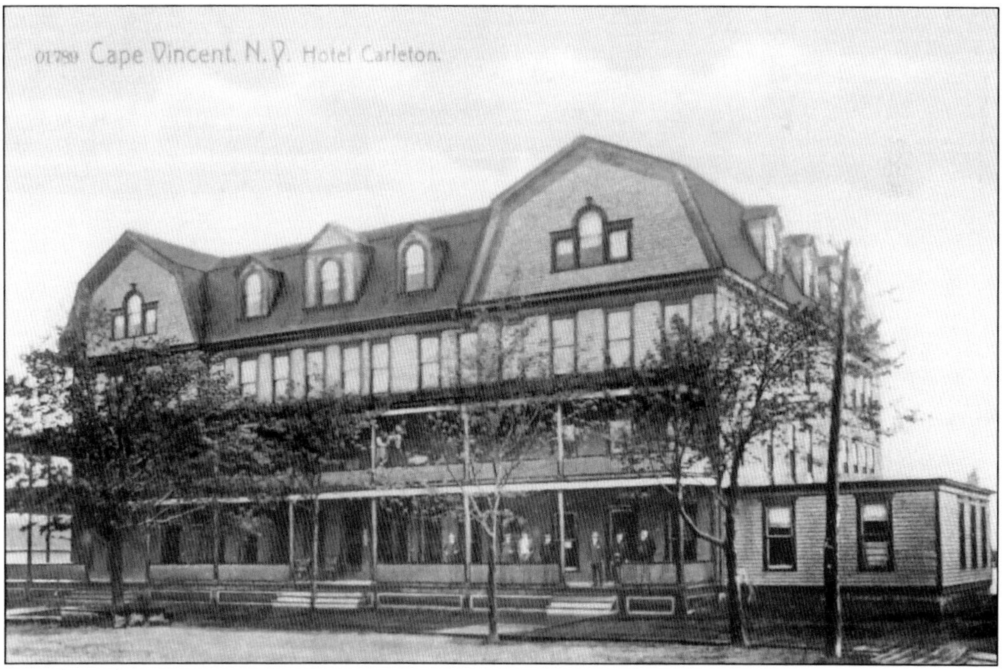

Hotel Carleton, Cape Vincent, *c.* 1908. The Hotel Carleton was built in 1898 and was considered one of the largest hotels in the river region prior to the construction of much bigger hotels built in Alexandria Bay.

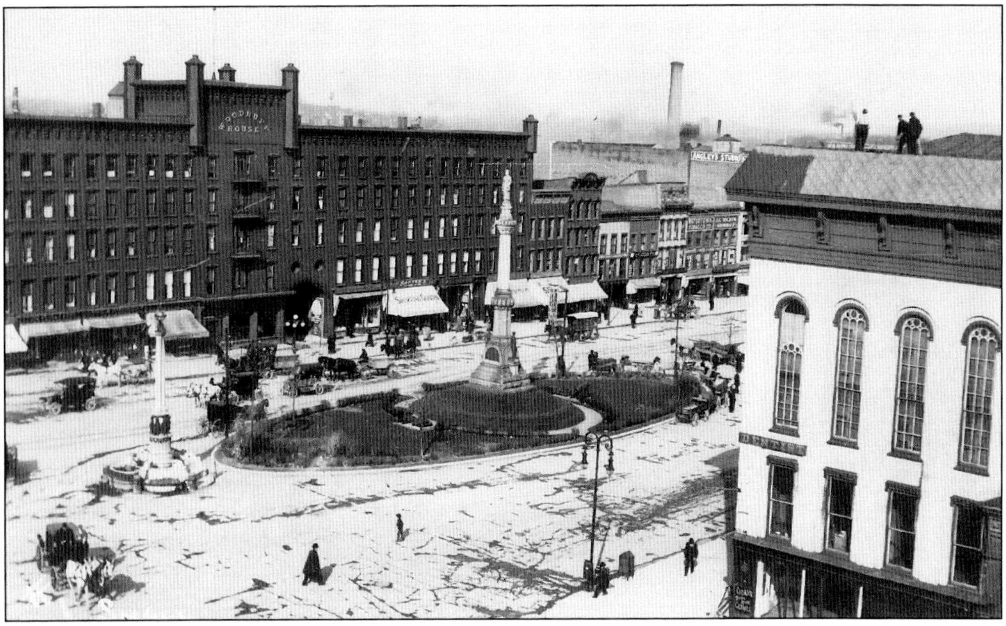

Woodruff Hotel, Watertown, *c.* 1905. The Woodruff House was considered one of the largest and most complete public houses in northern New York. Built in 1849 by Norris Woodruff, the hotel held a commanding location on the north side of Public Square in the city of Watertown, beside the railroad station.

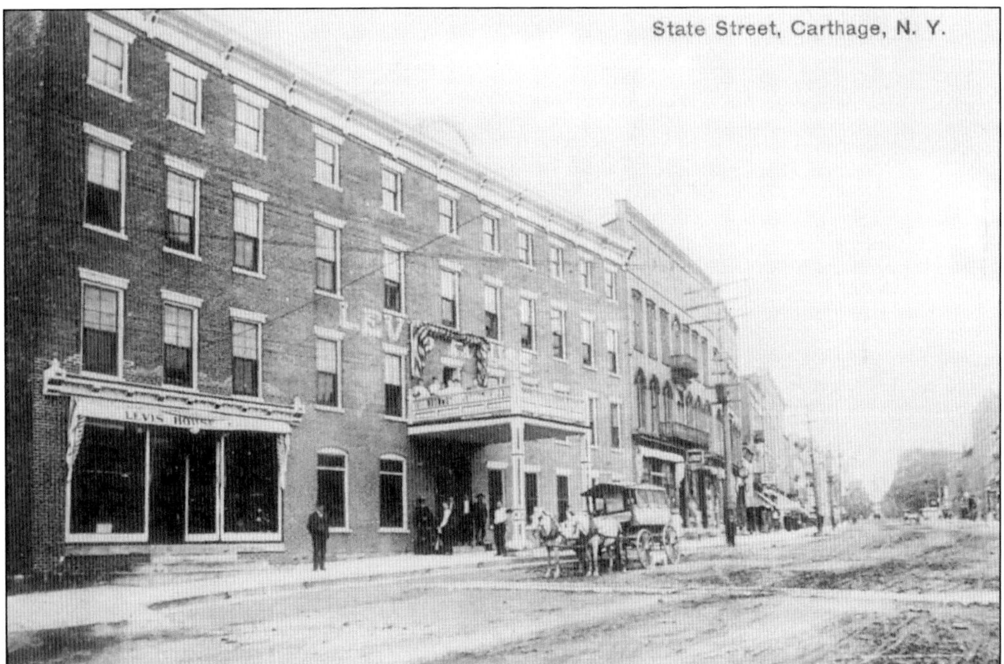

Levis House, Carthage. The historic Levis House was built by Remsen R. Brown around 1850. Brown was one of the early pioneer settlers to come to Carthage. The hotel had forty rooms, a restaurant, and grill.

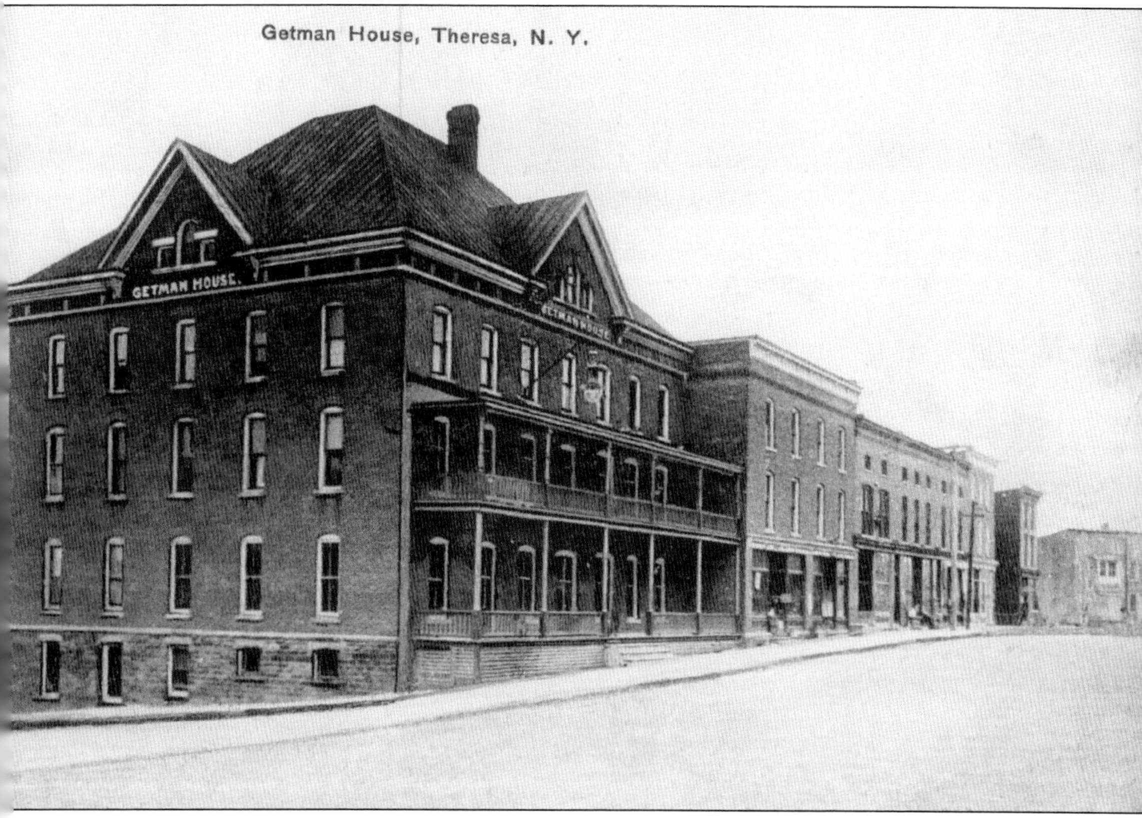

The Getman House, Theresa. Before the Getman House was built, there were two other hotels that occupied the site. In 1819 the first hotel in the village of Theresa was built by James LeRay de Chaumont. This hotel burned down in 1820. In 1824 the Brick Tavern was erected on the same site. Fire swept through and destroyed this building in 1890. It was replaced by the Getman House, which at one time was considered among the best appointed and managed country hotels in northern New York State.

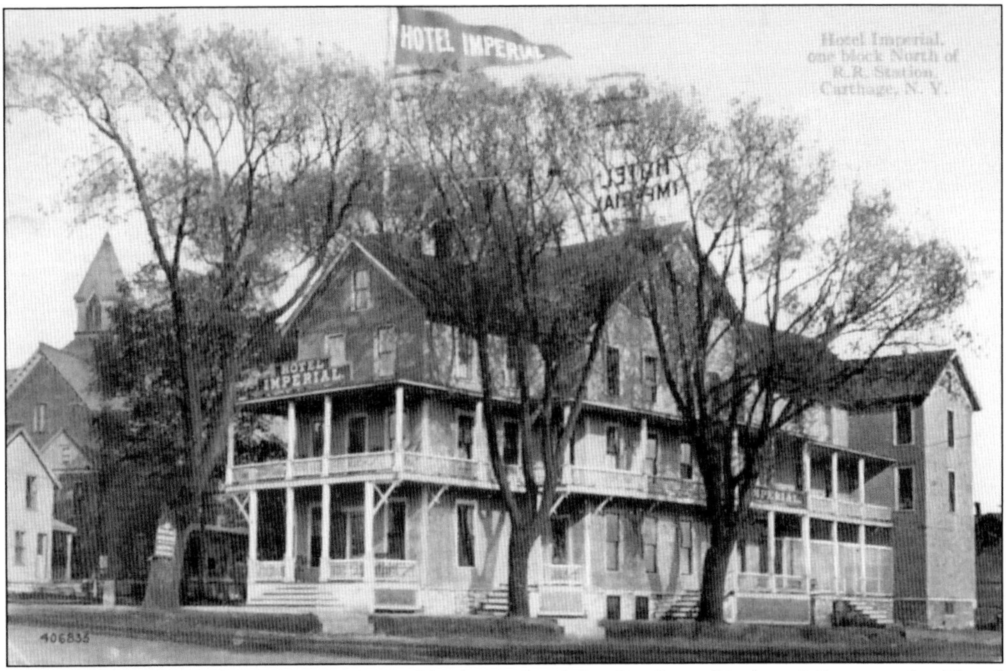

Hotel Imperial, Carthage. Located one block north of the Carthage Railroad Station, the Hotel Imperial was a convenient stop for weary travelers. It was built in 1867 and was recognized as a hotel of great distinction.

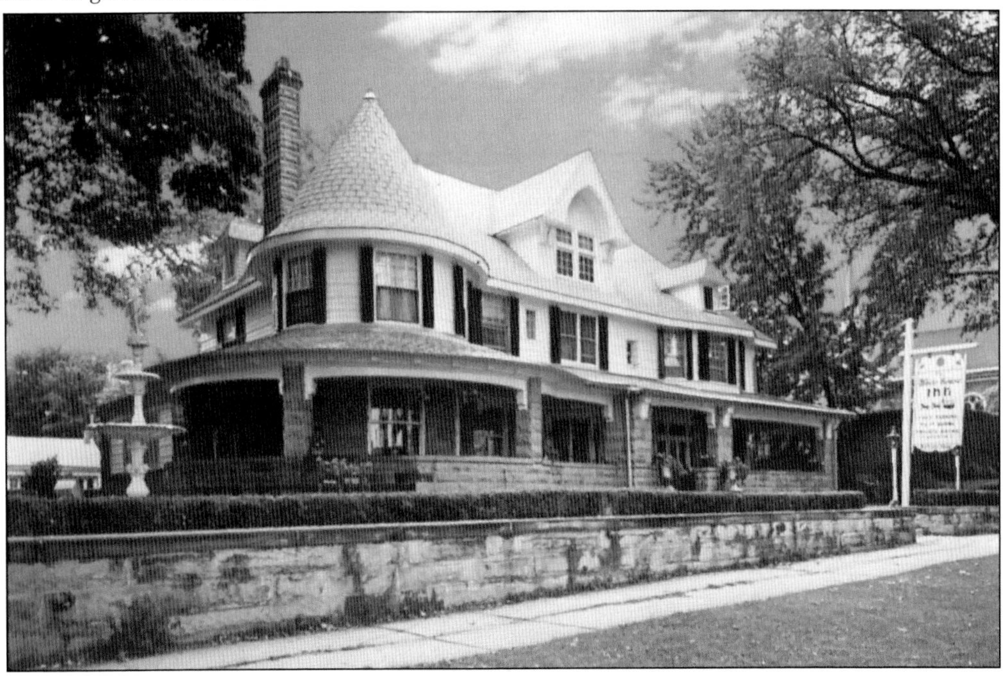

The White House Inn, Watertown. The White House Inn was a gracious structure located on the corner of Washington and Academy Streets in the city of Watertown. Built around 1885, it was originally the home of the Flower family. The inn was later razed to make room for the New York State Office Building.

Ten

Firefighting

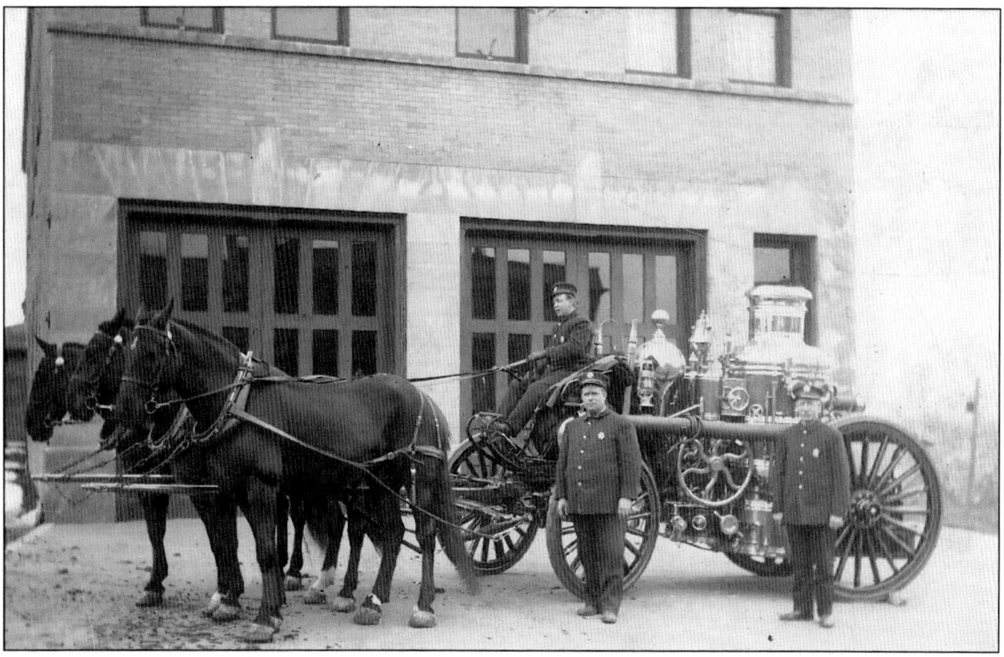

Watertown Fire Department. One of the oldest institutions in the city, the fire department held a meeting in 1816 that broke the city up into five wards and insured that each ward had a good and sufficient ladder. Five different hose companies were organized for the different districts. At the same meeting, the fire department decided to require each owner or occupant of a dwelling, office, factory, or workshop to have at least one leather bucket.

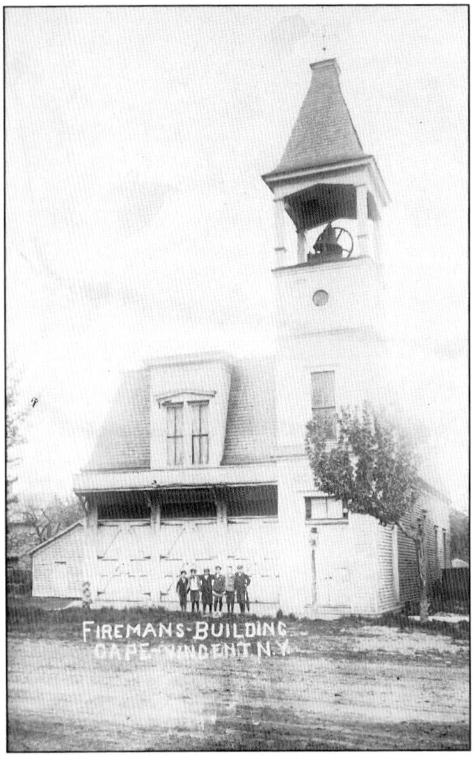

Cape Vincent Fire Department. In 1859 the subject of providing apparatus to extinguish fires was discussed. It was then voted to purchase leather buckets.

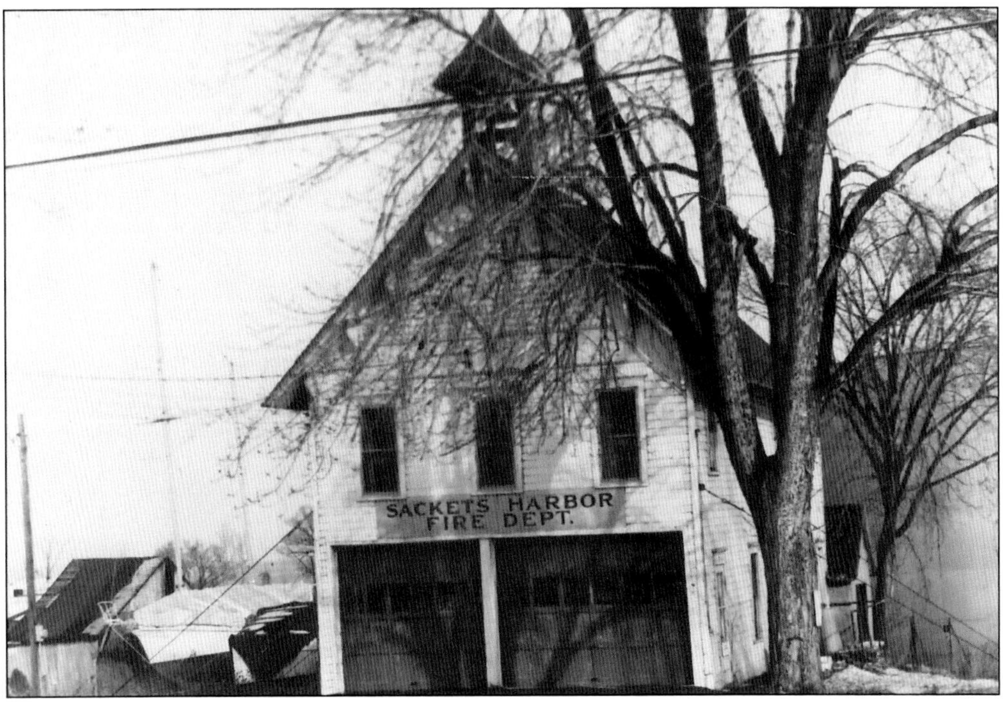

Sackets Harbor Fire Department. The Sackets Harbor Fire Department started out as what was known as the bucket brigade shortly after the War of 1812. After the big fire of 1843, a hand engine was purchased, and in 1889 a hose cart and brake engine were acquired.

John Hancock Hook & Ladder Company, Watertown. The John Hancock Hook & Ladder Company also shared the Firemen's Hall on Stone Street with the Jefferson Hose Company No. 3. This fireman, with his fire helmet in hand and standing at full attention, was one of the brave and proud crew who fought fires throughout the city of Watertown in the 1890s.

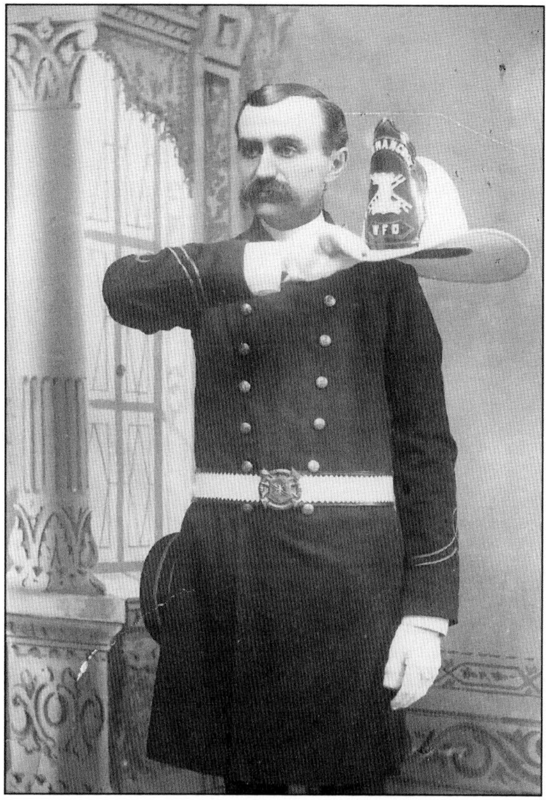

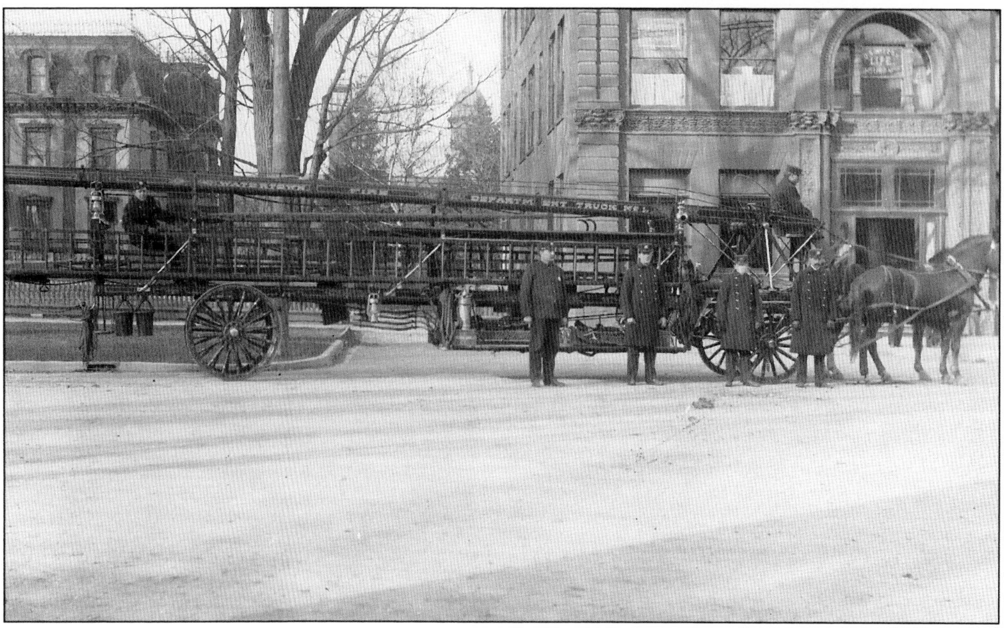

Watertown Fire Department. Leather buckets soon gave way to hose carts and hand engines. Fires broke out in factories, churches, hotels, and mercantile stores in Watertown. One thing that the citizens of Watertown could always be assured of, however, was that their fire department would come to the rescue.

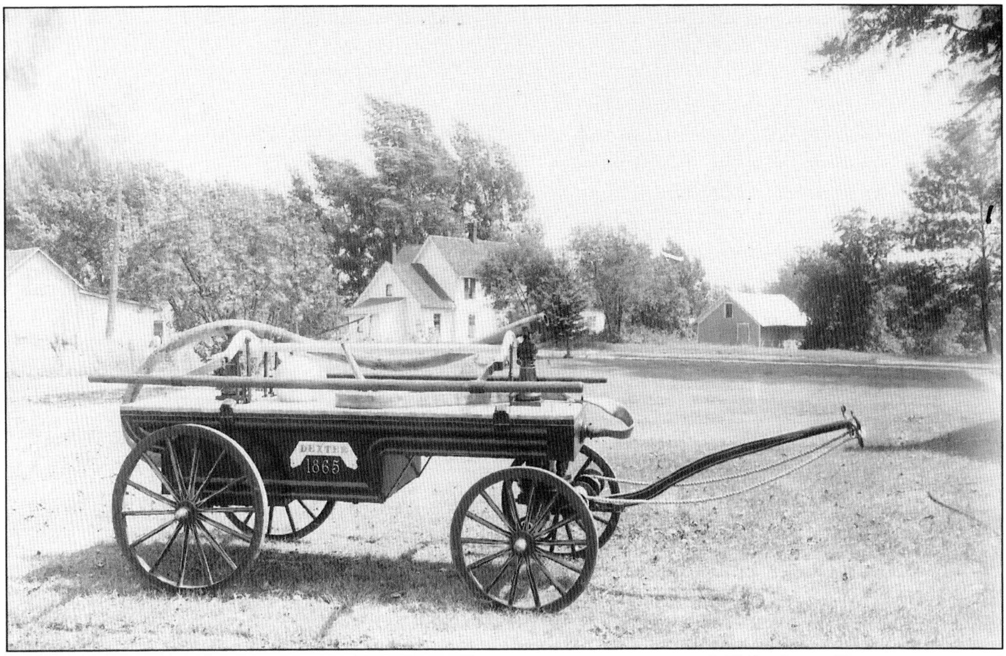

Dexter Fire Department. Soon after the village incorporation in 1855, the village petitioned to raise funds for the purchase of a fire engine. It was not until 1887 that the Dexter Fire Department had their own building.

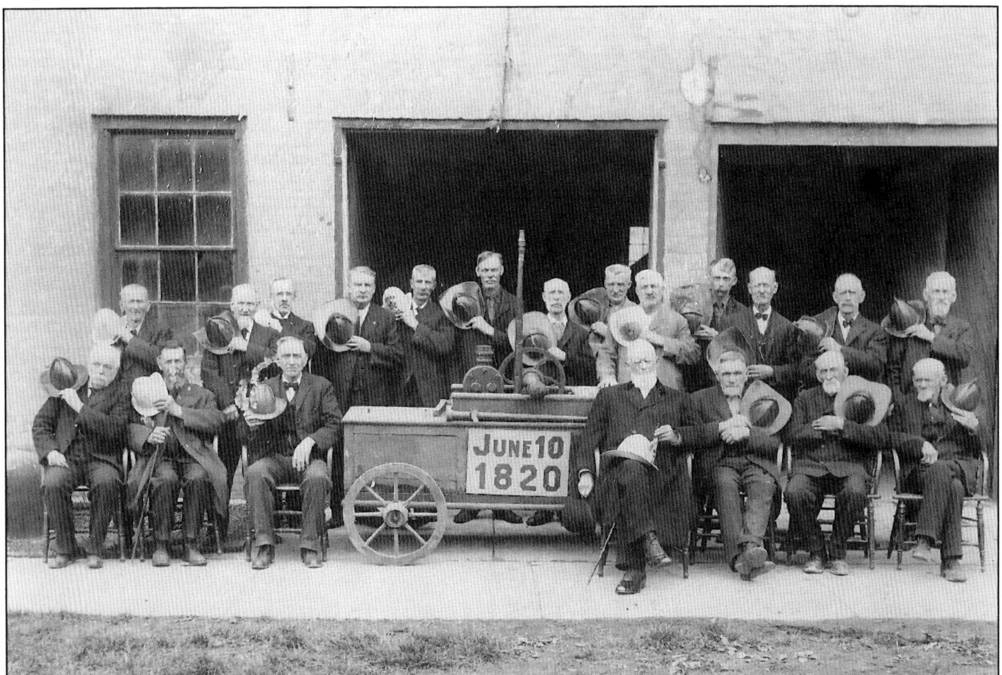

Adams Fire Department. Until 1860 the village of Adams had very few fires to fight. The major fires of 1860 and 1866 led the village of Adams to organize a fire department and purchase firefighting equipment.

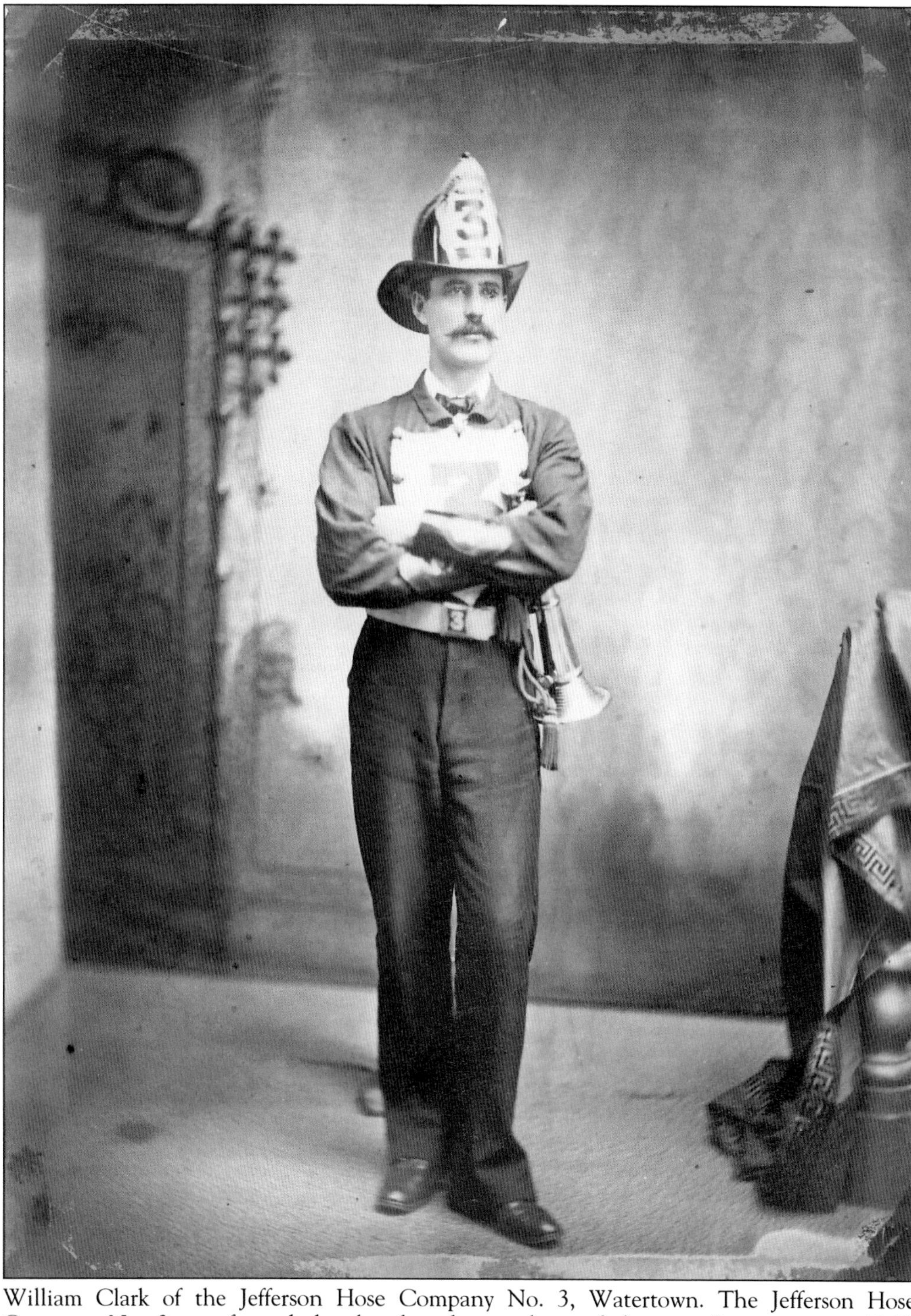

William Clark of the Jefferson Hose Company No. 3, Watertown. The Jefferson Hose Company No. 3 was formed shortly after the purchase of the new fire engine in 1845. The company occupied Firemen's Hall on Stone Street, which was built in 1854. Roswell P. Flower, the governor of New York State, once belonged to the Jefferson Hose Company as a young man.

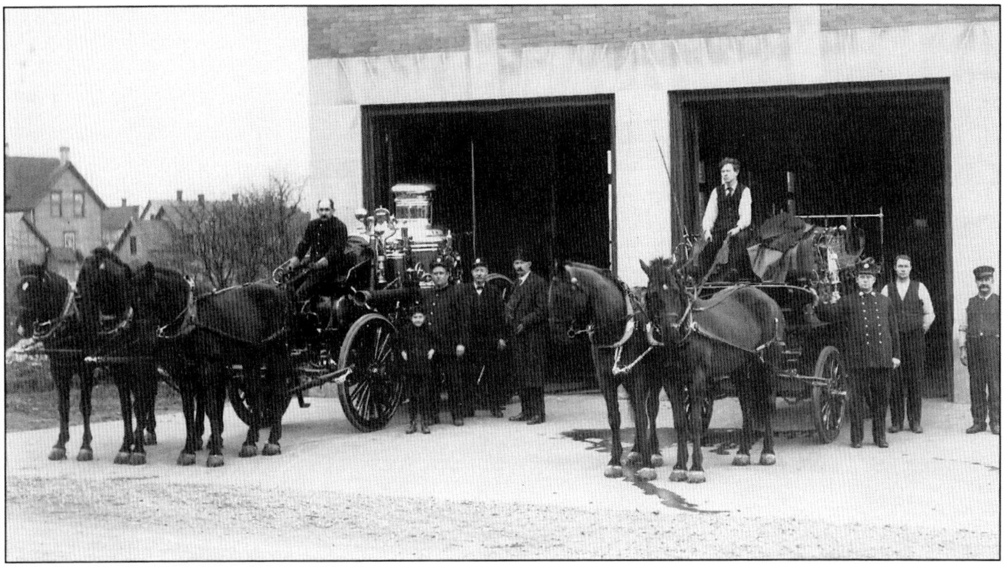

Watertown Fire Department. Watertown Fire Department and its equipment were very well known. The men and equipment of Watertown Fire Department were thought to greatly surpass that of any city of its size in the state of New York. It was a good thing too, because Watertown had repeatedly been devastated by fires. The hose carts and hand engines were put to good use extinguishing fires throughout the city in the late 1840s and early 1850s.

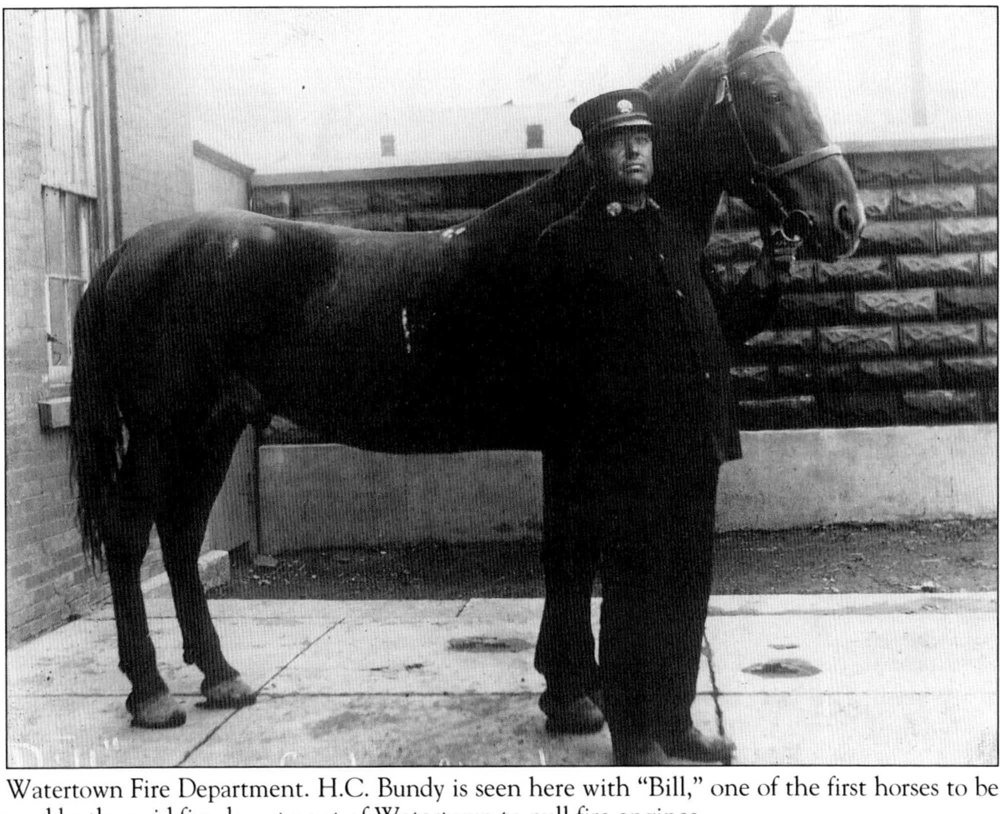

Watertown Fire Department. H.C. Bundy is seen here with "Bill," one of the first horses to be used by the paid fire department of Watertown to pull fire engines.

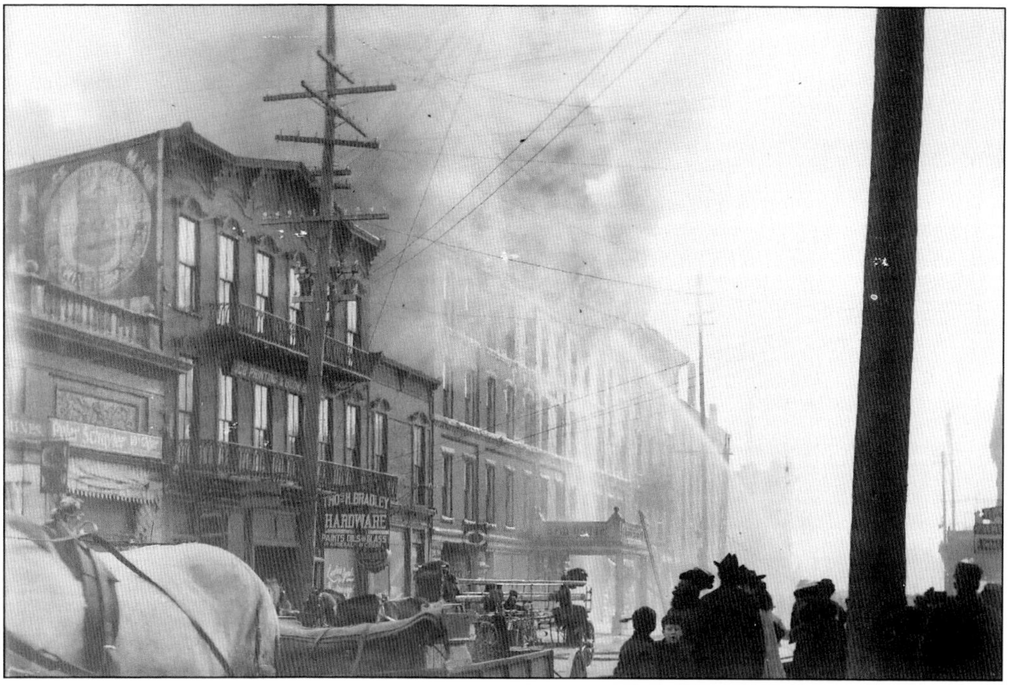

Watertown Fire Department. Throughout the first half of the 1800s Watertown was subjected to many serious and disastrous fires. Fifty years later, on March 6, 1903, a fire nearly threatened the downtown business district again. The Otis House, an elaborate structure located on Arsenal Street within a block of Public Square, was hit with a destructive fire. The morning after the fire little was left standing along the first block of Arsenal Street from Public Square.

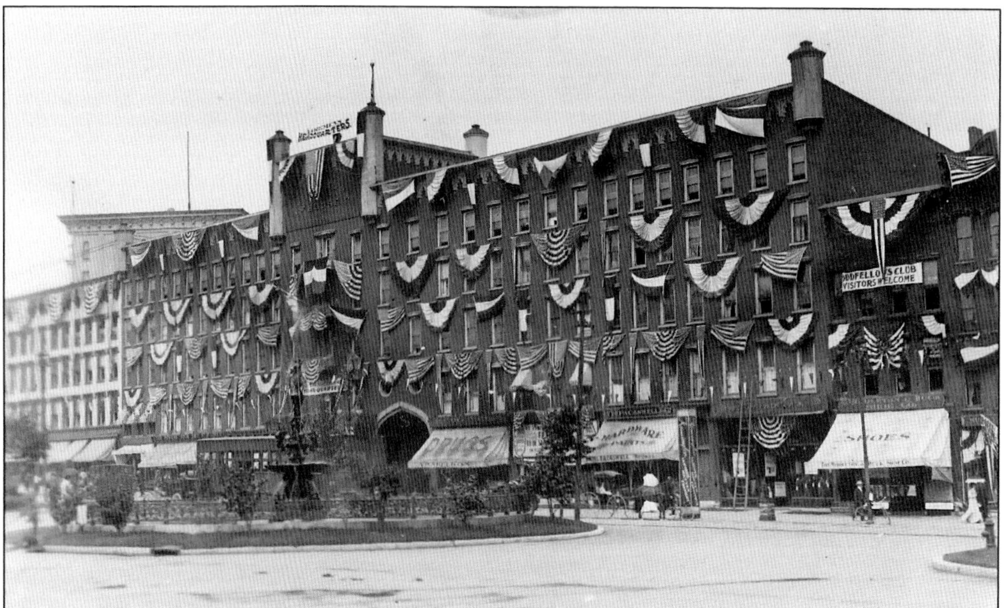

Watertown Fire Department. The Firemen's Convention of August 1910 included a circus parade complete with elephants and banners flying from every available window in Public Square.

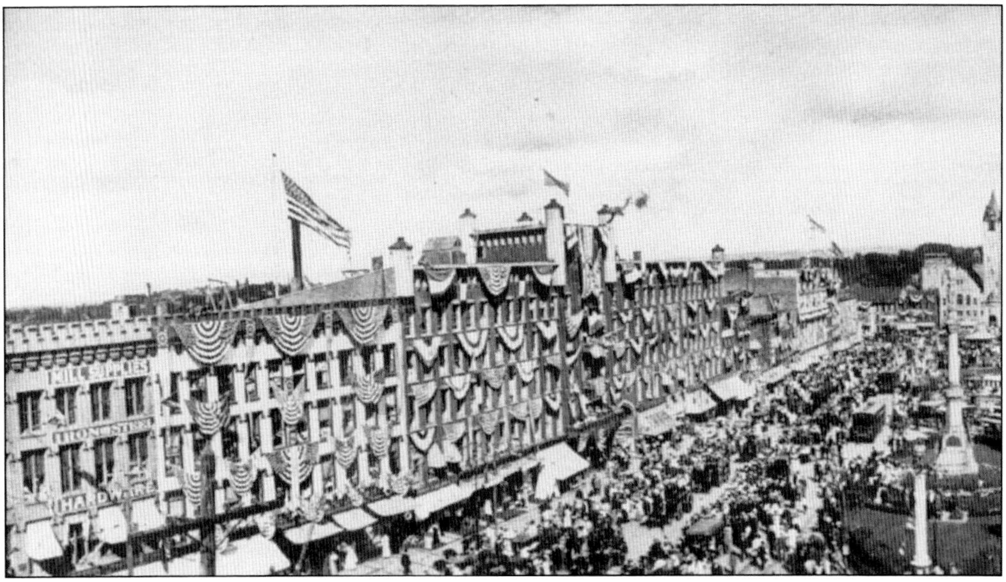

Watertown Fire Department. The Firemen's Convention, which began in 1853 as an annual parade, turned into quite a production by the early 1900s.

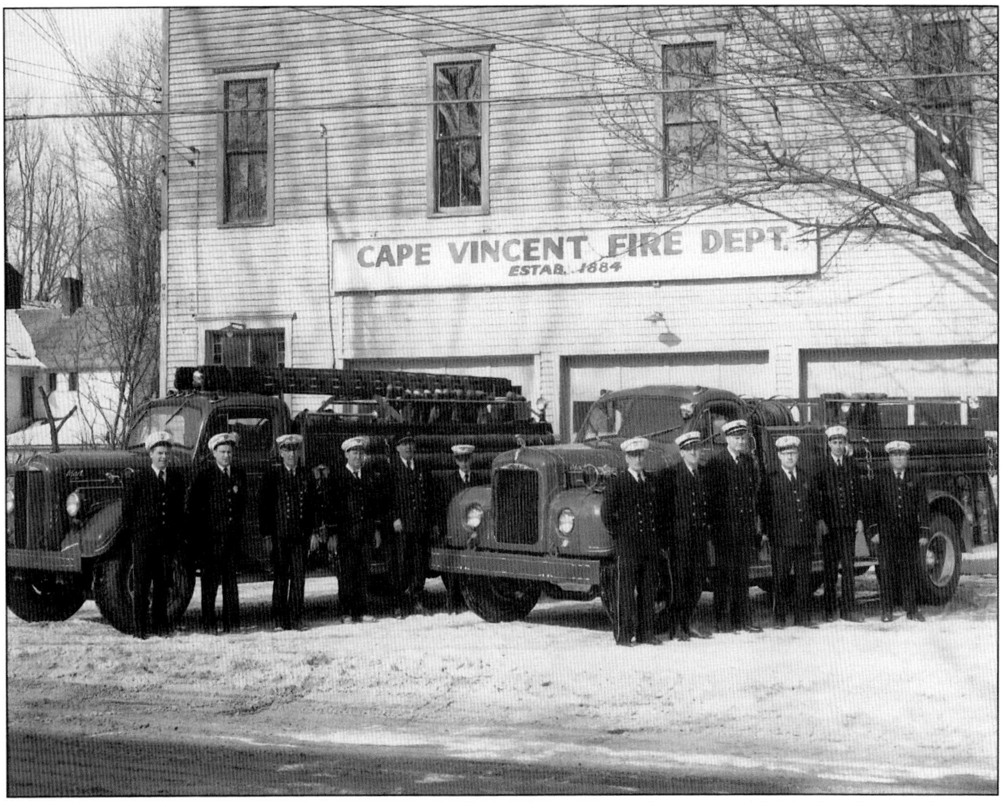

Cape Vincent Fire Department. While not formally organized prior to 1884, the Cape Vincent Fire Department had been in existence for nearly forty years. It was considered one of the most efficient firefighting bodies in the county.

Eleven

Residences

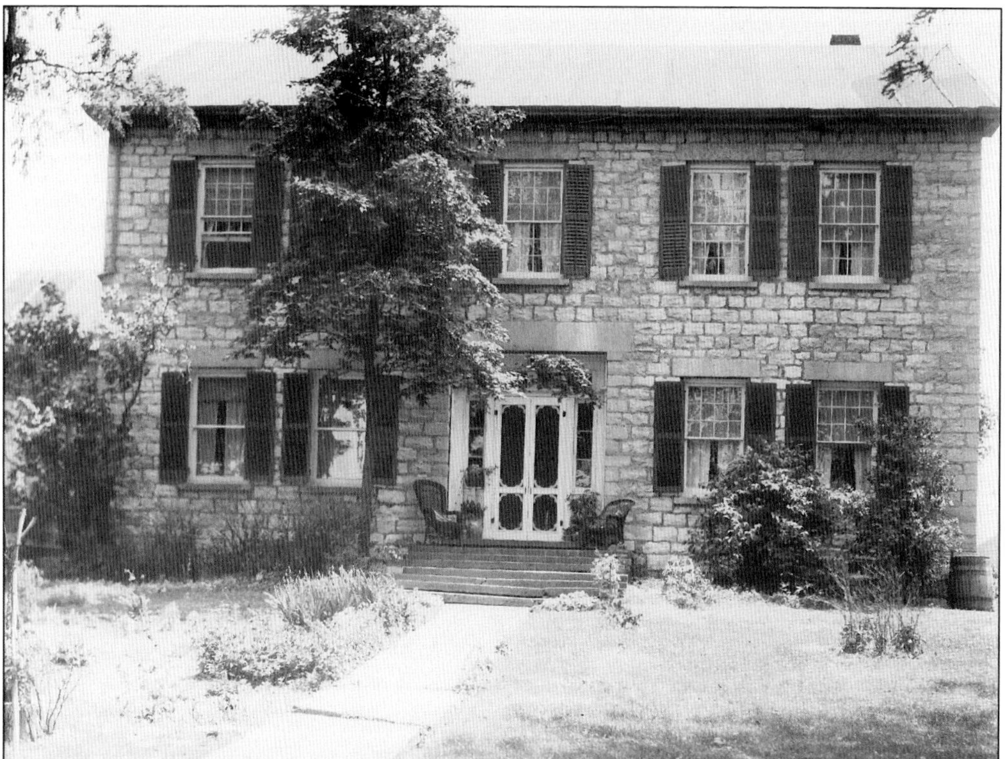

Noadiah Hubbard residence, Champion. One of the earliest New England pioneers to settle in Champion, Noadiah Hubbard became the town's merchant and innkeeper. (Photograph courtesy of David Lane.)

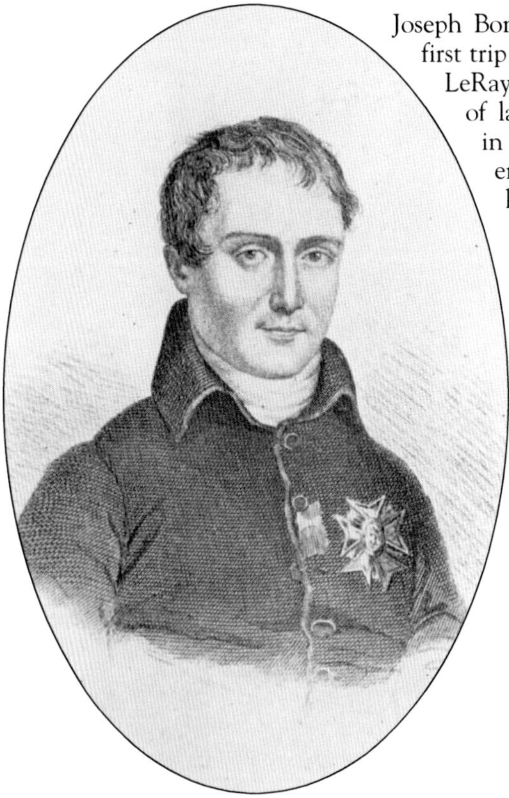

Joseph Bonaparte. In 1818 Joseph Bonaparte made his first trip to northern New York. He visited with James LeRay de Chaumont, who had sold him a large tract of land three years earlier. Bonaparte's summers in the North Country were spent lavishly entertaining guests while also mingling with the local residents.

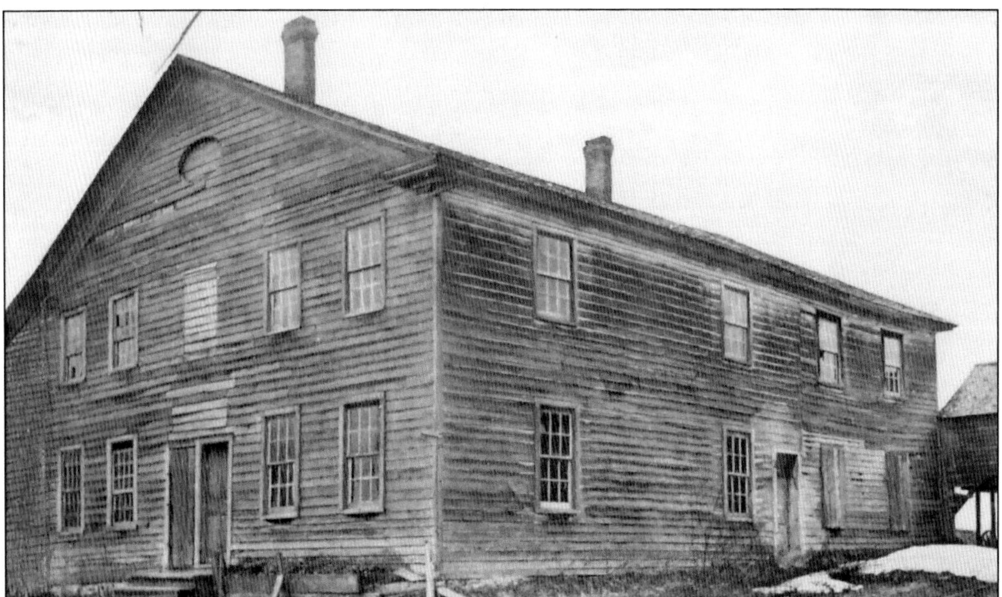

Joseph Bonaparte residence, Natural Bridge. Brother of Napoleon Bonaparte and ex-king of Spain, Joseph Bonaparte built a home in Natural Bridge, which he owned for several years. He later moved to Bordentown, New Jersey, but would spend his summers in Jefferson County.

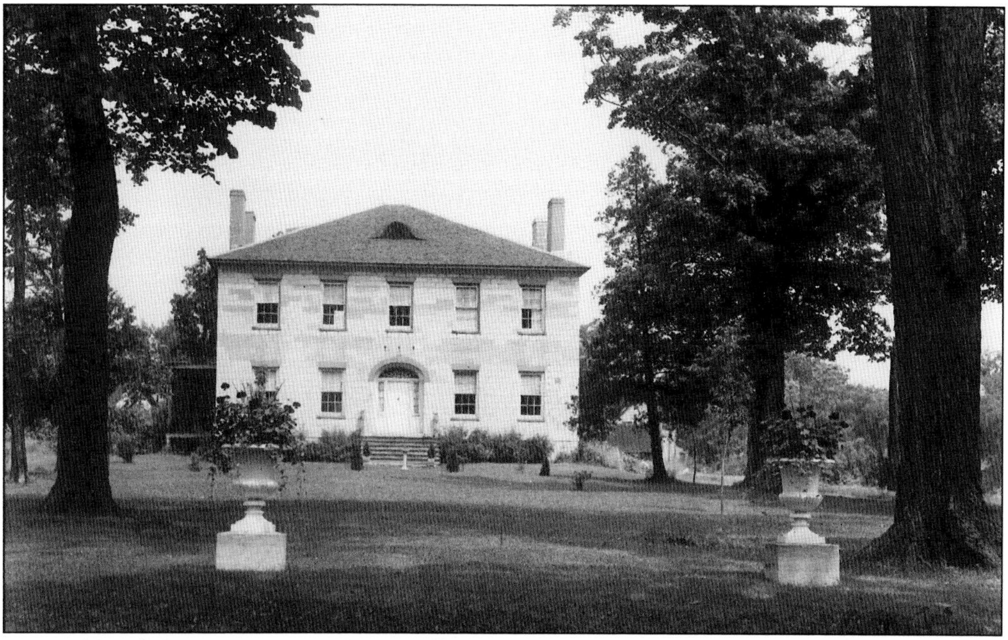

General Jacob Brown Mansion, Brownville. In 1799 Jacob Brown was the first pioneer to settle in Brownville. By the outbreak of the War of 1812, Brown was the militia general and was placed in command of the northern frontier. His power and influence organized and held together the militia forces of Jefferson, St. Lawrence, and Lewis Counties.

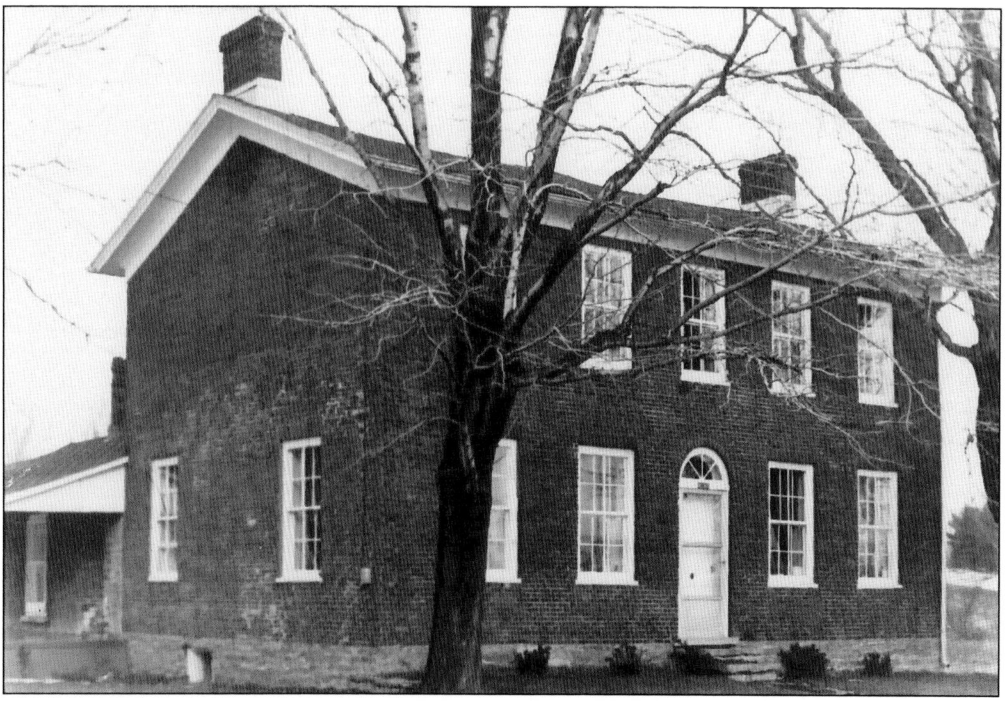

Samuel Guthrie residence, Sackets Harbor. Samuel Guthrie discovered not only chloroform, a popular anesthetic used during the Civil War, but also invented the percussion cap used in the firing of guns.

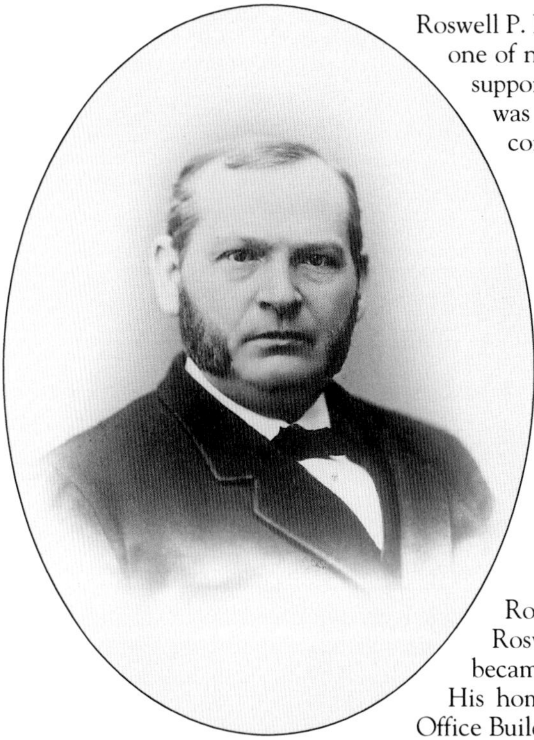

Roswell P. Flower. Born in 1835 in Theresa, Flower was one of nine children. At the age of eight he helped support his family after his father's death. Flower was a teacher before becoming a prominent congressman and governor of New York State.

Roswell P. Flower residence, Watertown. Roswell P. Flower, a native of Jefferson County, became the governor of New York State in 1892. His home was later used as the Jefferson County Office Building on Arsenal Street.

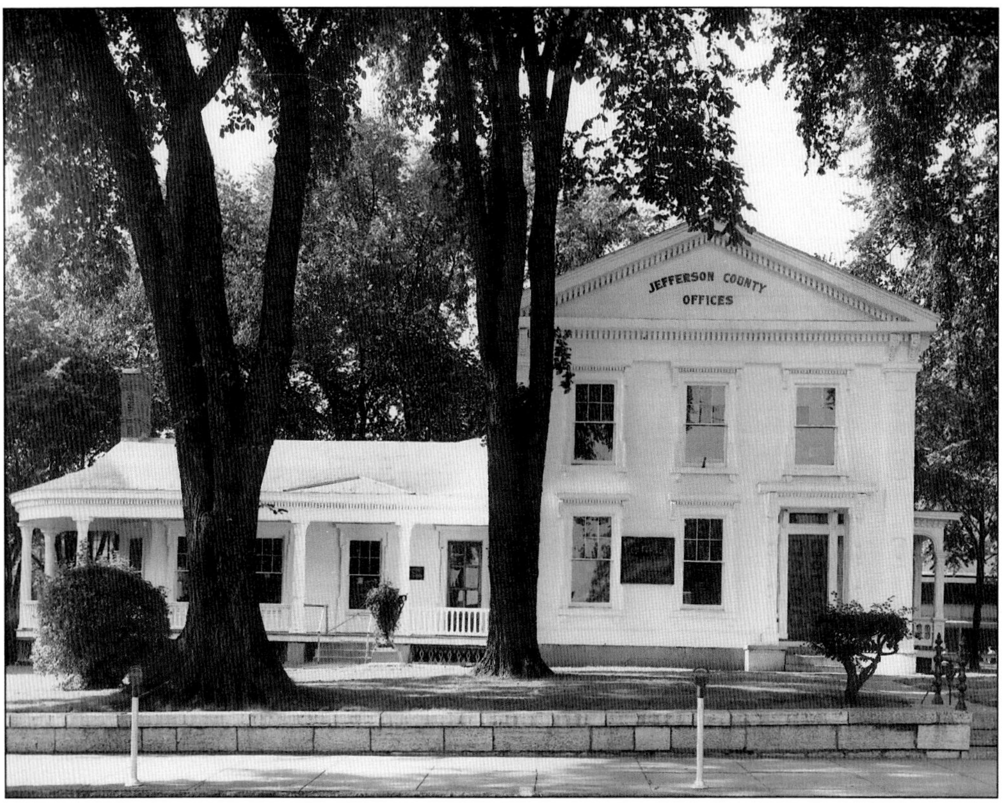

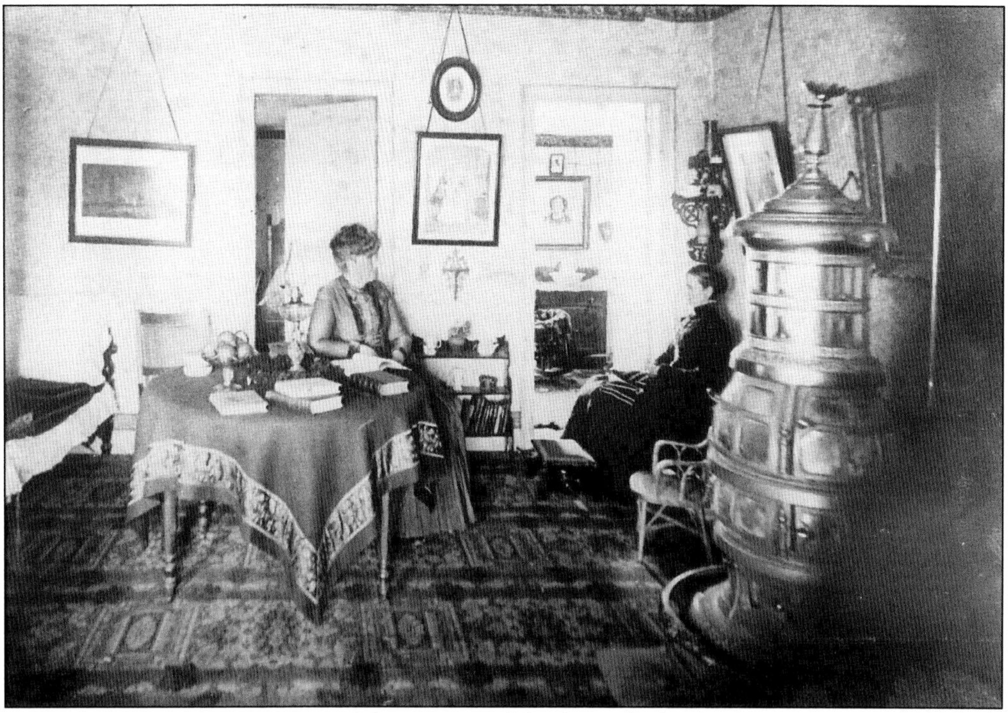

Bonnie View, Pierrepont Manor. The interior of this home looks quite as you would expect it to in the Victorian Age. Marietta Holley visits with a friend inside her home.

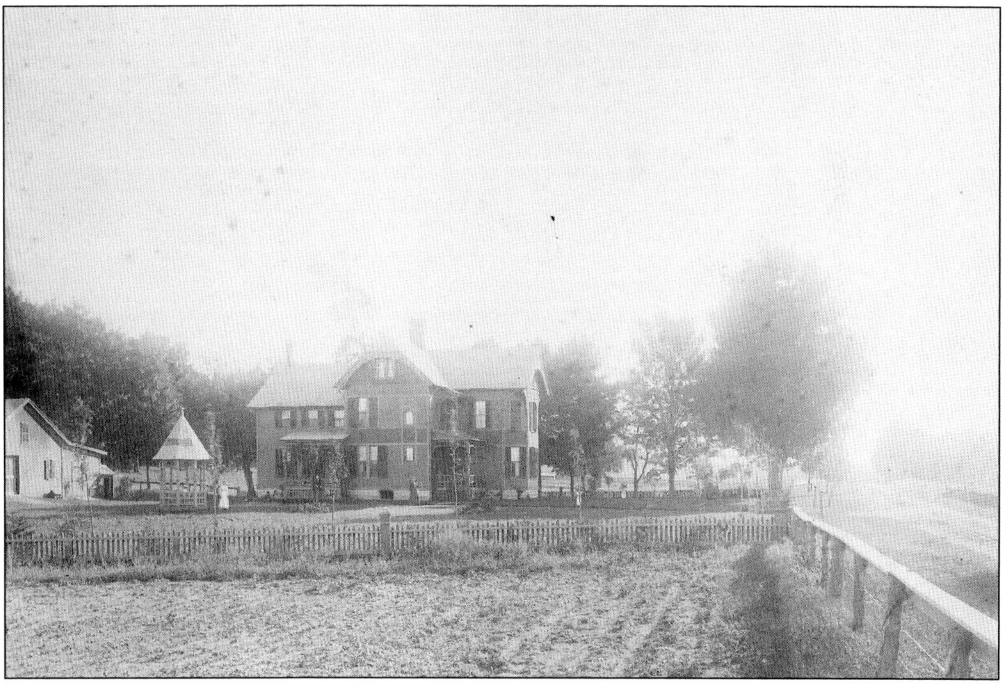

Bonnie View, Pierrepont Manor. This was the home of Marietta Holley, an accomplished writer, who is today considered a feminist, and suffragist. Holley represented a new era for women and women's rights in the United States.

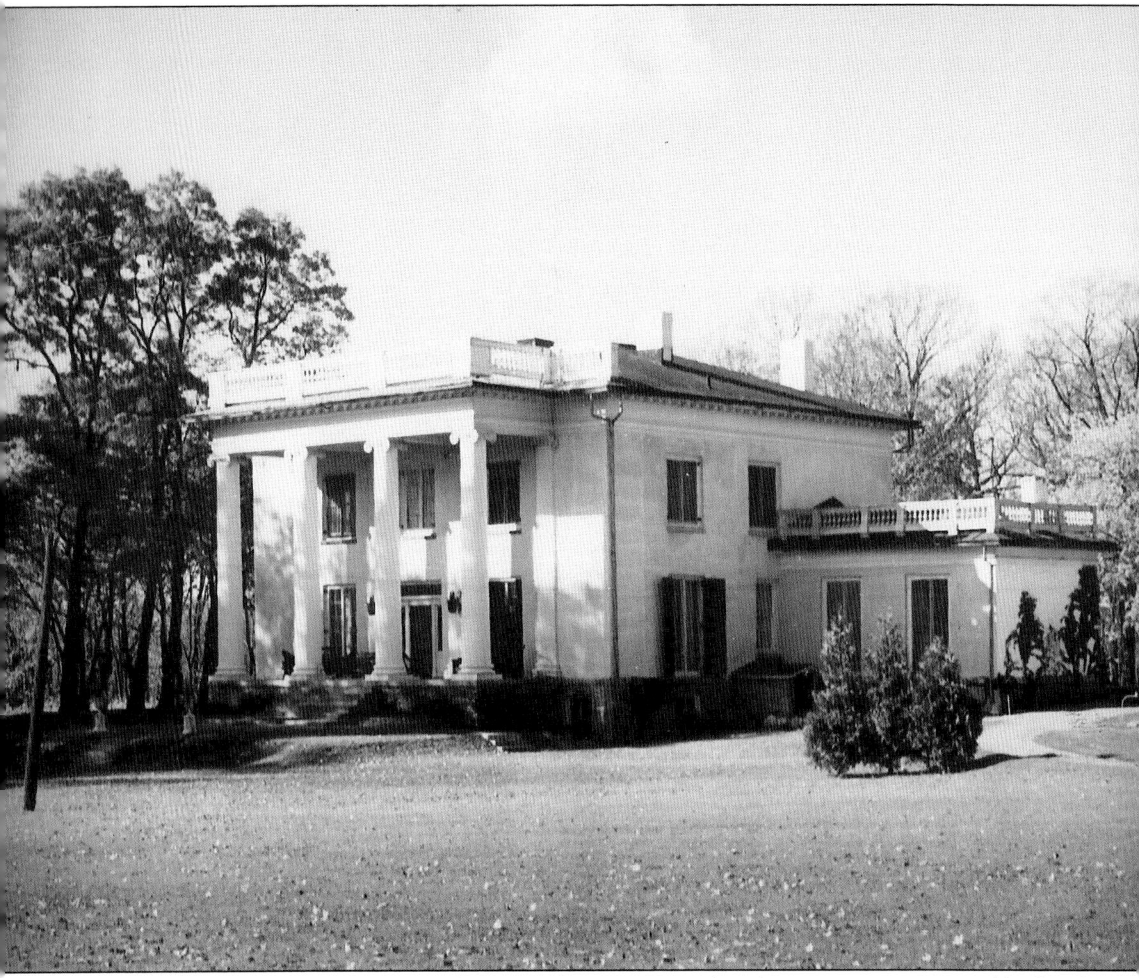

LeRay Mansion, LeRay. A French émigré James LeRay de Chaumont was responsible for the initial settlement and development of a large part of Jefferson County. His home reflected the refined hospitality and affluence of a French nobleman.

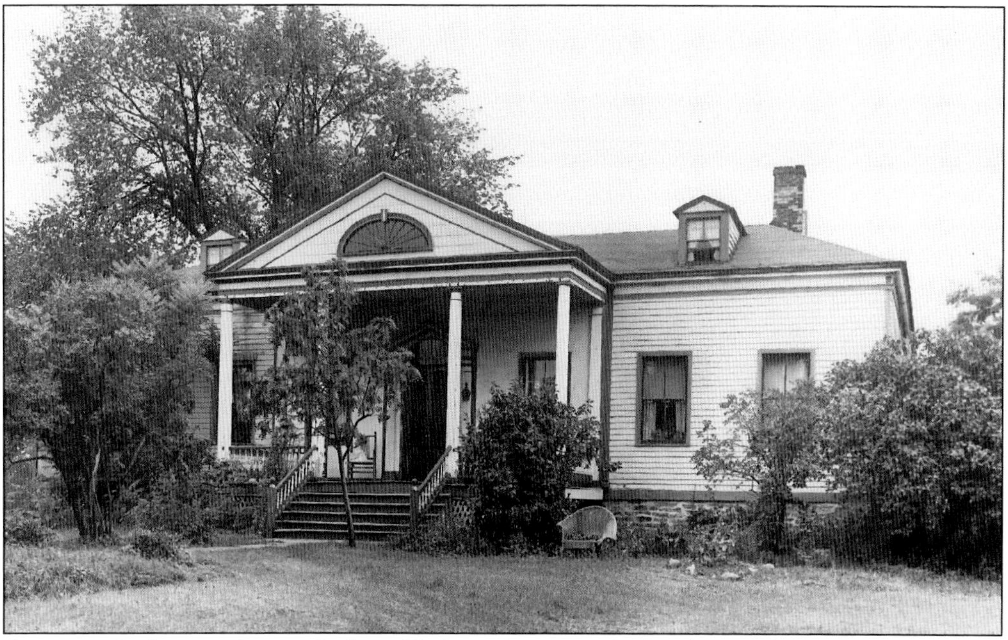

Augustus Sacket residence, Sackets Harbor. Augustus Sacket began the first settlement of Sackets Harbor Village. He built the sawmill that was used to saw lumber for the construction of the first homes in the village.

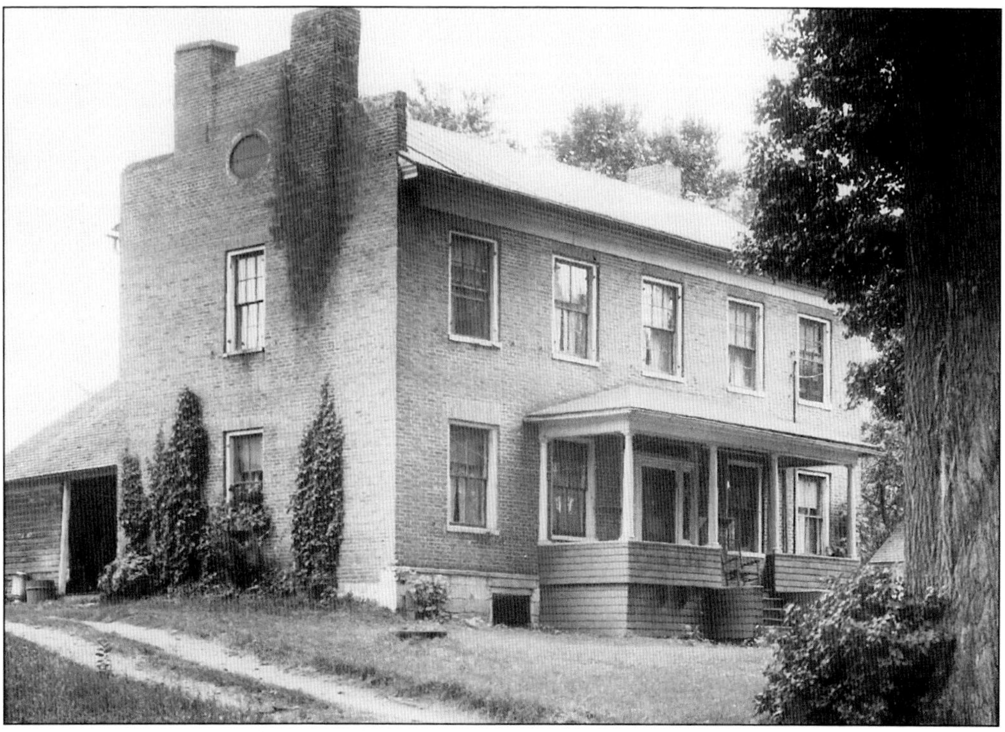

Dr. Abner Benton residence, Oxbow. Dr. Abner Benton was the first physician to settle in Oxbow. Dr. Benton also became the town's postmaster in 1819, when the first post office was established.

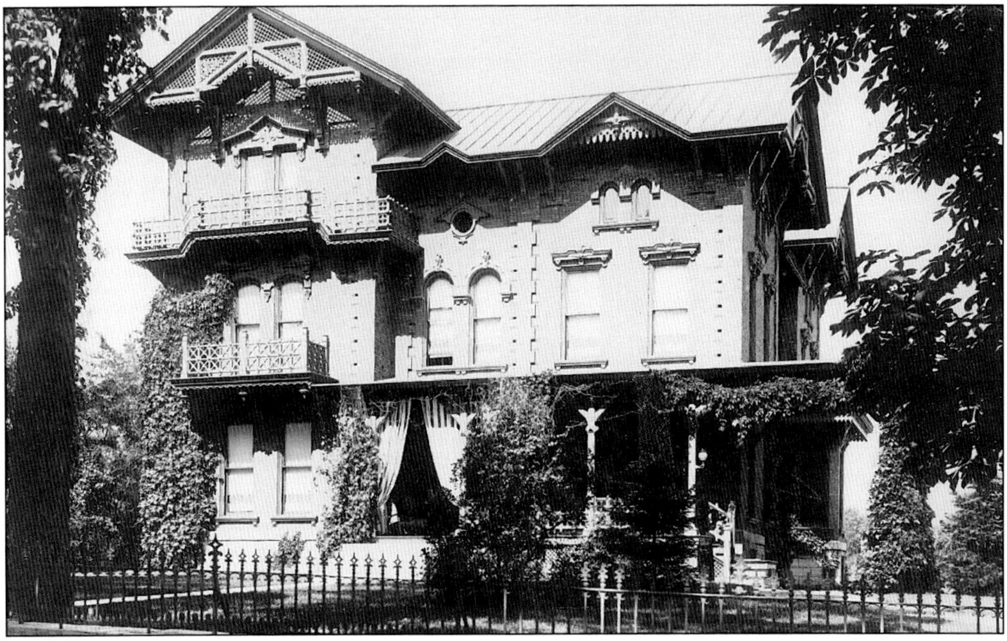

Paddock Mansion, Watertown. The Paddock Mansion is an impressive modified Tuscan villa surrounded by elaborate balconies. It was designed by John Hose, the same individual who designed the Jefferson County Court House and many other public and private structures in the county. It was built in 1878 for Edwin and Olive Paddock, and bequeathed to the Jefferson County Historical Society in 1922.

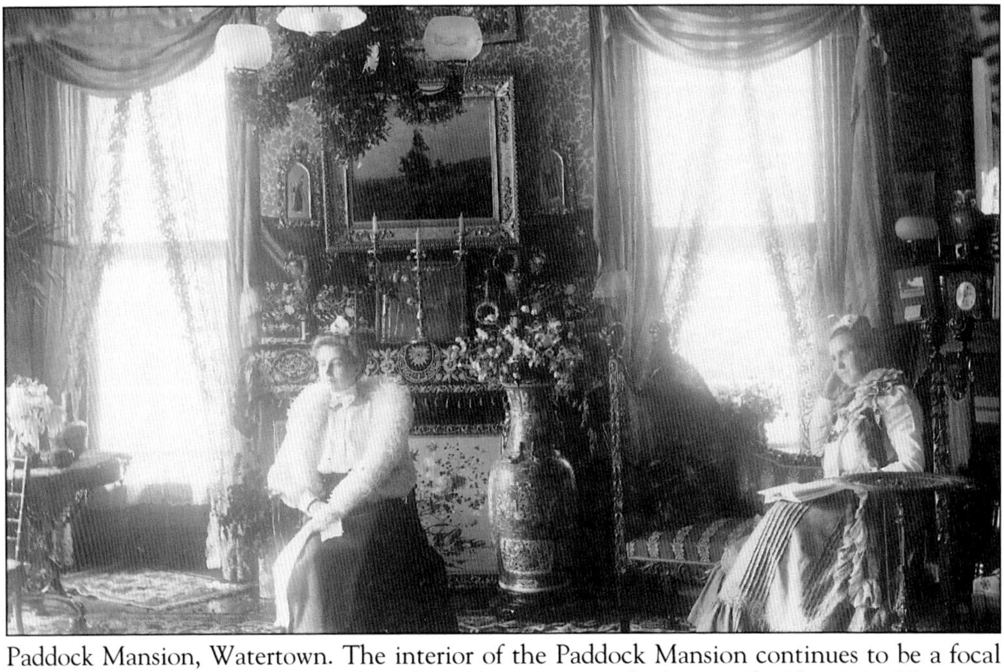

Paddock Mansion, Watertown. The interior of the Paddock Mansion continues to be a focal point for anyone visiting the museum. Its parlors are ornately decorated with original furniture acquired by the Paddocks at the 1876 Philadelphia Centennial Exposition. All of the woodwork in the museum is black walnut, oak, and ash and is original to the house.

Orville Hungerford. Hungerford, who came to Watertown in 1804, was instrumental in the establishment of the railroad in Jefferson County. He had many careers but was certainly recognized as one of Watertown's most distinguished citizens. He was a mercantilist, the first president of Watertown when it was only a village, founder of Jefferson County Bank, and the first president of the Rome, Watertown & Ogdensburg Railroad. He was also a prominent democratic politician and congressman.

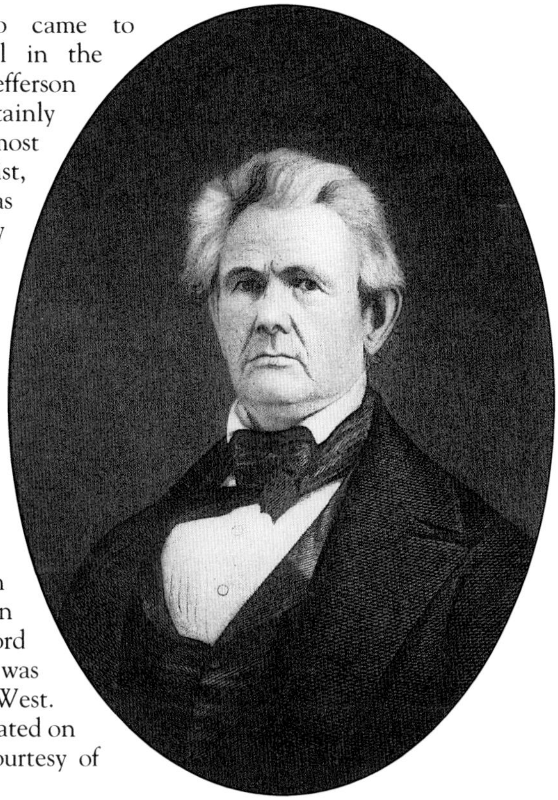

Orville Hungerford residence, Watertown. Constructed by Orville Hungerford in 1824, the home was located on Washington Street, and it remained in the Hungerford family for 130 years. In the 1960s it was moved, stone by stone, to Flower Avenue West. The Carriage House Motor Inn is now located on the home's original site. (Photograph courtesy of David Lane.)

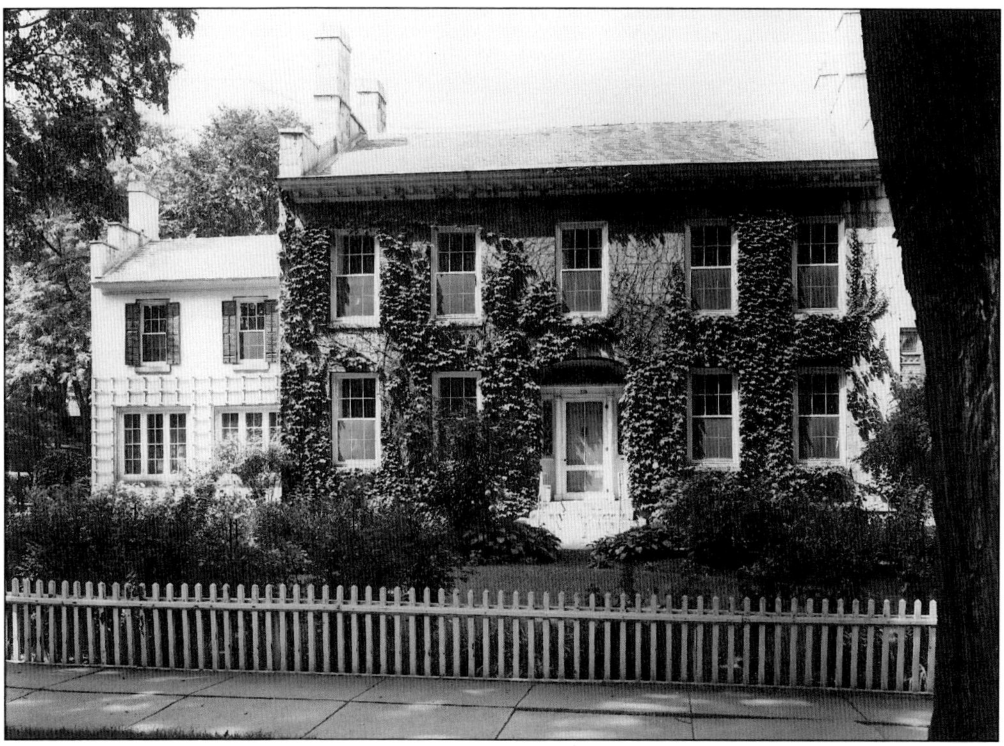

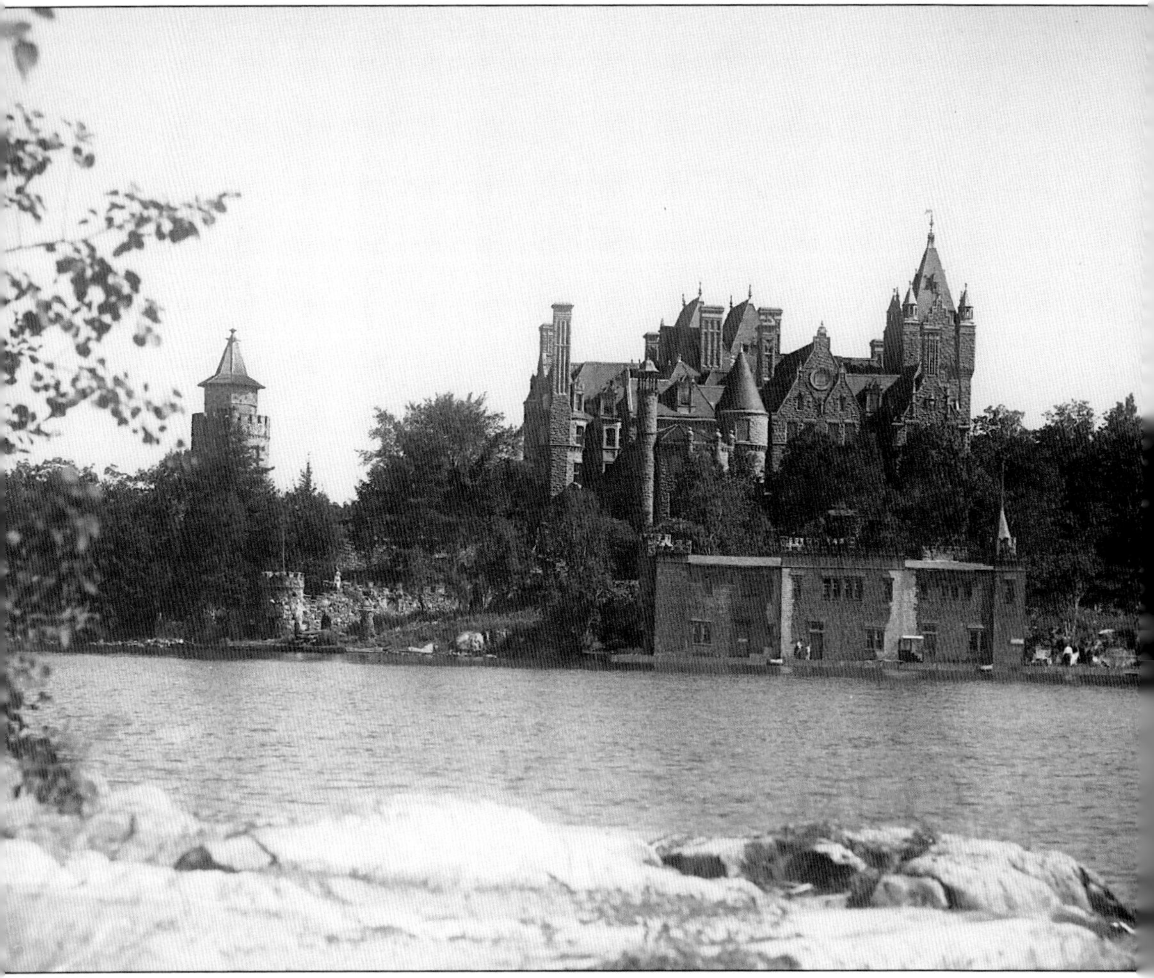

George C. Boldt, Heart Island, Alexandria Bay. In 1900 George C. Boldt purchased an island located just off the shoreline of Alexandria Bay. Boldt was the proprietor of the Waldorf Astoria Hotel in New York City, but planned to make the Thousand Islands region a summer retreat for his wife, son, and daughter. Four years later in 1904, after the death of his wife, all work at the castle stopped permanently.

Twelve

Fort Drum and Madison Barracks

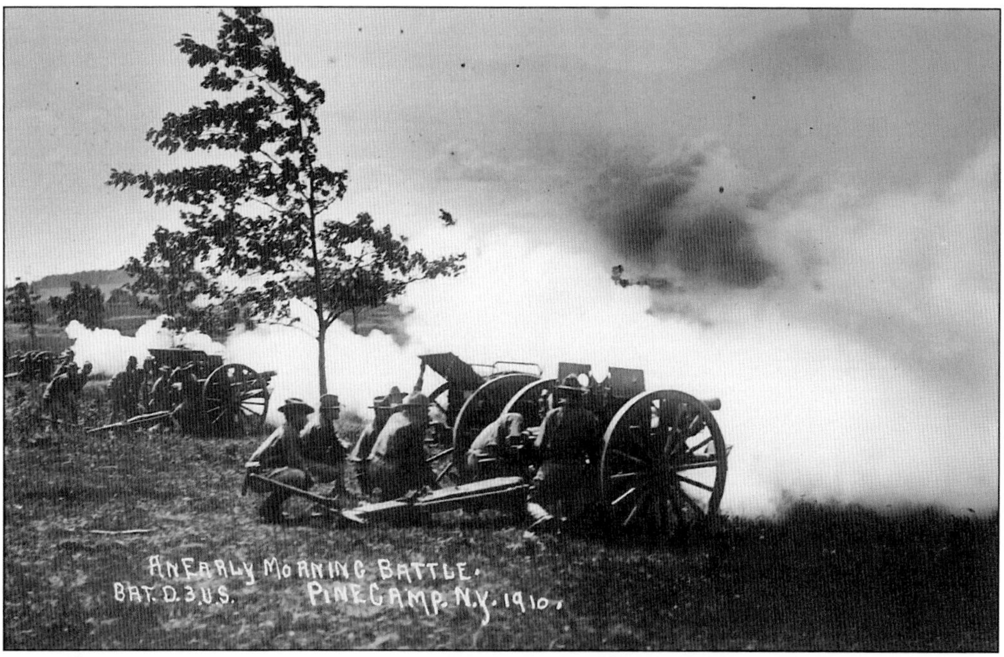

Pine Plains to Fort Drum, c. 1910. In 1908 land in Jefferson County was purchased by the federal government. This land was established as a training area for the National Guard. The many small towns and houses located within the Fort Drum boundaries were soon obliterated to give way to the military base.

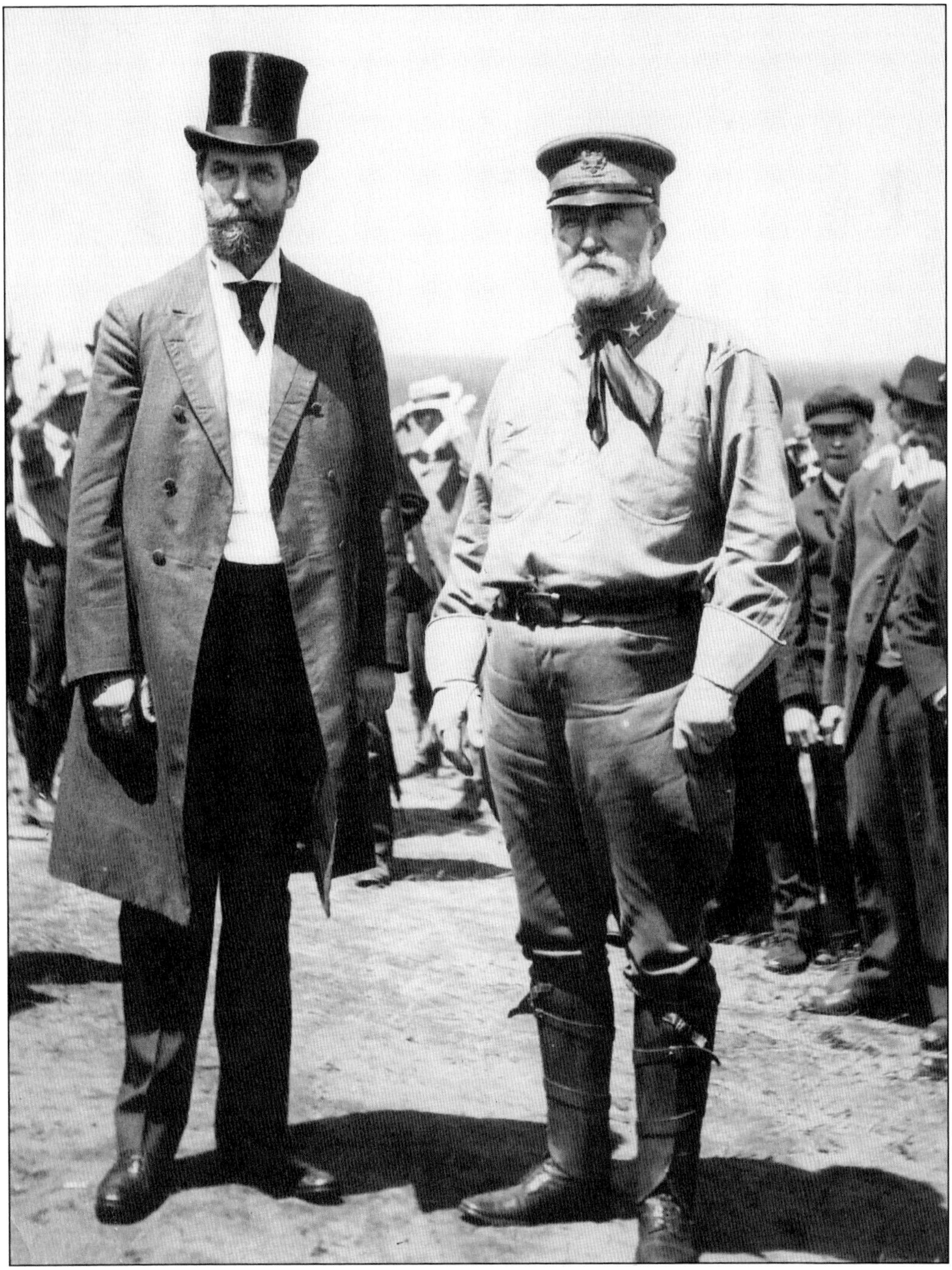

Pine Plains to Fort Drum. It was an eventful day when the governor of New York State, Charles Evans Hughs, visited Pine Camp. With General Fredrick D. Grant by his side, the two witness military operations on the base.

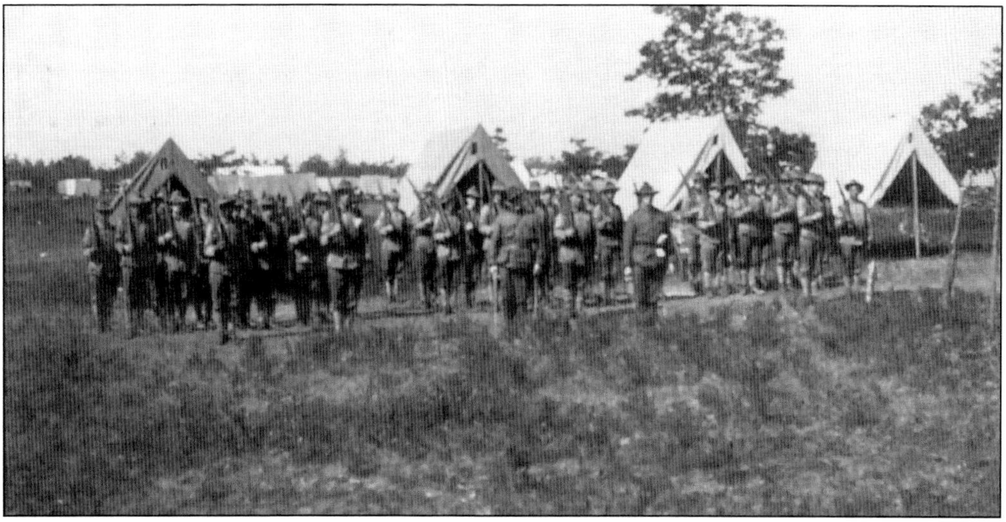

Pine Plains to Fort Drum, *c*. 1908. Fort Drum has actually had several name changes since its inception. What began as a small military establishment named Pine Plains later became Pine Camp, Camp Drum, and then finally Fort Drum.

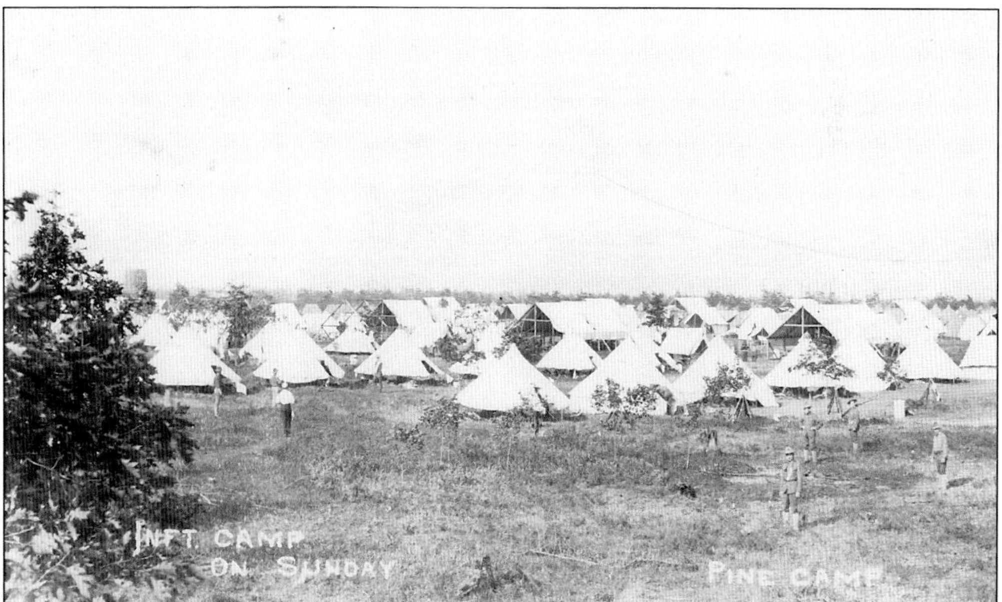

Pine Plains to Fort Drum, *c*. 1908. It was common to see encampments such as this one within the boundaries of the base. Training of troops continued here throughout the century.

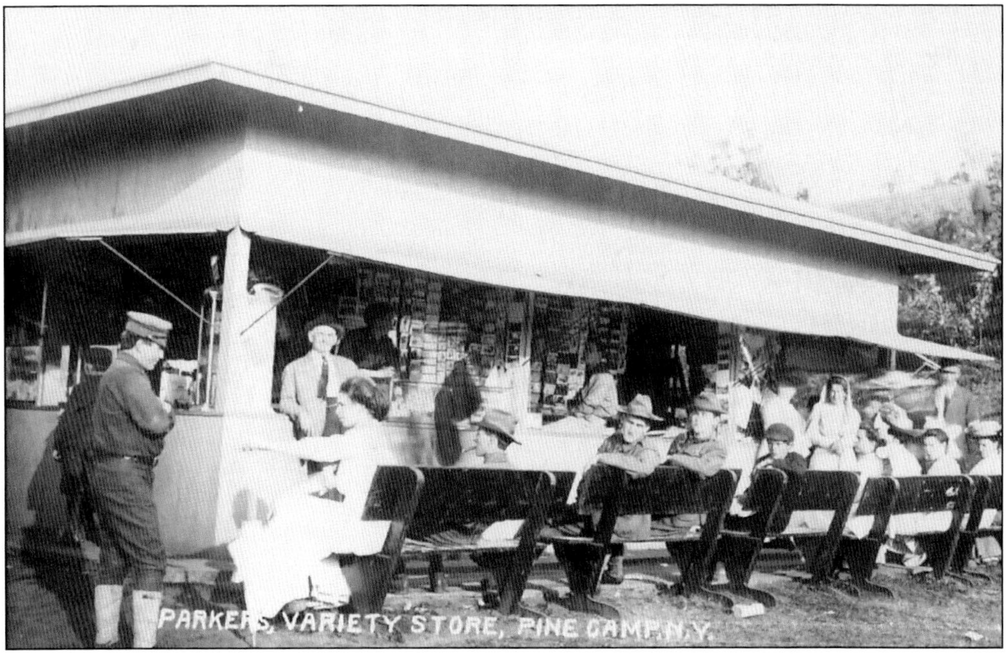

Pine Plains to Fort Drum, c. 1910. Pine Camp had all the amenities of any other town in Jefferson County. The Parker's Variety Store was one of the "essential" places frequented on the base.

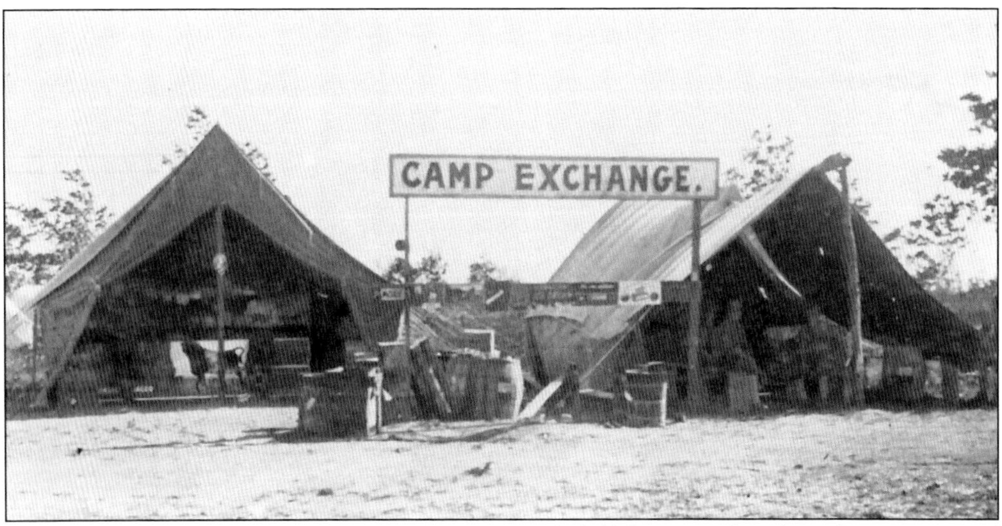

Pine Plains to Fort Drum. The Camp Exchange provided all the items that the military personnel and their families needed in 1910.

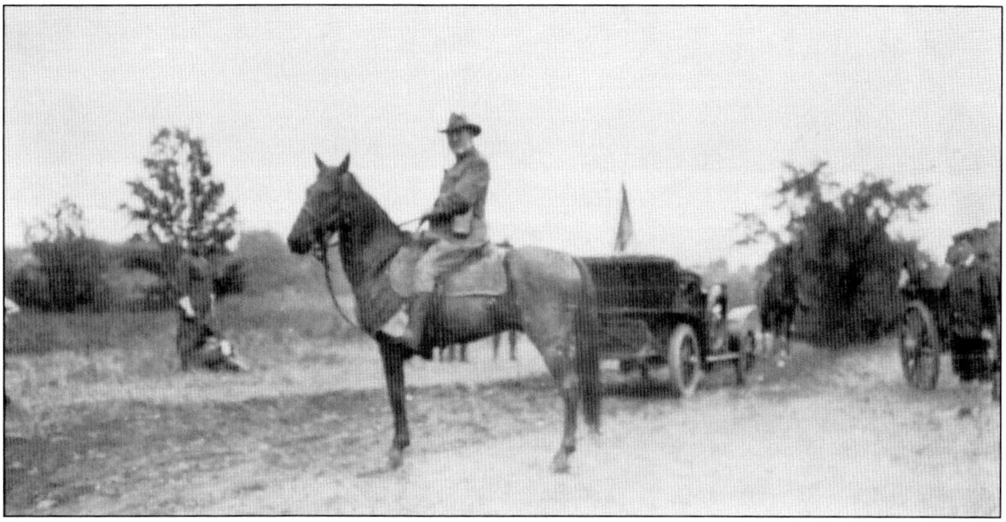

Pine Plains to Fort Drum. At one point Pine Camp military maneuvers were led by General Frederick D. Grant, son of the former president. This picture shows the general on horseback during field maneuvers.

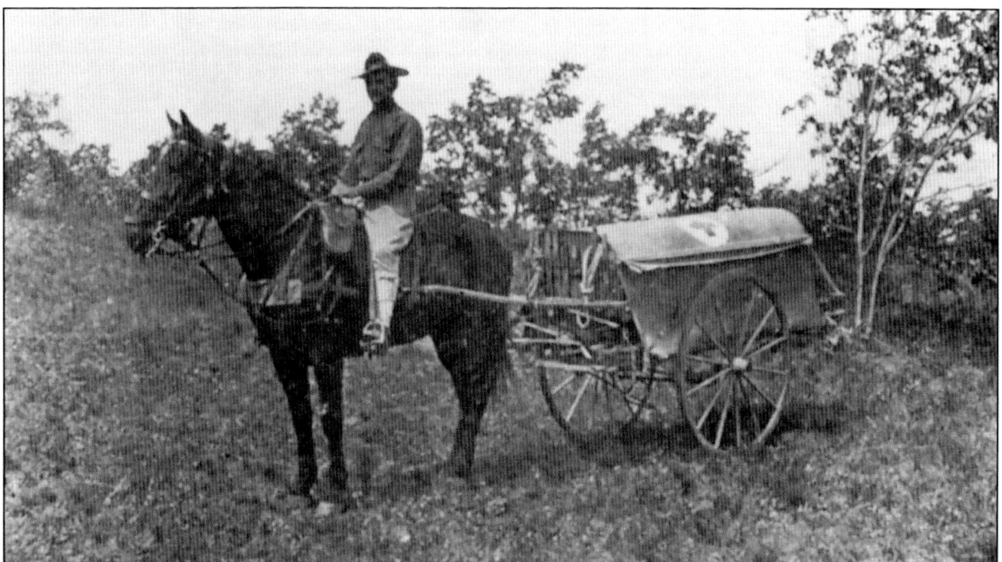

Pine Plains to Fort Drum, *c.* 1900. Pine Camp soldiers were not without injury. A field ambulance was certainly a necessity—whether horse drawn or mobilized.

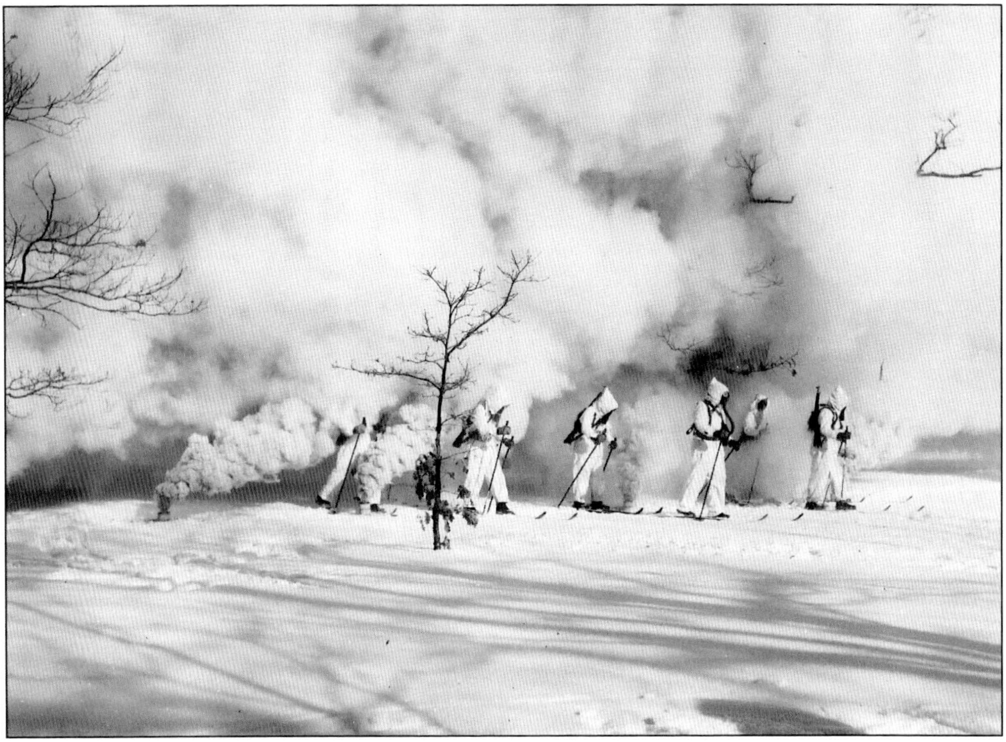

Pine Plains to Fort Drum. Training on the base did not stop when the snow started falling. With skis and warm outerwear, these dedicated soldiers continued to carry out the tasks expected of them in a winter exercise.

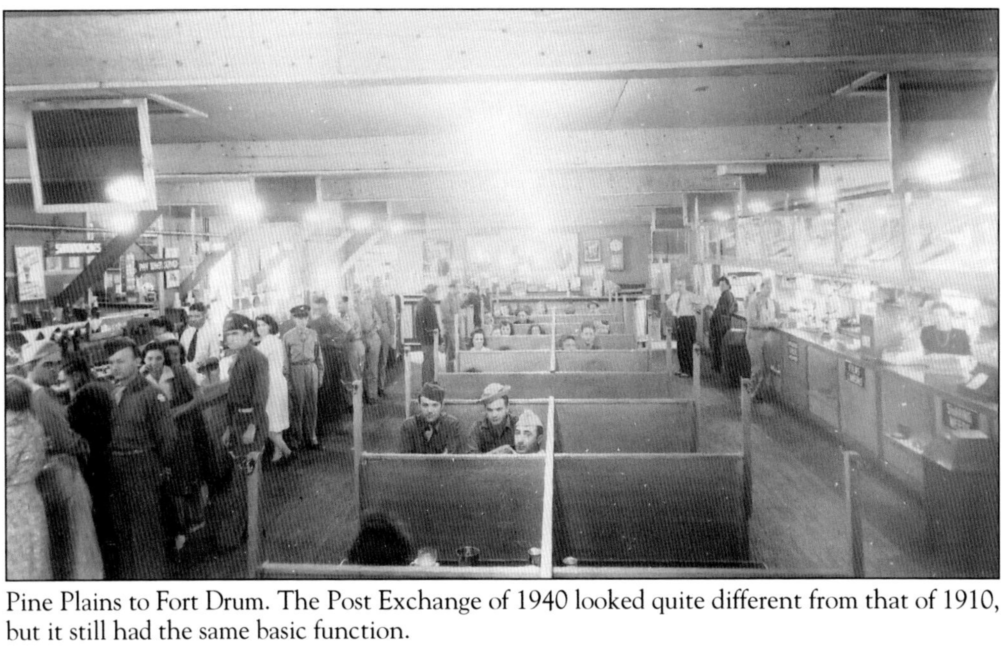

Pine Plains to Fort Drum. The Post Exchange of 1940 looked quite different from that of 1910, but it still had the same basic function.

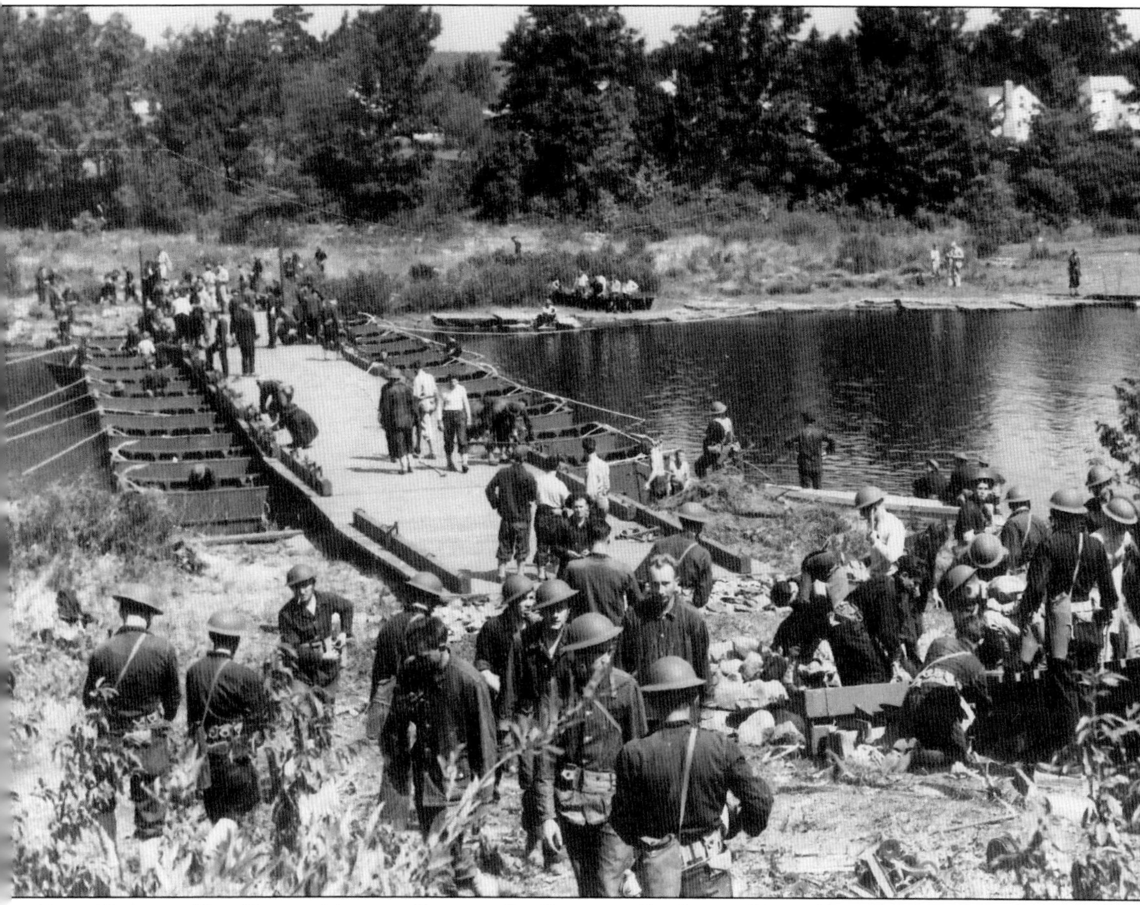

Pine Plains to Fort Drum. Visitors Day on the Pontoon Bridge at Camp Drum was a time for families and friends to converge on the training grounds. Seen in the 1930s, the soldiers are all in their World War I vintage uniforms.

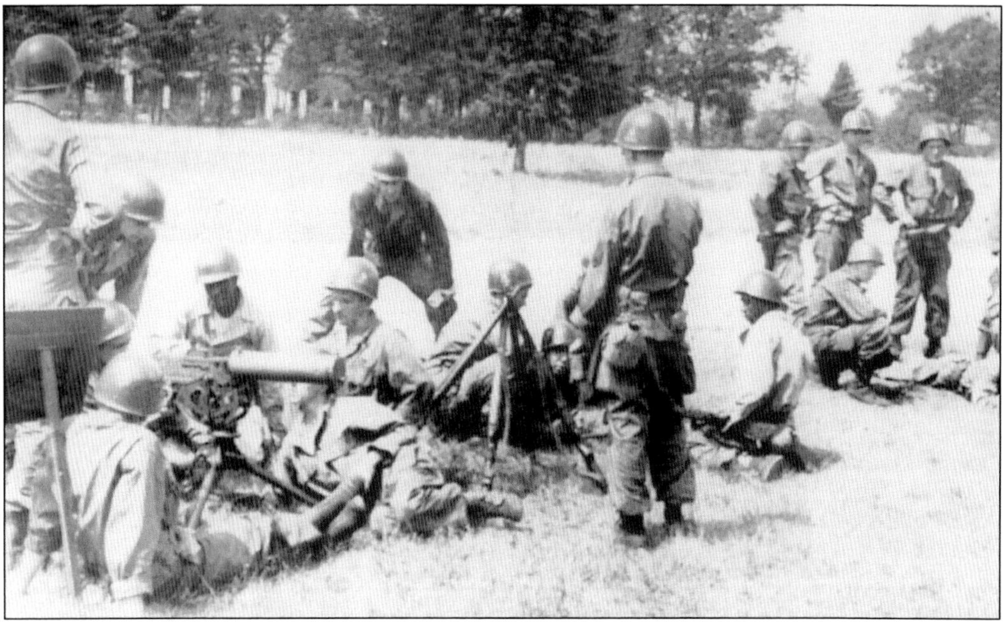

Pine Plains to Fort Drum, *c.* 1940. Shortly before the second World War the importance of Fort Drum was documented for the public. Starting in 1939, the military base became a training facility for newly organized divisions.

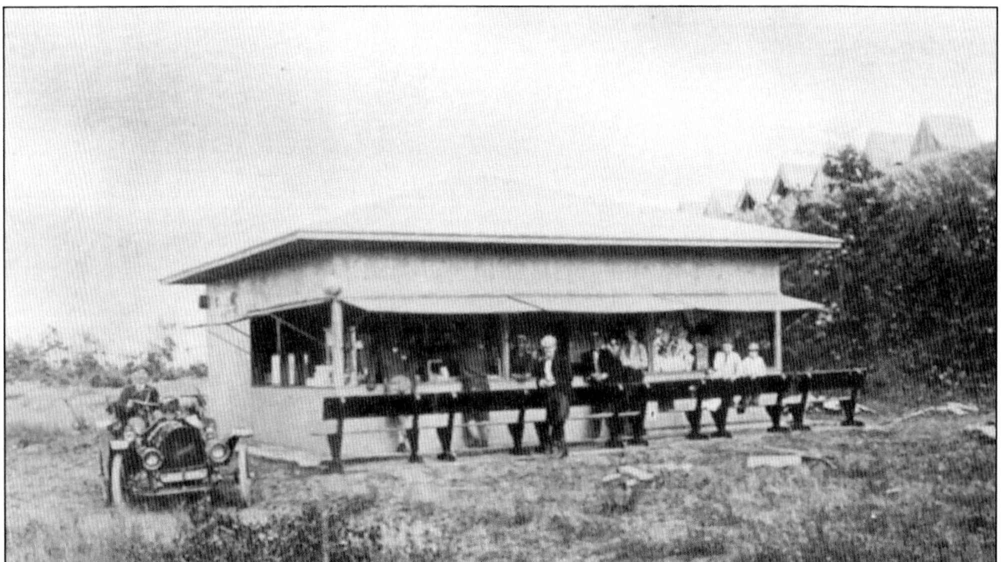

Pine Plains to Fort Drum. The post office at Pine Camp around 1910 served the needs of the military personnel on the base. It is certain that hundreds of letters destined for the soldiers' sweethearts and family were processed here.

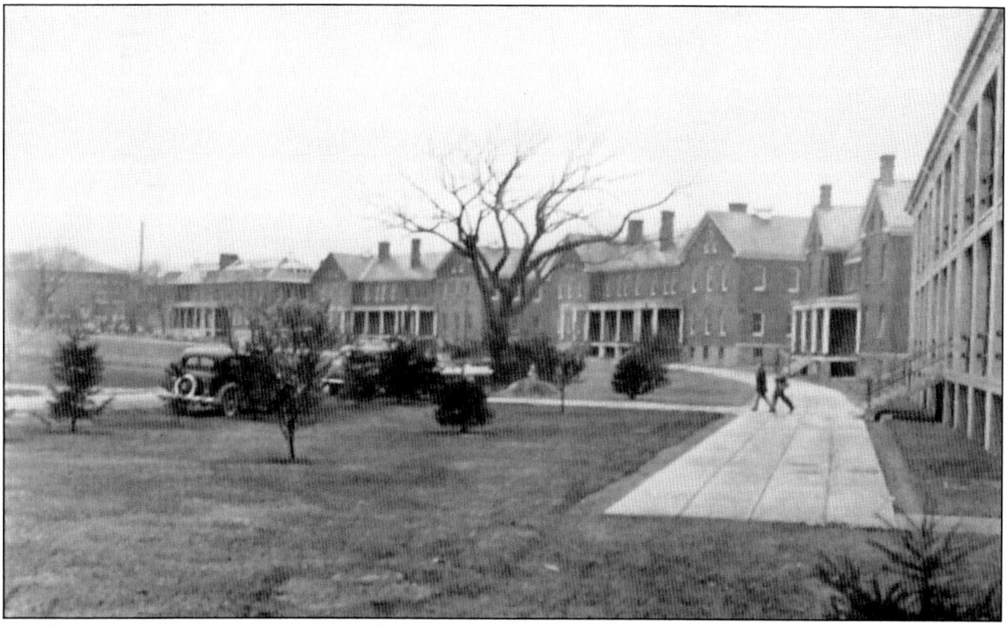

Madison Barracks. Madison Barracks, located on Lake Ontario's shoreline by the present-day village of Sackets Harbor, is one of the nation's oldest border posts. Sackets Harbor, before the War of 1812, was without defenses. Shortly after the attack on June 19, 1812, a log blockade was built around the village.

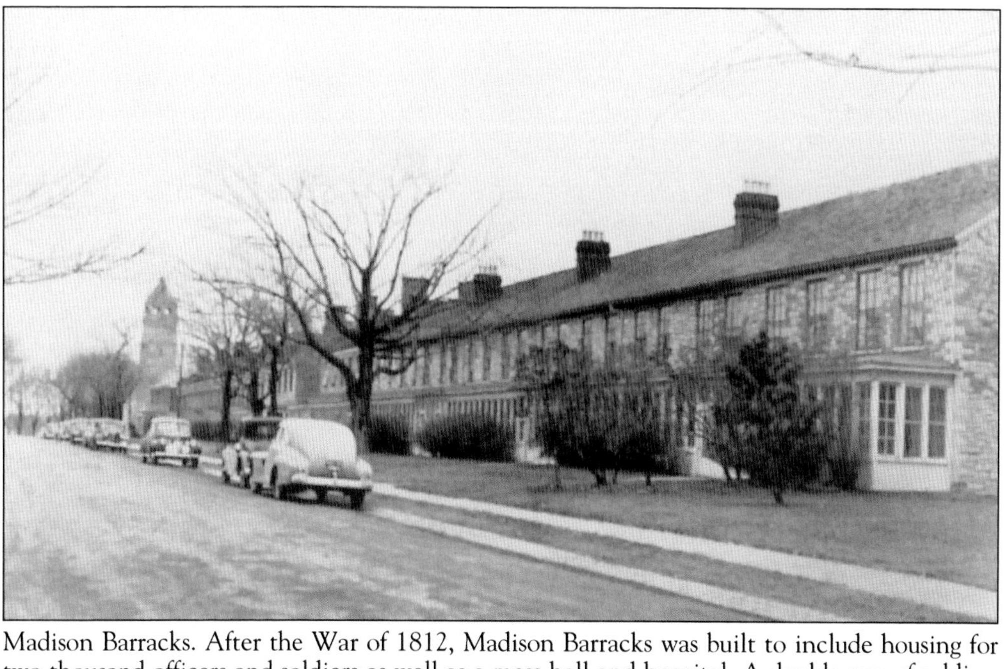

Madison Barracks. After the War of 1812, Madison Barracks was built to include housing for two thousand officers and soldiers as well as a mess hall and hospital. A double row of soldiers quarters, made of stone, were erected at a cost of $85,000. When completed, Madison Barracks was considered the most complete and desirable of any barracks in the land.

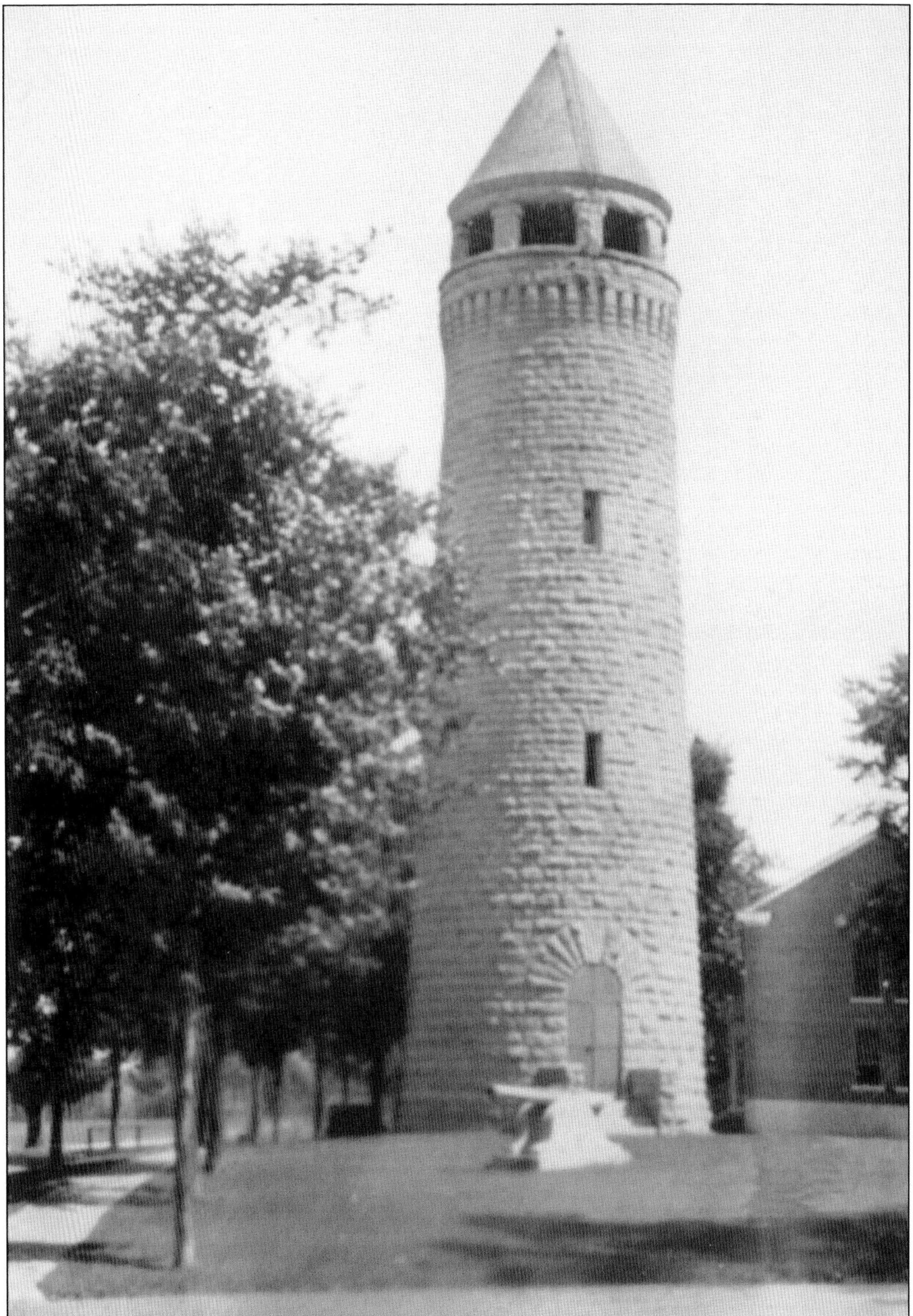

Madison Barracks, water tower. At Madison Barracks, a water tower was erected for the post. This tower stands 127 feet tall and is made of cut stone that encloses a 55,000-gallon steel tank.